THE MISSION

Names Are For Tombstones Baby

THE MISSION

NAMES ARE FOR TOMBSTONES, BABY

by **Martin Roach**
with Neil Perry

Independent Music Press
London

First Published in 1993 by
INDEPENDENT MUSIC PRESS

This work is Copyright © Independent Music Press 1993

The right of Martin Roach and Neil Perry to be identified as the authors of this work has been asserted by them in accordance with the Copyright, Designs and Patents Act, 1988

All Rights Reserved

This book is sold subject to the condition that it shall not, by way of trade or otherwise, be lent, re-sold, hired out or otherwise circulated without the publisher's prior consent in any form of binding or cover other than that which it is published and without a similar condition being imposed on the subsequent purchaser.

No part of this publication may be reproduced, stored in a retrieval system, or transmitted in any form or by any means, electronic, mechanical, photocopying, recording or otherwise, without the prior permission of the copyright owner.

British Library Cataloguing-in-Publication Data
A catalogue for this book is available from The British Library

ISBN 1-89-7783-01-9

Distributed by Omnibus Press.
c/o Book Sales Ltd.,
New Market Road,
Bury St.Edmunds,
Suffolk. IP33 3YB
Order No. MR55555

Printed and bound in Great Britain by Cox & Wyman Ltd, Reading

Designed at Grand Union Design.

ACKNOWLEDGMENTS:

Wayne Hussey, Mick Brown, Simon Hinkler, Craig Adams.

Tony Perrin, Joe Gibb, Kelly, Ric Carter, Mark Gemini Thwaite, Andy Cousins.

Miles Hunt, Dave Crook, Stephen Bradley, Harold Parsons, Stuart, Joe, Kaye, Stevos, E2's, Andrew and Richard.

Special Thanks to Mom and Dad.

CONTENTS:

CHAPTER ONE:	9
CHAPTER TWO:	26
CHAPTER THREE:	47
CHAPTER FOUR:	63
CHAPTER FIVE:	79
CHAPTER SIX:	93
CHAPTER SEVEN:	120
CHAPTER EIGHT:	134
CHAPTER NINE:	158
CHAPTER TEN:	171
CHAPTER ELEVEN:	202
CHAPTER TWELVE:	215
CHAPTER THIRTEEN:	224
CHAPTER FOURTEEN:	235
CHAPTER FIFTEEN:	247
CHAPTER SIXTEEN:	257
DISCOGRAPHY	269
VIDEOGRAPHY	275

CHAPTER ONE

"There are basically three kinds of people who 'perform'. There are those who do it naturally, those who want to possess that ability but don't have that touch, and there are those who want to and don't give a damn either way.

I'm part of that last category."

Iggy Pop 1975

"You should try everything once except incest and folk dancing".

Sir Arnold Bax

THE wind howled coldly down Camden High Street picking up a tide of paper cups and scraps of discarded gig flyers on its way, carrying them past the busy Underground entrance and on towards the murky waters of the Lock. Halfway along the journey the wave of litter bumped into two hundred pairs of legs huddled impatiently outside The Electric Ballroom, where the gathered crowd restlessly flicked to their watches every five minutes as if to will the eight o'clock opening time nearer. When the doors finally opened to welcome the crowd into the darkness beyond, they pushed under the broken neon sign as cold hands fumbled for the £5 entrance fee and filed past the small dog-eared poster announcing that evening's show: 'The Sisterhood. Ballroom. 27th February'. By 8.40 the venue was bulging and the same doors creaked shut to bottle the atmosphere inside into a cauldron of expectation. The two support bands The Mekons and Skeletal Family were afforded a warm and generous reception, but it was clear that this was nothing more than a polite distraction. The room buzzed with conversation and lurking within the misty shrouds of dry ice that hung in the air were many notables including Andrew Eldritch, front man for the legendary cult band The Sisters of Mercy, huddled furtively in a corner draped in his customary black robes. Finally at around 10pm, strains of Francis Ford Coppola's classic film track 'Apocalypse Now' washed over the swaying crowd who watched in fascination as four men swathed in black strode onto the stage. As the drummer settled behind his expansive kit the bass player adjusted his black military style hat, whilst across the small stage a third man was yielding under the thick strap of his cherry red Gibson double-neck guitar. Centre stage the lead singer of The Sisterhood, hiding behind a pair of dark glasses and a wide brimmed black felt hat, sauntered up to the microphone through the smoke that enveloped his features as the air of grandeur and pomposity grew. The crowd hushed and the singer spoke:

'I can't see a fookin' thing up here, this bloody dry ice
tastes fookin' horrible, why can't it taste like strawberries?'

Forty five minutes later, after a blistering set which left the crowd breathless, the singer once more quietened the crowd down and drew attention to himself. After pausing to adjust his glasses he said: 'Thanks to Andrew Eldritch we are no longer called The Sisterhood and as he spoke the large plain backdrop fell from the wall to reveal their new moniker, but comically it snagged halfway and wouldn't budge. As Ian Astbury and Billy Duffy of The Cult staggered on to the stage and drunkenly announced that this band were 'The future of rock 'n' roll', the nimble hands of a watchful roadie untied the backdrop to finally reveal the new name emblazoned across the wall: The Mission.

* * *

Wendy and Arthur Hussey were pleased with the way their first born child Jerry was progressing both at school and the local Mormon Church where the family were regular contributors. They hoped that one day he would grow up to be a missionary in the fashion of the great Joseph Smith whose teachings they followed with the zeal and devotion that befitted practising Mormons. The youngster, who preferred to go by his second name of Wayne, continued to show admirable application at his studies, despite being bullied for his fragile build and round glasses, and left the Ridings Secondary in Winterbourne with five 'O' levels to his credit, his first love already under his belt in the shape of one Rosalind Jones and a failed but valiant attempt at winning the Butlins 'Tarzan of the Apes Contest' in 1968. Much to his parents delight, throughout his formative years Hussey eagerly attended services at the local Mormon church, and was especially willing to participate in the many shows and dances that the church organised - in one instance as a 12 year old he spoke with consummate ease in front of a conference of over 700 people. Despite his religious enthusiasm and the possibility of continuing his education at the Yate Church of Jesus Christ Of Latter Day Saints, Hussey was anxious to sample life outside of the Mormon community and thus left school at 16, having signed up for a Management trainee scheme with the Co-Operative Bank.

One of the features which so attracted him to Mormon teachings was the active encouragement and use of music in various services and social events. However, as a teenager this musical interest gradually began to eclipse his religious commitments - Hussey increasingly spent more time with his guitar and listening to records than he did at Church. The trainee job did not progress well and soon Hussey found himself going through various occupations, but never achieving anything more glamourous than dipping kettle filaments in acid at the Russell Hobbs factory in Bristol town centre. All this time his knowledge and exposure to music was growing and at 16 he joined The Sweet Fan Club to compliment his burgeoning record collection. Although the first single he bought was 'Back Home' by the 1970 England World Cup Squad, his tastes improved and his dubious initial choice was soon complimented by the rather more tasteful likes of Mott the Hoople, T Rex, Slade, Bowie and Led Zeppelin, although there were momentary losses of concentration with choices such as Benny Hill's 'Ernie - He Drives The Fastest Milk Float In The West'. He also started going to live shows and was exhilarated at one Mott The Hoople concert when the band's singer Ian Hunter had pointed him out to the crowd because of the dark glasses he was wearing in a pitch black club, a habit that would stay with him for many years to come. All the time his own musical ability was developing - after a brief dalliance with piano lessons (and an ill-fated drum kit as a 6 year old) he had been bought his first guitar for £6 at the age of 13 as a holiday gift on his parents return from Barcelona. He advanced quickly enough for his local guitar teacher to send him home one evening with his new Woolworths guitar in one hand and a written message for his mother in the other, telling her that he had taught the boy all he could.

It was around 1975 that his enthusiasm for music began to dominate everything else. At home his father had noticed the eagerness with which his son would come back from school and practice his guitar and listen to his records: "He'd play for hours, come back after school, and play for ages, I'd find him with his fingers bleeding sometimes but he wouldn't stop. One day I came back from work and told him to give it a rest, so he stopped. About ten minutes later I thought I could hear him again, and I could - he was in the shed down the bottom of the garden." This fascination with his own musical ability was complemented by the emergence of a whole new musical movement that was shaking the very foundations of British music - punk. Hussey soon became embroiled in this phenomenon, though never at the expense of his much loved early '70's heroes such as Marc Bolan, posters of whom still held pride of place on his bedroom wall. His musical preferences remained firmly rooted in the days of The Metal Guru but there was an attitude in punk that appealed to his youthful sense of adventure, and removed the mysticism and elitism that had shrouded the music business and its stars up until that point. "I was a glam kid really, but when punk came along I was still dead excited by it and I'm pretty sure I wouldn't have gone on to what I did if it wasn't for punk. All of a sudden you didn't need to be a great guitarist or singer to go out and make records - it was more of a spiritual thing than anything else. When you listen to those records now, much of it doesn't stand up at all, but that was only part of it. Being involved in it and going into punk clubs meant that you could play three chord songs and still succeed, you didn't have to be like Genesis and Yes. Musically, I was more into the New York end of it, like Television, Blondie and Talking Heads but the spirit was the main attraction."

Against this backdrop of punk sensibilities mixed with glam rock, it was perhaps inevitable that the Church would struggle to captivate Hussey much longer. By the time he was 17 his mother felt that Mormon practice was no longer the priority in his life: "He was active until about 17 or 18, but those are always the difficult years. If they get through that period when they want to explore and experiment you've got them - we lose so many at that age. We did music festivals, arts and crafts, and Wayne would always take part as did all our kids. He would have made a good missionary but by now music was his love". Ironically it was at one of these Church shows that Hussey would make his first step away from this close-knit family. He fell for one of the girls in a Church band, Pat, and began commuting to Liverpool to see her. When his parents returned from a holiday that year he informed them of a decision he had made, as his mother recalls: "We went on holiday and when we came back he really shocked us, he said 'I'm not going to church anymore. If you make me I'll leave home'. He didn't want to hurt us. This was all the more difficult because a month or two earlier he'd said to us that he'd decided to go on his Church mission after all and we'd been busy getting all his missionary books and bits and pieces. So it was a shock when he phoned up and said he'd changed his mind again, and that he was going to join this band called The Walkie Talkies and that Church-wise that was it."

Partly due to his infatuation with this girl, and partly because of his excitement at the life he had caught glimpses of during his brief visits to Liverpool, Hussey made the brave decision to uproot from his Bristol home and move to the city on Merseyside, even though ironically Pat's group soon disbanded because the respective members took up their missions for the Church. Being away from his family was strange but was partly balanced by the hive of activity which the 18 year old suddenly found himself surrounded by. Punk was thriving and there was enormous scope to satiate his voracious musical curiosity and interest. "When I moved to Liverpool I used to go down to Eric's Club, to see Joy Division, Wire, The Teardrop Explodes, Echo and the Bunnymen, Big In Japan, all sorts of bands. All those people were really big stars to me because they were playing Eric's. Then one night I met some people there, who were in a band called The Dead Byrds. I played with them for a while, most notably at the Twilight when we supported Ultravox - before Midge Ure - and even supported The Pretenders on their first tour. We made an independent single but had to change our name so the record came out as The Walkie Talkies. There were so many bands around though, it was all very transient - I soon left and started working with a band called Hambii and The Dance. It was a very incestuous scene, but quite exciting. My predominant memory of it is that it was sunny all the time although I'm sure it wasn't."

By 1979 Wayne had established himself in the local music scene in Liverpool - he would play with other musicians regularly, such as Budgie who went on to join Siouxie and the Banshees, and generally became embroiled in the life of bands and clubs. By now music was his absolute priority, as his mother recalls:"There were several years in Liverpool when I think he went hungry. He was on the dole and rather than buy food he'd buy a couple of strings for his guitar or something. Many would have have given up but I realised that he sensed he could do something as far as music was concerned if he just kept at it."

* * *

Around the same time but across the Penines in Leeds, a new band had just been formed who called themselves The Sisters Of Mercy, with the enigmatic Andrew Eldritch on vocals and Gary Marx on guitar. Despite Eldritch having been a drummer in numerous Leeds punk bands, the decision was made to use a drum machine - with the mechanical rhythmn section christened Dr. Avalanche, the band were now actively looking for a bass player. They would not have to look for long - pretty soon Eldritch had met somebody in a club whom he thought was perfect for the role, a man by the name of Craig Adams.

Originally from Otley in West Yorkshire, but since the age of two an inhabitant of Leeds itself, Adams was the elder of the two children of Ken and Ann Adams, born in 1962. He had an excellent grounding in live bands and was as much a part of the music scene in Leeds as Hussey was proving to be in Liverpool - he very much identified with the punk spirit and was heavily involved in the actual music of the movement as well. His first band had been a gang of 14 year olds called The Village Green Preservation Society at his school in 1976, but this was a short lived affair: "We were hippy punk rock and basically did cover versions at school discos but we were exciting. I left for some reason, an argument - I seem to remember Jack Daniels was involved." After leaving school and being offered a job as a park keeper by the Job Centre, Adams started to take his music and bands much more seriously. Using his formal training on the piano, he became the keyboard player in the infamous Leeds band The Expelaires, who hailed from the independent Zoo label and claimed such stablemates as Echo and the Bunnymen and The Teardrop Explodes, bands who were at the forefront of the new youth vanguard of music along with labels such as Factory, Postcard and Fast. The nucleus of The Expelaires was the trio of Adams on keyboards, with a guitarist called Dave 'Wolfie' Wolfenden and a singer called Paul 'Grape' Gregory. Despite Grape claiming that the band were no more than "a gentlemen's drinking club on wheels" Zoo deemed them fit to invest the modest sum of £440 in a debut single, which was released in September 1979 as 'To See You/Frequency'. Fairly soon the band found themselves with an ardent local following and a series of notable gigs, including regular supports with The Bunnymen and an appearance at The Futurama Festival with PiL, Joy Division, The Fall and OMD. Perhaps most notably of all, after their second single, John Peel invited them on to his show to record a much-sought after radio session.

Progress was clearly being made but Adams was not entirely happy with the direction of the band: "At the time the bassist of The Expelaires played all this funky bass even though he had one of these amps with distortion built in. When he used to go out for a cup of tea at rehearsals I used to sneak over to his bass and play it with the distortion full on. He'd come back and say 'That sounds crap does that', whereas I always thought it sounded really good. We'd got a good following so it was no surprise when we were then offered a major deal, but to my immense frustration they wanted to do another indie single - I told them they were stupid and left." Somewhat disappointed but not discouraged, Adams formed another band called The Exchange which had all the trappings of a classic early '80's synth duo - their demo's were produced by John Langford, of the legendary The Three Johns, who was also the prime mover behind The Mekons, a band The Expelaires had regularly supported. Pretty soon however the restless Adams bored of wanting to be Gary Numan and decided he wanted to be a 'rock 'n' roller', and it was then that he met Andrew Eldritch, as he recalls: "One night I was down the F Club in Leeds. I was bored with The Exchange and I met this guy by the bar. It turned out to be Eldritch, and we got talking. We had similar musical ideas and fortunately he liked the idea of having distorted bass which helped me no end because I couldn't play a note. Also, Eldritch's girlfriend at the time was the DJ, so when I started in The Sisters of Mercy I used to stand with her because at least that way I had somewhere I could go without getting punched."

So using the shelter of the DJ booth, Adams had joined Eldritch and Marx as the final member of The Sisters line-up. Although Eldritch toyed with the idea of using a keyboard as well, it was not followed through, so save for a change hair colour by the blond front man, the completed band was ready to unleash itself on an unsuspecting pop world. Clearly they had something worthwhile. Very soon the band had started to attract a faithful audience of leather-clad post-punks who were increasingly associated with the rise of the 'goth' movement in the early '80's. They had revered predecessors: previously the movement had been led in Britain by Northampton's Bauhaus, who's nine minute brooding single 'Bela Lugosi's Dead' in 1979 had already acquired a classic status. Their contribution was mirrored perhaps most notably by Alien Sex Fiend from The Batcave Club in London, whose ghoulish act revolved around the thick white make-up and stage persona of the alien sex fiend himself, alias Nick Wade. Overseas there was even more revered company for goths - L.A's The Cramps had formed in Ohio back in 1976 but had come to dominate the unique scene that sprang up around New York's CBGB's club in the tail end of the decade. Although all of these bands had healthy cult followings and had been the leaders of what was becoming a whole new street fashion as well as music culture, The Sisters gradually came to be seen as the focus of goth attention. Soon the umbrella of goth covered many more bands including Luton's UK Decay, Barnsley's Danse Society, Oxford's Play Dead and Bradford's Southern Death Cult (later The Cult with a singer called Ian Astbury), but it was to The Sisters that the throne belonged. Largely due to Eldritch's deliberate alienation from his audience, a barrier which punk had fought so hard to break down, The Sisters and Eldritch in particular came to acquire colossal cult status by the end of 1982, with Leeds very much the base of their notoriously amphetamine-fuelled success. Their first single, the rapidly deleted 'The Damage Done' on their own Merciful Release label, was recorded through a 3 Watt practice amp, but by the second release 'Body Electric/ Adrenochrome' in April 1982 the band had developed enough to achieve the Melody Maker Single of the Week and by now held the hopes on their shoulders of thousands of followers disillusioned by the artificiality of the New Romantics.

The internal politics of The Sisters had from day one been a very highly strung and idiosyncratic affair - this was very much Eldritch's show, or so he would have people believe, and he manipulated circumstances with an ability that earned him a respected reputation for being in charge. Adams was aware of this when he joined the band but never fully accepted that it was the ideal environment in which to operate. His five years in the band saw a love-hate relationship develop between himself and Eldritch, the signs of which were evident even early on. In 1982, just after recording a single on the Leeds-based CNT label run by Adrian Collins and John Langford, Adams left the band and flew to the Canary Islands to take up a position as a photographer's assistant, only to return to the fold after only missing one gig back at home. Nonetheless, there was clearly mileage in this artistic tension created by such personality clashes because The Sisters' rise continued unchecked - by 1984 as well as their own massively successful tours, they had also toured with The Psychedelic Furs, supported The Clash, Birthday Party and Nico, and recorded a John Peel session. Most notably, their third single 'Alice' had been received to major critical acclaim and generally come to be acknowledged as a goth classic. The politics did not improve however, and at the end of that year despite the band's ever-growing popularity and the impending release of a new epic called 'Temple of Love', the rhythmn guitarist Ben Gunn quit the band. Eldritch immediately began scouting the music clubs and venues for a suitable replacement.

* * *

Whilst The Sisters Of Mercy were establishing one of the strongest cult followings Britain had ever seen, Hussey himself had also been very busy back in Liverpool. His work and perserverance had paid off in 1982 when he had won his first involvement with a major band, Pauline Murray & The Invisible Girls, from an advert he had seen in Melody Maker. After passing the audition successfully he joined the band on tour in both Britain and Europe, and the group enjoyed a degree of critical acclaim and a sizeable live following. Hussey featured on their popular 'Dream Sequence' single and was able to cut his teeth to a certain extent with this group, but it was to be his next band that really threw him into the den of the music business and showed him the possibilities that were open to somebody with talent and drive. Pauline Murray moved to Newcastle and decided to retire for a while, so with that band on ice Hussey was looking once again for a project he could work with. Soon after the European tour he received a phonecall from an enigmatic and uniquely talented character by the name of Pete Burns who had a band called Dead or Alive, and was looking for a guitarist for a recording session on a forthcoming single. Hussey got the job, played guitar on the record and ended up staying for two years.

It was during this period that Hussey first started to seriously defer from his strict upbringing as a Mormon - he had not been practising the religion for some time now but initially there was a very real guilt evident in his lifestyle. At the start of his life in Liverpool he was very much cocooned in his abstinent background - by the end of his Dead or Alive days he had taken to wearing dresses and make-up and had the single word 'Drug' scratched into the body of his battered guitar. The essence of Dead Or Alive focussed very much on the androgynous persona of Pete Burns himself, and Hussey was very influenced by this. As a result, this was also to be the first time that he grew apart from his family, as his mother explains: "There was a time when he went through a strange patch - he didn't ring us up and I think that's because he was doing a lot of things that he knew we were dead against, and I think it gave him a guilty conscience. Wayne and I have always talked and he's always told me things, sometimes things that I hadn't really wanted to know about. When he was in Dead or Alive he'd phone up but there wasn't that closeness and I felt he couldn't talk to me."

Even so, Dead Or Alive were attracting much public attention and Hussey began to enjoy his first taste of mainstream success. Having said that, despite the popularity of the band they played only six gigs in the two years when Hussey was a member, and this eventually frustrated him enough that he decided to leave. In one instance Dead Or Alive supported Killing Joke but most notable perhaps was their slot at the Futurama festival, where they were second on the bill to The Damned, with the rest of the line-up consisting of Sex Fiend, Sex Gang, Dance Society and Southern Death Cult. Hussey has fond memories of his days with Pete Burns: "The first two years of that were great, the feeling of camaraderie between us was very tangible, we actually believed we were the best band in the world, and there was a point where I thought we could do something brilliant but it went too far the other way. Everything I wrote was put into a sequencer, I ended up doing just backing vocals and nothing else. Also, with the first LP, there were so many session people coming in - this added to the lack of live shows caused me to lose interest so I felt I had to leave. It was quite amicable, but I think at the time Pete felt betrayed and let down because my heart wasn't in it anymore, which is understandable. He is somebody who demands loyalty and devotion. Nobody could have said a bad word about him." Ironically, Hussey left just after recording his last set of backing vocals (a-ha, a-ha) for Dead or Alive's cover of K.C and the Sunshine Band's classic 'That's the Way I Like It', which gave Dead Or Alive their first Top 30 success - Hussey was spared a dubious Top of the Pops debut by his premature departure.

A week of dubious band offers later, having already turned down an offer to play in a new band with Holly Johnson, Hussey's phone rang once again with yet another proposition. This one was different, the band were serious and the offer was too good to miss. The caller was Andrew Eldritch, and the vacancy was in The Sisters Of Mercy. A meeting was arranged in Leeds, The Sisters home town, and Hussey found himself immediately attracted to their guitar-based version of The Rolling Stones' 'Gimme Shelter' which was being released at the time, and served as an exact antithesis of the overly sequenced music he had been involved in, and ultimately become disillusioned with in Dead Or Alive. After discussing arrangements Eldritch rang Hussey up again, offered him the job and said 'Have you thought about changing your name?'

* * *

Declining the suggestion of a name change, the new member soon realised how the band's power structure operated: "I started rehearsing with Craig and Gary in the cellar of Eldritch's place. It was very primitive, we did a lot of rehearsing but never with Andrew. The first time we played together was at our first gig - he used to sit up in the living room and when we'd come up after rehearsal he'd just say 'You trashed that song as well.' Gary was becoming disillusioned and after I'd been in the band only about three weeks, he asked me to leave with him and Craig. I think from that point on I held the band together in many ways. When I arrived Andrew pretty much ran the whole show, but while I was there it did become more democratic - it was mine and Gary's tunes that were actually used. To be honest though, the thing about The Sisters was largely down to the whole lifestyle as well, not just the music."

Central to this lifestyle and the appeal of The Sisters to their fans was the culture that was based in Leeds, but by now had spread across the country. Leeds had a notorious reputation for being the speed capital of the UK and the whole scene in the city at that time was very close knit and unique - John Langford of The Three Johns remembers the atmosphere well: "It was amazing in Leeds, the way it all clicked. It was a real community at one time, The Faversham Arms pub, The Warehouse, The Phono, all these great places, and there were people around like Clare, Goth Queen of Leeds who used to do the sound for The Mekons. Headingley had cheap housing so you got all the bands there plus there's a lot of pubs. It was a very close scene at one point, and everybody seemed to have a nickname. There was a joke about The Faversham Arms pub that you could draw a map around all the bands in their own little corners in there. It was great when it was Goth Central, people never got up until it was dark. You'd walk around Leeds 6 and you'd see all these rows of houses emptying as it got to dusk. There were more goths per square mile than anywhere else. I could never muster up the energy to be one myself, but they were really into it and they'd never give you any hassle". Dave Hall, a local promoter and an integral part of the whole scene remembers it much the same: "There was a load of music and bands, but noticeably, all the people who were actually achieving anything tended not to do much locally in Leeds. The groups that played around the small pubs never actually achieved anything much, but the bands who sat down and thought about what they should do more clinically were the ones that got somewhere."

In this environment The Sisters of Mercy proved the case that it was the band who could isolate themselves enough from a unique but limiting local phenomenon who could go on to succeed nationally - The Sisters worked hard nurturing a live following nationwide, and when they gigged they took all the speed haze of Leeds with them on the road, becoming almost legendary for their drug intake. Wayne Hussey by now was definitely not a by-stander - his partner in crime in the many stories of excess that The Sisters of Mercy became famed for was Adams, with whom Hussey had rapidly struck up a very close and warm friendship. As a result the pair frequently dominated the tour tales, as Adams recalls: "Me and Wayne spent most of our time together. Eldritch was always sat in the front seat of the van and us two and Gary in the back. It was only Wayne and I who drank heavily so we always got into all sorts of shit together. We were due to do this festival in Frankfurt once but we woke up at 9am on the day of the gig in this house about 100 miles away from the venue. How we got there...well, we'd been out with somebody or other. We had to get back by 2, no money on us, nothing. We both looked like pieces of shit. I just automatically got on with Wayne, even though we were forced into that situation because of Eldritch's personality, but we did instantly get on. Although we'd gone through some pretty weird paranoid situations thinking we didn't like each other, it always came back down to a really great friendship." At one gig in Liverpool, Hussey and Adams greedily drank a bottle of home-made wine proffered by a fan's father. The following morning Hussey woke up in a strange room stark naked except for a ribbon around his dick. Another date saw the manager of an unsuspecting hotel being told that the pair had had some trouble with a wardrobe; his reply that 'It's no problem whatsoever Sir, which room is it in?' was met by the admission 'Well, it's not exactly in a room, it's in a tree outside.'

Apart from a handful of reviews criticising them for being Doors rip-offs and overly serious The Sisters continued to grow, with Eldritch correctly and succinctly undermining accusations that the band were beginning to take themselves more seriously than the monstrous and ruthless rock band they had set out to be. Even during goth's infancy the humour of The Cramps had been lost on many, and Eldritch was justified in pointing out that this misconception was now a heavy millstone around the neck of the goth movement: "The trouble with the press is that they won't recognise that the rock format still has an enormous amount to contribute as long as it is approached with the right attitude and an awareness that certain things just can't be taken seriously. People are ready to recognise a smartness and a sense of humour in pop but not rock, which is just as suitable a vehicle."[1] Adams put it on a more practical level, citing his reason for wearing so much black being that it facilitated less washing whilst on tour.

* * *

Across town from The Sisters of Mercy camp, a band called Red Lorry Yellow Lorry was beginning to acquire a considerable following for their own brand of post-punk gothic music. Their single 'Hollow

Eyes' taken from the debut album 'Talk About The Weather' had become a goth favourite, helped by the generous air play it received after being championed by John Peel. The backbone of the band was provided by the drumming of a character called Mick Brown, who despite their growing success, was a little disillusioned with the band's increased use of a drum machine, but resolved to continue undeterred.

Further afield, forty miles away in Sheffield, the guitarist with a loose experimental outfit called Artery, whose post-punk prog-rock had won the band much critical acclaim, was becoming restless. As a blond haired youngster, Simon Hinkler had played drums and later keyboards with the band Pulp, who themselves pursued a highly experimental course which appealed to his creative nature. Once in Artery, Hinkler played on two of the band's four albums and toured three. He had already produced an album of his own called 'Flight Commander, Solitude and the Snake' in 1984 as an outlet for his more experimental tendencies, and despite Artery's massive local following he was becoming unsettled and feeling restricted once more. As a result, Hinkler had accepted an offer to produce some local bands who shared their manager Tony Perrin with Artery. Whilst Hinkler was at a Hull studio working on these demos, the resident engineer mentioned that The Sisters of Mercy were having yet more personnel troubles, and that their disillusioned guitarist Gary Marx was going to leave and had been in to record some solo material. Hinkler convinced the engineer to give him a contact number for the Sisters and he subsequently rang their sound man, one Pete Turner about the impending vacancy. He was politely told that the band would not be needing a new member. The matter was closed.

* * *

Back in Leeds, the situation of 'us and him' in The Sisters camp had finally caused Gary Marx to quit, leaving the band still divided, except now it was a definite two way split: on the one hand was Eldritch and on the other were the two good friends Hussey and Adams. Such frustrations and arguments were not always present though. Hussey remembers two years of the band as exceptional: "I loved The Sisters, I thought we were the best group in the world, there was such a belief in that band". This belief was shared by the public and there were many times when The Sisters were a complete unit of colossal potential despite the lack of chart success, and the more unsavoury side of affairs was not what the public saw. They watched a band on a seemingly inexorable rise to fame and fortune, and the rapid and large sales of their debut album 'First and Last and Always' confirmed their unique appeal. However, the greatest irony of The Sisters' career was that the more they achieved the more they became destined to implode amongst internal wranglings. When it was announced that The Sisters of Mercy were to play the Royal Albert Hall on June 18th, 1985, to a sell-out crowd, it was widely acknowledged as the band's greatest moment - yet eight weeks after the Albert Hall date The Sisters of Mercy as it was known then was dead.

The two weeks immediately after their triumphant appearance at The Albert Hall The Sisters went to New York to shoot the video for the next single, and then almost as a last attempt at reconciliation, Hussey and Eldritch went to Hamburg for a month to write new material. Their efforts were doomed and it was apparent that the differences were by now irreconcilable, as Hussey explains: "It got to the stage where every time Andrew left the room we'd have a go at one of our songs." He told the press at the time "As far as Craig and I were concerned, we'd resigned ourselves...we'd not been enjoying it for a while, but we'd resigned ourselves to sticking it out, and maybe it would've got better, but in fact it was getting worse." On returning from their ill-fated trip to Hamburg, Eldritch refused outright to sing any of Hussey's songs, and thereby sealed the fate of the band. "When he said that Craig walked out of rehearsals and a day later I did. He was listening to things like Fleetwood Mac, Stevie Nicks, Foreigner, and there was us listening to Motorhead or whatever. And it showed." He went on "We started taking ourselves too seriously, thinking we were more important than we were. It was all contrived for effect really the culmination of all the rock and roll clichés."[2] To both him and Adams the original spirit and humour of the band had essentially been lost, and this combined with the personality clashes with Eldritch made the whole situation untenable.

"I left two days later, even though Eldritch wanted me to play guitar on the next record. At that point, it was quite amicable but then all the legal stuff started..."

CHAPTER TWO

"Sharon was managing the chips and Jimmy was taking the other stuff out of the fryer. He thought he had the knack of it. He dropped the cod into the small greaseproof bag and Sharon took it and put it into the big brown bag, along with the chips. They worked well together, Sharon and Jimmy Snr. They didn't bump into each other. It was like they were two parts of the same machine".

Roddy Doyle: The Van

THE demise of a great band also frequently sounds the death knell of the careers of the respective members, who in many cases flounder, directionless, under their new found musical freedom, vainly searching for a firm identity. Towards the end of The Sisters Of Mercy the more Hussey's ideas polarised with Eldritch's, the closer he and Adams became, both musically and personally, as a result of which when the band finally split the two friends automatically resolved to continue their close association. Within four months they had recruited two more members to complete the line-up of a new outfit and played their debut show in London.

In many ways the break up of The Sisters was a final release from the artistic stranglehold that public preconceptions confine a popular band within, but the two friends had no definite plans at this stage, only a shared enthusiasm and determination to succeed. "When me and Craig split we didn't really know what we wanted to do. We had songs, all of which Eldritch had rejected. I became singer simply because Craig didn't want to and didn't write lyrics." They knew what they didn't want to do, and that was to follow the path that had ultimately destroyed their previous band - The Sisters had effectively achieved what it had set out to do and then lost the original essence of its very existence: "That was part of the problem, we'd done it. In the process of doing that we'd lost the joke of it, that was what it was meant to be, a joke. We started thinking we were more important than we actually were - we started thinking in terms of rock 'n' roll history. But The Sisters were a great rock 'n' roll band, there's no doubt about that".

The nationwide mourning of the worshipping and devoted Sisters fans was intense, but was not matched by a similar grieving on the part of the two departed members. Hussey and Adams went straight to The Slaughterhouse Studios in Driffield to demo some of the ideas that Eldritch has so flippantly rejected. Although their musical ideas were as yet untried, the warming relationship between them affirmed that the fractured personal environment that had finally destroyed The Sisters was never going to trouble their new association, even though it was as yet incomplete. On the way back from the first session at Driffield a drunken Adams put his arm around Hussey in the van and said 'You're me best mate in the whole world and this is going to be a great group.' Since there were only two of them at this stage, with no real direction or plan, this in itself was an incredible show of faith.

Whilst Hussey and Eldritch had been in Hamburg overseeing the death-throes of The Sisters, Adams had been busy. After accepting an invitation to join a fortnight's tour of Holland with The Dead Vaynes, Adams headed off in an orange van with 'Fozzies Mobile Disco' sprayed down the rusting side panel. After the first gig The Dead Vaynes retired to their allotted accommodation - this was no four star hotel however, but a wooden shack in the middle of a pine forest. Steve Vayne had fallen asleep in the van on the way back from the gig but wouldn't wake up - eventually Adams wrenched open the door he was leaning against, but Vayne fell out and broke his collarbone. They still had five gigs left so Vayne simply grabbed a roll of parcel tape and stuck his injured arm to his battered leather jacket, said 'That should do the trick' and headed for the shack. They finished the tour with Vayne leaving his arm in its temporary sling until they returned home to Britain, where he finally received some proper medical attention.

Once back at home, Adams quickly bored of his inactivity and so formed a cover band in Leeds to fill his time, the fiercely non-serious Elvis Presleys From Hell. Alongside Adams were Grape (former Expelaires) on vocals and a guitarist called John from the local band The Batfish Boys. Completing the line-up on drums was Mick Brown from the now widely acclaimed Red Lorry Yellow Lorry. Described by one observer as "like one of those sixth-formers you loved to avoid...with his long straggly hair, battered denim jacket embroidered with Led Zeppelin and the standard collection of motorcycle badges"[1] Brown roomed with Adam's friend and Lorries guitarist Dave Wolfie Wolfenden, who knew Adams himself from their earlier days together in The Expelaires. The Presleys was a loose outfit formed by this group of close friends looking for some easy gigs and easier money - Adams and Brown both enjoyed the relaxed atmosphere of these cover shows. It was at one of these Presleys gigs that the idea first struck Adams that Brown would be the ideal drummer to collaborate on the demos he and Hussey were recording: "I was living with some of the Lorries and gigs were hard to come by. So we formed The Presleys, just doing cover versions for beer money. That was when Mick and I realised we were both just going through the motions in our own bands. The Presley's wasn't the best band ever, but we did do a steaming version of 'Crazy Horses'." Mick took a similar relaxed approach to his music: "The Presley's asked me to play drums, we just did covers and stuff. We supported a band in Bradford and Craig and I were talking afterwards about how good it was just playing, without all the other things that go on being in a band and stuff like that." Once the idea of Brown helping out had been considered, Adams suggested it to Hussey and the pair found themselves more and more attracted to it. His recruitment however, was not that simple, as Hussey recalls: "We spent ages trying to persuade Mick. Craig and I went to London to see the Lorries at The Clarendon and drove back to Leeds in their van with Mick and Wolfie in the front. I thought 'He's a good chap' so Craig decided to ask him if he'd drum for us. I think Mick wanted to do it, but his loyalty understandably lay with Red Lorry Yellow Lorry." Brown agreed to play the session, did so and was then offered the position permanently - he remembers the proposition well: "After we'd done a few of those Presleys gigs, Craig and Wayne were going to record the first EP. They just asked me to do it. I was with them for five days, I hitched back home with Craig after, we had plenty to talk about then. The night they finished the recording they came round my house - I think it was all meant to be very subtle, because I was still in the Lorries, but they came in and Craig just walked straight up to me and said 'Are you joining then?"

Brown liked the idea of playing alongside Hussey and Adams but he had a strong loyalty to the Lorries, with whom he had been for four years, and this made the decision more difficult than he at first imagined. Eventually, in the first week of December 1985, encouraged by his girlfriend, Brown decided to make the break: "I was kind of coming to the end of the Lorries really, and because they'd started to use a drum machine more and more I didn't like being second fiddle. I was thinking about leaving and Wayne and Craig effectively forced the decision for me. At that time the Lorries were just about to get a small deal and finally come off the dole, so the irony was that I was passing up the chance of what we had been working towards over four years, but there just seemed to be a confidence about these two that I went for." It was this confidence and atmosphere that appealed to Brown the most - his priority had always been to enjoy his drumming and here there seemed to be a similar emphasis, on this frequently neglected element of music: "I thought Wayne was talented, with strong ideas. The stuff that he played, along with his and Craig's attitude on what was going to happen, I could get off on it, I liked them."

Brown's career in music had always been firmly based around enjoying himself first and foremost. Originally after leaving school at 16 with no qualifications, he had gone to college for three years and studied a furniture and interior design course, initially hoping to progress to a commercial art course. He left college however and took up various trucking jobs, and this was when his musical interest really flourished, although his penchant for the drums had manifested itself at an early age: "I used to sit on our settee, pull up the cushions, get the kitchen buffets out and play on them. I'd got as good as you can get on a settee and kitchen buffets, so I thought it would be a piece of piss to transform from a three piece suite to a proper drum kit."[2] Far from being a child prodigy, as such assaults on his mother's furniture suggested, Brown's choice of drums was not an automatic one: "One time when I was changing jobs I'd just got my pay. I was down the pub and this kid walked in with a guitar. He had no money so I bought it off him. Then another mate came in and I was stood there drinking me pint with this guitar in my hand. This second guy was a guitarist but he only had a drum kit, so as I thought I could play drums we ended up swapping. My first band was with a friend called Ray and we used to practice three times a week and play once a year. We even made a single but I remember getting it back, rushing home, putting it on my turntable and nearly crying, it were that crap - by the time it had been cut and pressed it had deteriorated tenfold and the demo was far superior. Ray had a mate called Chris who formed Red Lorry Yellow Lorry and I ended up joining them - I stumbled my way into it really." Now he had stumbled on to Hussey and Adams and inadvertently become involved in a group which was to become one of the biggest bands in British music.

*   *   *

With the role of drummer filled relatively easily, and with Christmas rapidly approaching, the three members of this very embryonic outfit began scouting for a guitarist, as Hussey could clearly not accommodate all the vocals and guitar work simultaneously. Their fears about auditioning hundreds of hopefuls for the job were apparently relieved when their friend and ex-Sisters sound man Pete Turner dug out the phone number of a guitarist who had called him a year earlier about the vacancy in The Sisters left open by Gary Marx. So the name of Simon Hinkler was put forward as a suitable candidate and an ideal way of avoiding the lengthy and tiresome experience of auditions. Hinkler was duly phoned up, and drove to Leeds under the impression that he was auditioning for The Sisters of Mercy, unaware that Eldritch's band had split up. Once there he proceeded to fail the audition with complete and utter abandon, as Hussey explains: "The first thing Simon said when he came through the door was 'Alright lads, shall I skin up?' I thought 'Oh no...' He ended up staying the whole weekend. He didn't think he was up to it himself, he arrived in a not-quite-Afghan coat, we sat down watched a film but Simon really cocked it up because he was so stoned we weren't sure if he could play at all." Hinkler decided himself that he was not good enough and left despondent and annoyed. So the band would have to audition after all. Brown takes up the story: "We put an ad in Melody Maker and started auditioning. We tried Vince White from The Clash - you definitely knew you were in the room with him. He came in chewing gum rather fast, and when Wayne was showing him the chords he said 'Nah, nah, let's just jam.' But there was one guy in particular who left just as much an impression on me in a different way. He came in wearing this massive grey overcoat which he never took off, and his guitar still had the price tag hanging off it. I think he'd just lifted it from some shop and come straight to the audition. I think he walked off with one of our guitar straps as well...We held all these auditions and got some real fruitcakes - even guitar teachers, but it wasn't just a matter of someone who could play." Hussey continues: "One of the people I auditioned was a bloke from Bristol who actually taught me guitar down there in my early days; when I left Bristol to go to Liverpool I remember telling him 'I'm going to Liverpool to be a pop star, I'm going to make it' and he just said 'Nah, you're nothing' and just laughed at me." The auditions were getting nowhere and the potential guitarists were getting worse. Then one evening after they'd finished auditioning another batch of probably-nots, they received a message from a frustrated Hinkler to the effect that he regretted what he'd done earlier, that he was the man they needed after all, and could he have another shot. This time it was different. He blew everyone else away.

With the pieces of the jigsaw gradually fitting into place, the new band's ideas about where they were heading also began to crystalize. The calculated nature of their plans was never more evident than in their choice of name - The Sisterhood. Coming so soon after the death of The Sisters of Mercy, whose own fan club had celebrated under that very moniker, many saw this as an inflammatory gesture of the most blatant kind, none more so than Eldritch himself. Moreover, despite the personal friction which precipitated the fall of The Sisters, the split had initially been an amicable one, with the idea being mooted of Hussey contributing some sessions on the forthcoming second Sisters album. With Eldritch bringing in Patricia Morrison from The Gun

Club he had managed to keep The Sisters afloat. With the announcement of his ex-colleague's new line-up under The Sisterhood name any remaining charitable feelings rapidly dissipated and the two camps became embroiled in an unprecedented bitter, personal and legal wrangle which was to dominate the pages of the music press for the ensuing months.

* * *

The start of 1986 was to prove an eventful period for the fledgling band The Sisterhood - it would host their first ever gig and tour, and even witness personnel problems of their own. It would also see the start of a prolonged and often vicious public conflagration between the two camps that had once been united as The Sisters of Mercy. When The Sisterhood announced their formation to a blast of criticism from several camps, none more so than Eldritch, it looked a distinct possibility that this tepid reception, along with their own bluster and cockiness would turn round and destroy them before they had even started. Resolutely, they introduced the new group to the public, revealed their priorities and aims and left people hankering after proof of their confident claims that The Sisterhood were a band of massive potential.

In many of their early interviews, it is clear that the new band were very confident of both their music and their ability to play the music industry at its own game. Stepping into this high profile environment was something of a shock at first for Hinkler - although Artery had been very popular locally, this was a different game altogether: "I immediately hit it off with Mick and we became big pals. With Craig and Wayne it was slightly different. I'd never known anybody who'd been in such a big band before so I was unsure of how to react. They were both incredibly focussed on making a success out of the new band at all costs. It operated on a very different level right from the start. In addition, every band I'd ever been in had worked out songs in rehearsal, so it was different to have Wayne bringing in a Portastudio demo and saying 'This is what we should be playing'."

The freedom that the break from The Sisters gave to Hussey and

Adams was also very evident - The Sisterhood offered them songs that could be developed without the complication of the omnipresent Sisters' drum machine Dr.Avalanche: "These songs are good in the very first instance, and having a drummer helps. If we wrote a song in the soundcheck with The Sisters, it would take us three days to program the drum machine. With a drummer it's difficult in one sense knowing whether he's going to stay on his stool or not, but it's good for spontaneity. We had to, it would have been a mistake not to have a drummer." In addition, there was a genuine belief that these songs were altogether more accessible and melodic than their predecessors. At the same time Hussey was eager to acknowledge the influences on this new material and tempered the band's public cockiness with a respectful glance back to an earlier era: "What I do is contrived, we all are in our own little way...you have all these visions of people who've gone before you who are your heroes, and part of the contrivance is all those images. You are essentially a conglomeration of all those people who have gone before but at the same time it is your personal interpretation of all this that is the individual factor." He continued in this honest vein: "We know what we're good at..I don't think we've got it in us to be innovative. What we are good at is dealing with cliches, and making them seem absurd and ridiculous, which is what, I think, we are."[3]

With the public forewarned that The Sisterhood were to be a band proud of their influences and unashamedly absurd, even ridiculous, the new line-up began the delicate and lengthy process of gelling together as a complete unit, with Jim Reid of Record Mirror already christening them as "the first indie supergroup." It was to his credit that Hussey acknowledged the problems which might arise as a result of the new band's members' previous careers: "Simon's got the hardest job. Primarily I'm a guitarist so I've got my eagle eye on him. Left to his own devices he comes up with some lovely stuff, although when I ask him to play something of mine he has problems with it." This attitude was to be indicative of the whole new environment, and emphasised the fact that they fully intended to heed the three key lessons which the painful split from The Sisters had taught them. Firstly, that the band would not be ruled by the self-indulgent iron-fist of one leader and that it would be fully democratic - although Hussey provided all the musical material initially there was a full democracy working inside the band camp; secondly, they honed their awareness of the business element of the music industry which The Sisters had used to such great effect, and armed with this were fully prepared to inflict their pre-meditated plan on the press and public; and thirdly, they determined that the mayhem and excess that had so notoriously dominated The Sisters tour days was to be continued with complete and utter abandon.

So with this dichotomous approach of a pre-meditated business angle and a completely spontaneous musical direction, The Sisterhood booked their first ever gig, at The Alice in Wonderland venue in Dean Street in London's Soho. The event was bound to attract frenzied music press attention, but this situation was exacerbated by one mischievous fan spreading the rumour that it was a reformed Sisters of Mercy that would actually be appearing. And so it was to a packed club that The Sisterhood stumbled on sometime after midnight, bathed in meagre lighting and sandwiched between the tiny stage and the low ceiling. Hussey launched into the opening number 'Wasteland' at completely the wrong rhythm causing the others to stumble in when they saw fit, and leaving Dave Vanian of The Damned who was watching from the DJ booth, clutching his belly and rolling around in tears of laughter. In addition to this rather ignominious entrance, most of the audience had by now realised that the rumoured Sisters re-union was not going to materialise and disgruntled noises began to escape from all corners, with shouts for old Sisters songs growing ever more incessant. "We don't play that stuff anymore" retorted Hussey and stormed on regardless, but the gig was ultimately doomed to peter out after only forty minutes, mostly because they were all helplessly drunk. However, behind the dry ice and drunkenness there was a hint that The Sisterhood had something different and unique. The set had its share of shambolic points, but it also had some highlights which suggested a potential way beyond the mediocre blues and club bands that the venue normally featured. There was a song called 'Serpent's Kiss' which silenced the doubters in the crowd with its thunderous momentum, and the opener 'Wasteland' seemed to transform the band away from the seedy surroundings onto an enormous musical landscape. There was still the ominous tone of The Sisters of Mercy on many songs, but there was another element, a pop side to this new band, which peaked in a brief song called 'Severina', when all the chaos seemed to evaporate and the group suddenly made a lot of sense. Refreshingly, there was no distance between the band and their audience - Hussey handled the crowd with an instinctive ease throughout, contrasted by the ever-present swirling guitar which created an impressive atmosphere matched perfectly by the dark and romantic imagery of the band themselves. Eldritch and much of the press had instantly dismissed The Sisterhood before they had even played one gig - as the crowd disappeared into the dingy streets of London on that night the thought that played on many of their minds was simple: 'Maybe The Sisterhood have something special after all?'

And so despite a calamitous debut ("We were fortunate that we actually stood up for 45 minutes"), the foursome headed for the most famous of rock and roll hotels, The Columbia, which was to witness the first manifestation of their soon-to-be-notorious collective approach to after-gig entertainment, perhaps best voiced by Mick: "It was a complete and unmitigated disaster that gig, but we celebrated like The Rolling Stones afterwards. You know, back at The Columbia, completely rat-arsed."

This dubious start was followed a week later by the first airing the band had on national radio, when they recorded a session for the Janice Long Show on BBC Radio 1, appearing as The Wayne Hussey and Craig Adams Band, rather than under The Sisterhood banner. This was most people's first chance to hear the music of the much-publicised new group. Tracks included were 'And the Dance Goes On', 'Severina', 'Sacrilege', as well as a pomped-up version of Neil Young's epic 'Like a Hurricane'. Although the session was brief, there was an air of confidence about the band - already they seemed to know where they were heading. With the show completed and off air, the switchboard was flooded with phonecalls from excited listeners asking about the band and where they could hear them next - the word was spreading. With this session behind them the band were eagerly scouting for gigs to satiate this rapidly growing curiosity from a intrigued public who had now heard the quality of their songs away from the drunken Alice in Wonderland debacle. They would not have to wait long. Whilst staying at Hussey's house, Billy Duffy, guitarist from The Cult and long time friend of The Sisterhood's singer, asked them whether they would like to support his outfit across Europe in February - such an opportunity for a band only three weeks old was not one to be missed. However, there were two major obstacles in their way which threatened to sabotage their chance of getting off to a flying start. Firstly they didn't have a manager - at this stage the administration of the band was mostly done by Hussey and was already becoming a major distraction from his challenging new role as singer, guitarist and frontman. Secondly, the band needed £5000 to cover the expenses of The Cult tour, and they had only eight days before the deadline. On the Monday before the tour things looked bleak with neither a manager nor any money in sight.

Enter Tony Perrin, former manager and flatmate of Hinkler, and well-known local music entrepreneur. After dropping out of his degree course he had become involved in an independent music label in Sheffield and eventually manager of one of the acts on that label, Artery. Having left the label to manage them for four years he had good experience with the politics of looking after a band. The Sisterhood had a shortlist of three managers' names but Hinkler knew them all and also knew that Perrin could do a much better job, so he was contacted. Perrin was confident of his ability but freely admitted that the scale The Sisterhood were already working on was a new area to him: "With Artery I never really tried to deal with major record companies and big business, but when these guys came along it was immediately obvious that this was a completely different league and that this was probably my opportunity to make things work and step up into this big league. Although they were only looking at one album at this stage, it was always in the back of my mind that these guys were different - I didn't analyse it that coldly, there was just something about them, it was more a case of the bus was leaving for Europe, let's get on it and go."

Before they could do that there was the small matter of finding £5000 to finance the tour. The band were introduced to Perrin through Hinkler and immediately liked what they saw. They offered him the job as manager on condition that he find the money for the tour - this was only eight days before the bus was pulling off to leave. Not one to be pressured, Perrin took stock of the situation in his own time: "They wanted me for the job and basically said 'You can have it if you can get us £5000 by Friday to do this Cult tour'. So I said I'd think about it over the weekend and phone them on Sunday at rehearsals before 5 o'clock. I went to Dave Hall, whom I had done flyposters for over the years in Sheffield - he was trying to get a new merchandise company off the ground so I told him we needed £10,000 and £5000 of it in cash by the end of the week. He agreed to buy our merchandise rights, principally because he knew all about The Sisters and that they sold shitloads of T-shirts."

So on the Sunday before the proposed tour, The Sisterhood tried to rehearse in a small studio but were distracted by wondering whether Perrin had managed to find the money or not. There was a big tour at stake and he had promised to call them on Sunday afternoon. The tension mounted. Back at his house, Perrin was sunk into his favourite armchair, sipping a beer and watching the 'Lord of the Rings' film on television, which he had never seen before. In the back of his mind he knew he was supposed to phone The Sisterhood and inform them of his decision, but it was a great film. He vowed to call as soon as it was finished. Two hours passed and whilst Frodo and Bilbo Baggins were still fighting the warlords of Mordor, The Sisterhood were becoming increasingly anxious waiting on the phone. Finally, the phone rang, Hussey jumped on it and relayed the good news that Perrin had the cash - the tour was on. Perrin takes up the story: "Wayne said 'You're a bit bloody late...' Anyway, I got the job and we met up with Dave Hall in a motorway service station on the way to the ferry to join The Cult tour. He handed over a plastic bag containing £5000 in used fivers in the middle of the night on the M1, we jumped on the bus and before I knew what had happened I was on tour with The Sisterhood in Europe".

*   *   *

If the Columbia Hotel in London was to be the first witness of their excess after a single gig at Alice in Wonderland, Europe was to be the first to see them let loose over a whole tour, even though this one was only twelve days long in total. It was to be a major testing ground for the new group and threw them in front of relatively large audiences, irreverent of their infancy - their second ever gig in Utrecht's Muzik Zentrum was to a packed crowd of 2000. The Cult were solidly established with a loyal following but this did not intimidate The Sisterhood - they launched into the tour with all the confidence that their earlier press declarations had hinted at; The Cult found themselves supported by a virgin band who were threatening to distract their own hard-earned following. Hussey recognised this himself at the time: "I think The Cult have alienated a lot of their fans and that audience is there for the taking...Our criterion is that if it sounds good when we play it on an acoustic guitar in my living room then it's a good song...The majority of the songs we've been doing in the set so far are my songs that Andrew rejected for The Sisters' second album. It's ironic 'cos he saw us at Birmingham and told us how good he thought the songs were."

Despite some critical reviews from European press who failed to see past The Sisters Of Mercy legacy with any objectivity (the Noorderlicht club even billed them as 'The Sisterhood (ex-Sisters of Mercy)'), the tour was well received. The European audience were very open-minded to this new band and although the majority of the set was new material, the reactions were very enthusiastic. With many songs clearly in their infancy, there was much room for development, but at the same time there were already highlights of the 40 minute set (which never took more than 25 minutes because of the copious amounts of speed the band were using). 'Wasteland' was invariably well received and other brighter moments such as 'Severina', 'Sacrilege' and 'Garden of Delight', as well as the two covers of 'Like A Hurricane' and 'Wishing Well' were proving similarly popular.

As well as being well received by the audience, the tour was well enjoyed by the band. The group were clearly not unnerved by the prospect of playing to four figure houses every night - the bigger the crowd, the more they celebrated. With a copy of the American beatnik writer Hunter S. Thompson's 'Fear and Loathing in Las Vegas' under one arm, serving as a joint tour itinerary with the notorious Led Zeppelin history 'Hammer of the Gods' under the other, The Sisterhood introduced Europe to their own particular brand of touring, with their every move fuelled by vast quantities of speed.

They were not alone in their antics - when they had split from The

Sisters of Mercy, Hussey and Adams had taken the road crew with them, and in the words of John Langford "had sucked the best of the Leeds youth into their crew, like the chain gang". With Jez Webb on backline, Phil Wiffen on lights, Pete Turner on out-front sound and completed by Nipper, The Sisterhood had taken the community atmosphere from The Sisters and transplanted it straight into their camp. As well as the ex-Sisters crew there was also Eds, Steve 'Sex Pistol' Watson and Grape, who along with the rest of the crew lived the lifestyle as much as the band and were as essential to its very existence as the band themselves. After one show they went to an Irish bar and asked the barman for the hardest drink he had, something unusual. After his suggestions of various cocktails and other bizarre beverages were laughed off the bar, he finally bent down behind the counter and produced a small silver canister containing nitrous oxide, laughing gas. Suitably inebriated, the group spotted a drunken heavy metal type wandering around aimlessly outside the club, dragged him in by the hair and removed most of his clothes leaving him sprawled on the dance floor. By this stage the nitrous oxide had taken full effect and people were dropping like flies. The party stumbled to a 24-hour ten pin bowling alley which was fully computerised and only required the odd ball to be rolled down towards the skittles in the distance every five minutes in between the crates of beer they had purchased from a bewildered barman.

After another show, Webb and Grape decided to exact revenge on The Cult's drum roadie, who had displayed the audacity to decline an evening out with them in favour of an incredibly attractive German girl. Having placed a bucket full of water over his door frame, the two sneaked round to his balcony and opened fire with a large industrial fire hose. Understandably annoyed at being drenched when relations had been progressing very well with the girl, the roadie leapt up from the bed, pulled up his trousers and ripped open the door screaming violent threats at the two assailants who were fleeing down the corridor. The consequent downpour of water from the overhead bucket ruined metres of the hotel carpet as well as any remaining chance he'd had with the unfortunate girl. The next day the hotel receptionist saw two large unkempt men with their chins dropped and hands behind their backs like errant schoolboys, being lectured by The Cult tour manager, whose nagging forefinger accentuated his rhetorical question 'Am I right in saying you boys did a bit of damage last night?' They were fined half their wages for the entire tour. Not content with that, Hinkler, Adams and Ian Astbury were then arrested for stealing bikes after a gig in a club in Amsterdam which was previously a Nazi interrogation centre.

Perhaps the most striking feature of this tour however, was the colossal amount of drugs that the band were taking. The amphetamine haze of The Sisters was carried through into the first tour of this new group with increased vigour, and for Hinkler it was an incredible experience: "It was fucking mind blowing. To have gone from playing relatively small places with relatively small crowds to playing with The Cult to big audiences so quickly was amazing. I'd never done such vast quantities of speed and alcohol either, we did so much on that first tour it defied belief. It was something I'd never previously envisaged myself doing. I don't like to do things by halves, so I thought if I'm going to do this whole rock 'n' roll monster thing I've got to do it properly or not at all".

*   *   *

The aftermath of the European tour was very much a mixed bag. On the one hand they had enjoyed a wild time and had broken the band into the rigours of extensive touring. At the time Brown was very excited about it all: "Take it from me these lads are the fucking business, although they do nick absolutely everything - I came out with ten pairs of clean underpants and I've got one left". "We learnt in front of people, it was a good laugh. We travelled on their bus, it was the first time that any of us had been on a proper big rock 'n' roll coach. We had a good time, although we were indulging in things that maybe weren't too good for us." He continues "When we walked on at Utrecht for the first Cult gig, nobody knew anything about us because The Sisters of Mercy meant nothing in Holland - when we walked on there was a big cheer, and when we walked off there was still a big cheer. It was a case of 'Yes, we can do it'. It was fucking brilliant from start to finish, it gave us a great start". Hussey also suggested at the time that touring was something the band could easily accommodate: "Touring is partly a holiday, playing gigs is secondary. I could go onstage pissed out of my head and know I could play the songs inside out. Auto pilot." Hussey's feelings were shared by his colleagues, although Adam's memory was more selective: "The only thing I can remember is falling over at the last gig."

On the other hand there had been a degree of friction between the last member to join, Hinkler, and the other three musicians. The band took drastic action - the guitarist was sacked as soon as they landed back in Britain. Hussey probably best explains why they chose the dramatic course of sacking a member they had recently worked so hard to find "During that tour it all went to Simon's head because he'd not experienced it before whereas we had. The Cult were very busy with TV shows so we'd help get their bags but Simon would just pick his up and walk off to his room. He'd walk into the dressing rooms like a real idiot, a real pain. On the bus on the way back we were all doing speed and crying to each other saying 'We've got to sack him, we've got to sack him'. It had been such a good tour so this was all the worse for it." Tony Perrin, closest to Hinkler and displaying the objectivity that is such an essential prerequisite for any successful band manager, saw another angle on the episode: "The dismissal happened about ten minutes after we'd got back off the coach from The Cult tour. We had three UK shows lined up and the tour had gone well, but everybody was really quiet on the coach journey back. There had been a lot of discussion about whether we should play these three UK dates or not and Craig, for one reason or another, was dead against these shows. To this day I think that Craig forced the situation to try and avoid playing these gigs - it had as much to do with that as Simon himself. We walked in to the hotel back in London and Craig just told Simon he was sacked. There had been disagreements and they felt it wasn't working out. Simon told me later it was the lowest point in his life when he got back up to Sheffield after being sacked and went to his empty flat which hadn't been occupied for a month and was absolutely freezing".

"As it turned out, he needn't have worried, because after a brief interlude they re-instated him for the handful of UK dates. When I asked him to play on these shows, he asked me if they were using him, manipulating him and I lied and said 'No'. Maybe that event left him with a chip on his shoulder about his value to the band, maybe not, but I do think that it under-pinned the whole relationship from then on, although having said all that, it wasn't an issue that was bubbling under all the time, and it was forgotten about as soon as things started to work out." Indeed, Hussey was soon much happier about Hinkler's approach: "When we re-instated him it was still very temporary, but I think he realised you can't have an attitude with the people you work with. You have to make an effort to get on with people, and he'd mellowed out so that his real personality came through." Even though they had suffered a minor set-back with this personnel trouble, it was clear that their overriding perspective and optimism refused to be dampened, as Brown recalls: "Things still looked good.. Right from the beginning there's always been a good attitude over-riding generally. A good feeling, so whenever the shit hits the fan, there's been an ability to cope with it. It's part of the nature of the band." Similarly, Adams refused to let his new successes go to his head and relished memories of his return home: "When I came back from The Cult tour, I went to live with Jez and Grape. We had no money, so we slept all day and stayed up all night because there's nowhere to spend our money anyway - it works quite well as long as you've got some cigarettes, coffee and tea. We used to listen to local radio all night and enter the competitions so we could get free stickers. We used to call ourselves The Beaver Boys, and Mick used to come over because he only lived round the corner. We'd play cards and enter the competitions and get the DJ to say 'Hello to the Beaver Boys of Headingley'. One night he asked us what it meant and Grape said 'I can't really explain it over the air.'"

The Sisterhood had hit the ground running and were snapping up any opportunities that came their way to further the band's cause. One of these chances came in the form of the bitter press controversy with Eldritch. With Hinkler re-instated on guitar, the band were back on track and ready to play the three UK dates, which by now were much-anticipated media events as well as gigs. The reason for this was simple - in the first two months of the group's existence The Sisterhood became involved in one of the bitterest and most widely publicised arguments ever to grace the pages of the music press. Incensed by

Hussey and Adam's apparent disregard for his ownership of The Sisters of Mercy name, Eldritch had launched attack after attack against what he saw as the bastard sons of The Sisters, through the press and later via solicitors letters. He was supported or antagonised by a fierce and unprecedented battle of their respective followers in the letters pages of the Melody Maker and continually baited by The Sisterhood themselves. The dispute became known as the corporate wars, with Eldritch claiming he had seven counts on which to take them to court, that he had been betrayed by his former colleagues, and he continually issued press releases to the effect that The Sisterhood were a rogue outfit which would go away if they were ignored. The irony was that the more Eldritch denounced them, the more he perpetuated public awareness of the band and the less likely it was that they would indeed vanish as he had predicted. His own sword was turned against him and was backed up by the fact that while he was fighting a war of words, The Sisterhood were taking it on the road and playing to the masses. Every written accusation by Eldritch was best answered by a Sisterhood gig - in this fashion they won many Sisters fans over to their camp, people who had become disillusioned with the lack of live Sisters shows after Eldritch had decamped to Hamburg. In many cases the followers were as much into the lifestyle of the Sisters as the music itself and whilst Eldritch licked his wounds, inactive in Hamburg, here was a band who were living every minute of their lives as if it was their last, this was a real and genuine alternative. In addition, many of the more discerning fans realised how influential Hussey and Adams had been in The Sisters and that to a certain extent they had made the band what they were live. Furthermore, if these weren't reasons enough for The Sisterhood to prolong and exacerbate the press controversy, apart from the obvious good publicity, the name served as an ideal medium to extricate themselves from a poor contract and relationship with WEA, which was a legacy of Hussey and Adam's days under Eldritch's watchful eye. WEA could not release any records under that name so unless they released them they had a dead band and financial loss on their hands.

Whilst The Sisterhood blazed their way through Europe supporting The Cult the battle in the press raged on. Eldritch appeared in various magazines claiming they had fostered the impression they could play as The Sisters of Mercy (because of the rumour surrounding the Alice In Wonderland gig), that they only used his name to get press, that they were contractually obliged not to use his names, that they owed him varying large sums of money and that they had betrayed him and stole his road crew. He also eulogised about their musical ethics: "Their ability to bend over forwards in order to make progress appals me...I never sang a lyric of Wayne's, I never found one I could sing." He suggested that Hussey's songs were "particularly vacuous..the guy didn't have a clue - he'd just string buzz words together."[4] As part of the final insult he set up and ran a competition in the music press to find 'poor Wayne's band' a proper name. The phenomenon was not restricted to the UK alone - on The Cult tour The Sisterhood found foreign journalists especially infatuated by the controversy, and Brown and Hinkler were especially tired of the repeated questions about something they had no part in but had merely inherited. The press and public alike thrive on personal conflict and this controversy was tailor made for the papers - the majority of The Sisterhood's first interviews were nothing more than an autopsy on The Sisters of Mercy, and eventually the new band issued a directive that journalists were not to ask any more questions about The Sisters.

Eventually something had to give and it was The Sisterhood who appeared to capitulate, but on closer inspection not before they had bled the situation for all it was worth. Tony Perrin explains: "Fairly early on we were all enjoying causing mischief and flying in the face of it all. We had nothing they could have sued us for so we just went for it. We'd certainly figured out our plan of action long before we finally changed the name. Pretty early on we decided to ride the press and it was essentially quite calculated. But I think Eldritch perpetuated it longer than anyone else bothered. We'd still get letters from his lawyers ages after but nothing would ever come of it. The whole thing cost us legal bills and that's all, the rumours about big losses by us were all rubbish, it was never going to court. When I saw the contracts Wayne and Craig had signed in The Sisters I was appalled, but that was the way Eldritch worked. I was really an outsider to all this so it was a problem I inherited and Wayne made a lot of the decisions then anyway. We enjoyed it and when it was spent we left it there. Ultimately though it had a very positive effect on us in many ways.

Perhaps best of all, the whole episode set us up as the underdogs and there's nothing the British public love more than that."

The other Sisters splinter band, Gary Marx's Ghost Dance achieved nowhere near as much publicity and notoriety during the same period, even though they appeared to have more chance of success when Marx was joined by Anne Marie from Skeletal Family to form a band that seemed tailor-made to fit the demands of the burgeoning goth fraternity. However, Hussey clearly knew what he was doing and was unashamed about such manipulation of the business, and stated their case with clarity and honesty: "We are more willing as a group to play the game. With The Sisters of Mercy it was part of the psychology not to. I came from Dead Or Alive who were commercially very successful in Britain. The reason they were more successful, more than anything else is because they played the game. There are ways of doing that and keeping your dignity. Not playing the game is copping out. The accusation that most groups get once they've reached a certain level is that they've sold out - that's bullshit. The decision to sell out was made when you formed your first group. You're in a group, you want to sell records and get as big an audience as possible. It's a learning process. Being in a group is 75% being aware of the business and 25% being aware of the musical aspects of it."

The Sisterhood only played one full gig under that name in the UK - the three dates which awaited them on their return from Europe, including the notorious show at The Electric Ballroom, were chosen to be the vehicle with which to announce the final chapter of the name controversy that had so intrigued the public until now. A fortnight earlier Eldritch had released a single under the name The Sisterhood called 'Giving Ground' which topped the Indie charts even though Eldritch himself was not singing on the track - the release was nothing more than a spoiler, and it worked. Thus Hussey and his band were forced to change their name and chose to use these dates to announce The Mission publically. The shows themselves saw the foursome ready for whatever they faced, with their show honed by their dates on the Continent. They blasted out a set that had people seriously doubting any of the accusations that this band would be a passing phase, with highlights including the opener 'Wasteland', as well as tracks such as 'Garden of Delight', 'Hurricane', 'Serpents Kiss', 'Stay with

Me', and 'Sacrilege' and a rendition of the Sisters favourite '1969'. In a gesture that was to become their trademark, the band finished with the encore of 'Shelter from the Storm'. Apart from the obvious importance of the gig as far as the new name was concerned, the band themselves remember the actual music with some reservation, most of all Adams: "That was a disastrous gig. Mick had drunk vast quantities and then his bass drum pedal broke. We didn't have spares in those days so he had to play bass drum on the tom-tom and it got worse and worse. We all thought we'd really screwed that up." Brown was equally embarrassed: "Everything that could break did. I remember coming off, I ran straight outside and started banging my head against a wall. Billy Duffy came out and stood behind me going 'You should be more professional' and I'm braining myself thinking 'Tell me about it.'" Nevertheless the crowd and most notably, the attendant press were bowled over. Mat Smith from Melody Maker became an instant convert: "In the end all it took was musical differences. Tonight though it all made a perverse kind of sense - Eldritch lounging in the shadows attempting to retain his aura of myth and mystique while Wayne and Craig take it on the road. It was up there swathed in dry ice and white light that the legend was born."[5] Mr. Spencer of Sounds was equally enthusiastic: "It's such a happy discovery. This music stands head and shoulders above all competition. Well, I never."[6] After the dramatic unveiling of the name in London, the backdrop snagged yet again the following night in Birmingham - a writ prevented it from snagging at all in Leeds as Eldritch had the gig cancelled. The introduction of The Mission may not have been as glorious as planned but it had the desired effect. There would be no more shouts for 'Temple Of Love'.

CHAPTER THREE

"It started off as a fairly small thing. We just took it over because we managed to convince the guy that owned the pub that we could bring in more people than the local band he had playing there. He tried us out for a bit, and within two or three weeks there was a huge line outside until it became a huge event".

Keith Richards of The Rolling Stones

WITH a deliberate policy of prolific gigging in mind, The Mission set out to capture the legions of fans that their first shows had hinted at. After passing over the alternative name choices of Crystal Religion and Love Patrol the band had opted for The Mission, partly inspired by the brand name of Hussey's speakers and partly by the book his mother had bought him for his proposed Mormon adventures. In typical style there was even a hiccup before this could be clarified - there was a band called The Mission from Birmingham who caused some concern initially after it was discovered they had already appeared under that name on a compilation LP called 'Live at the Thames Poly' the previous autumn. Once this minor problem had been solved The Mission were free to take up the offer of a gig in Valencia, Spain, an ideal warm-up for their forthcoming twelve date British tour.

Not being in a position to afford a full crew, The Mission headed for the airport where Tony Perrin found himself filling in for the first and last time as Tour Manager, with Steve Sex Pistol working the lights and Grape ending up as backline roadie, simply because they couldn't afford anyone else. On arrival they were confronted by posters billing them as 'The Mission (Formerly the Sisters of Mercy)' and were promptly informed by the manager of the venue that there would be two shows, one at midnight and the second at 5 in the morning. Perrin takes up the story: "We debated it between us and then agreed that we'd do it if they'd find us a few grammes of wizz to keep us awake all night. The first show was electric, but as soon as we'd finished everybody buggered off, the venue totally emptied and I instantly thought they'd done a runner with the money and everything, and I was convinced we wouldn't see a penny". He needn't have worried - after spending an anxious four hours in a dingy dressing room contemplating the fate of the appearance fee, The Mission trudged towards the stage. Suddenly, as they were setting up, at five minutes to five, hordes of locals began to appear from the shadows, converging on the venue in vast numbers from nowhere. Suitably inspired and somewhat relieved, the set was blistering. The next night they were followed by a suspiciously young local girl, who was ecstatic when they offered her a drink more out of sympathy than anything else, hoping she would then leave them alone. Unfortunately, she took this as a gesture of friendship and followed them around every bar and club in town at a discreet distance. Towards the end of the evening a large and irate local woman, evidently the young girl's mother, stormed into the bar they were currently drinking dry and emptied glasses of beer over the band, hurling abuse at them and then dragging the girl out of the bar by a massive forearm. On leaving the bar, wet but relieved, the band and crew headed for the hotel but as they turned a corner the band noticed the same girl slinking through the shadows after them again, only this time she had started to remove all her clothes as she was walking. They legged it. Arriving back at the hotel they were greeted by the sight of their old tour backdrop fluttering from an eighth floor balcony high above. Making it at last to the safety of their room, they opened the curtains and were confronted by the one crew member who had stayed in, tight-rope walking along the balcony eight stories up, out of his head on acid.

The band returned home after this brief but eventful excursion and went straight into rehearsals. Unfortunately, because of the suffocating contracts Hussey and Adams had signed with WEA whilst in The Sisters of Mercy, they were now contractually obliged to continue any future projects with that label. Very soon however, it was evident that this would not be a fruitful relationship and the atmosphere was not helped by the bitter press controversy still raging with Eldritch. The record company would not give them any funding, nor would they release them out of what was a stifling and unworkable contract - The Mission found themselves in the immensely frustrating position of being a live working band with an audience there for the taking but unable to record, get the proper backing from WEA or even change companies, despite the many labels who had already approached the band. They faced a deadlock and possible suffocation. Previously the band had tried to provoke WEA into action but it had not worked and their relationship was rapidly deteriorating. Hussey remembers going to WEA with the finished demo of 'Serpent's Kiss': "I put down the guitar solo and all of a sudden it sounded like a song, but they said I couldn't sing. Great songs, Wayne, but we recommend you look up these people as singers, and they shoved a list under my nose that included Pete Murphy, Sal Solo, Gavin from the Virgin Prunes, and Andi Sex Gang. They had absolutely no perception of what we wanted to do at all. It showed you what they thought of The Sisters of Mercy as well...I knew then that we had to get off WEA. Mick was livid - that's when we decided to really antagonise them, and really that's what a lot of all the stuff about The Sisterhood was for. But those first few months really strengthened our resolve, formed the character of the band if you like." Even after a WEA representative had seen the storming Birmingham Powerhaus show in March, he was not impressed despite this healthy press reaction: "The Mission have the human touch. Hussey treats the stage as a few planks of wood rather than an ivory tower."[1] The WEA man still said they had no future, but would they like to reform The Sisters? Tunnel vision prevailed.

Such myopia was all the more frustrating because the band were being visited by so many other companies at this stage - at The Electric Ballroom show in February Dave Bates and Charlie Eyre from Phonogram had turned up with The Mission's agent Martin Horne, but since it looked for all intents and purposes that WEA were going to strangle them in a contract Perrin saw no reason to give them free tickets so he refused to let them in unless they bought one at the box office. Turning away prominent A&R men was not something that the band intended to do very often, so on the advice of a lawyer, they decided to independently release 'Serpent's Kiss' to force WEA's hand into action of some kind.

There was no guarantee that this would work however - indeed WEA were within their rights to sue the band, particularly as the single to be released had been recorded as part of the first session at Driffield at Warner's expense. Perrin recalls that even when the decision had been made to release 'Serpent's Kiss' on the Birmingham based Chapter 22 label (later home to Pop Will Eat Itself and Ned's Atomic Dustbin) all was not that simple: "I called the office at WEA and fully expected them to refuse my request for the master tapes - when I got there the tapes were lying on a desk, nobody else was there, they were just lying around. The decision wasn't too difficult to make. I just grabbed them and legged it." So in May 1986, The Mission released their first single even though they legally did not own the recording - they figured that if they were sued it would be yet more good press. There was no guarantee that the single would get any reaction and the band could be sued for breach of contract and find themselves forever locked into a bitter and fruitless wrangle with a totally disinterested label. It was a gamble.

'Serpent's Kiss' entered the Indie Charts at No.1, the first time this had ever happened with a debut single. It massively outsold its nearest rival that week and went on to easily become the biggest selling independent single of the year. The release even dented the Gallop charts at No.70, where it stayed for three weeks, was Indie No.1 in Germany and twelve months later still occasionally re-entered the charts. It was only knocked off the top spot by The Smiths 'Bigmouth Strikes Again' but Morrisey's band soon fell away whilst Serpents Kiss stayed at No. 2 for six more weeks. In short, the gamble had worked.

The song itself was supposedly based on Satanist Aleister Crowley's book 'Moonchild', where a serpent's kiss was an erotic greeting from a man who would bite into a woman's bottom lip, prompting ill-founded rumours that Hussey was a practising Satanist. The track displayed all the trademarks that had seen The Mission championed as the leading new goths - the adrenalin rush of the A-side was contrasted by the much darker flip side of 'Wake', but there was also a vibrancy that lifted it out of the excessive gloom that had suffocated so many Sisters' tracks. The infectious guitar arpeggios were complemented by Hussey's low-sung vocal until the chorus, when the song threw off any remnants of Eldritch's sombre tones, and Hussey displayed his capable incipient voice. Lyrically, there was still the particular focus associated with gothics:

"Candles flicker and the devil dances on the wall"
and "A serpent's kiss, on the witching hour,

A serpent's kiss, on that untouched flower"

The track did not however, lose itself amongst such dark imagery - Hussey's guitar detail was bursting with hook lines and melodies and the thundering drums and dexterous bass gave the song a driving momentum that would become associated with all Mission tracks. Hussey was very excited by the result: "We recorded 'Serpent's Kiss' in October and when we'd finished it was a real feeling of elation - I think that record has a really joyous sound." It was a remarkable debut.

The press, whose pages had been filled with so much controversy about this new band, gave the single a mixed reaction. Many remained non-committal: "I sat in a candle-lit room for this one, wanting to create the gloomy gothic atmosphere that surrounded The Sisters of Mercy. They can either suffocate in clinging, ungrateful cobwebs or come up for air. The decision's yours."[2] The less serious magazines were more forthcoming, such as Short who called it "moody, mildly malevolent with a definite touch of class"[3] - however, already it was evident that The Mission provoked a very definite response from some quarters, with the signs of a love/hate relationship developing. The NME were most uncharitable: "The Cult, er sorry, The Mission...screeching guitars and the drumbeat is more monotonous than a drum machine. Tinny and dull."[4]

The video for the single was a classic - the band knew three days in advance that the single was going to be Indie No.1 so they hastily scraped together £2000 and over a 72 hour panic filmed a home-made video featuring Adams dressed as the devil chasing the others around a park, with everybody playing soccer, pulling faces and generally behaving like a gang of schoolboys. It was completed just in time to rush it across London to The Whistle Test studio where the band, along with the public, saw the finished product for the first time. The light-hearted nature of the spoof video gave it an appeal that brought success. The fledgling Chart Show was in the middle of a dispute with BPI about the costs of videos and subsequently were not showing many promotionals. The independent effort by The Mission landed on their desk with a note saying 'You can show this as much as you want. Ta'. They did and the video featured on the show for weeks. Hinkler still feels that this was their best moment on video, a medium the band would struggle to come to terms with over the years: "I love that video so much, it showed what we are as people. When I'm 60 years old, I'm sure that it's that video that'll stand as a testament to this period of my life. It pretty much tells the whole story."

Despite the lashings of comedy some people still chose to interpret this release as pompous, serious and a confirmation of their status as the new messiahs of goth, just as The Sisters of Mercy had been warmly welcomed to the fold back in the early 1980's. The gothic tag was something that the band would carry with them for a long time, and despite their denials it is easy to see how the accusations arose. Presentation such as the early artwork by Sandy Ball, and concert programme texts all appeared to build a mythology around the band. The tours were given names such as 'Expedition 1' and the songs carried titles like 'Serpent's Kiss', 'Blood Brother' and 'Wasteland'. Lyrics such as 'Star Child' 'Sacrilege, burning on the funeral pyre, toss and turn on the cross to burn' all fuelled the conceived gothic status. In addition, the band's appearance was to many a confirmation of their suspicions, with the abundance of dark hair, black leather and flowing shirts, with Hussey hiding behind his now trademark dark glasses and wide brimmed hat. The band themselves argued that all this romantic imagery was very light-hearted and humourous - one interviewer was greeted by an empty room with a bat hanging from the ceiling and a sign saying 'Welcome to Goth City'. Adams choice of clothing was more by accident than anything else - his sombre military style black hat was given to him by the elderly landlord of a cheap bed and breakfast they had once stayed in for the night, after the old man had taken to the bass player and decided he wanted to offer him a gift. The band and their close followers knew it was all tongue-in-cheek, and that the 'doom and gloom' imagery of goth that many of their fans ardently pursued was not matched by the band themselves. Even so, the image of any band is essentially how the public perceives them, not how the band perceive themselves, and because many could not see the private joke that was The Mission, they became inevitably embroiled in the whole goth movement.

Gothic or not, 'Serpent's Kiss' had a massive effect on The Mission's popularity and finally nailed any derogatory Sisters remarks - Eldritch released 'Gift' as The Sisterhood and the first words on the record were '2,5,0,0,0' reputedly the amount he had won from The Mission in the courts (infact it was the amount of the advance that Eldritch had received from RCA on release of the album). Meanwhile, whilst he was busy arguing with himself, The Mission had set up a new group and had now taken the nation's youth by storm.

* * *

Hussey is convinced of the important effect that the catalyst of 'Serpent's' success was to have on the band's future career: "The impact of having a successful independent single is far greater than having a major single that just gets into the Top 100. That initial period was very good for us in terms of character building because we went through a lot of traumas and trouble, financially as much as anything." Now the band were very much in the driving seat as far as record companies were concerned. The attempt to force WEA's hand had worked - they were released from their contracts soon after they had made it clear that The Mission were going to release a second independent single. The band had now broken loose of the stranglehold WEA had held over their careers, and they exploited this newfound freedom to the full.

On 24th May, 1986, The Mission launched into a 12 date tour of the UK, known as Expedition 1, where incredibly they played to sold out crowds every night. The tour opened at Glasgow QMU and included nights at London's Town & Country Club, Manchester International and Nottingham Rock City with support from one of

Hussey's former bands, Pauline Murray and the Storm, as well as Leeds' favourites The Batfish Boys. The shows were well received by the press who acknowledged that The Mission had already established their own identity: "Like a Gothic Faces, The Mission can be pissed as rats but they'll play like demons. They can be almost incapable of standing up, yet they can still strut, sweat and sneer their way through a performance with an uncontrollable whiplash energy that is a pure joy to behold."[5] Unfortunately, there were signs that a section of the press had taken a disliking to the band and there were many viciously critical reviews, probably more so than complimentary ones. Roger Holland accused them of losing the humour that he felt had apparently been an integral part of The Sisters and went on to say "They churn out a curdling and soulless big time rock mediocrity, while a crowd, who probably never got the joke in the first place, sing along, oblivious. This is inexcusable."[6] Another reviewer was equally uncharitable: "Pompous 19th century opera-noise...(with) lyrics all about serpents and razor's edges and cracked mirrors and so forth"[7] whilst Andy Hughes was a little more succinct, saying The Mission reminded him of "the noise of someone rolling marbles down a coal shute."[8]

Despite the frequently severe criticism aimed at them in the press the band continued their tour frenzy unabated. After only the third gig Hussey was banned indefinitely from Leeds Warehouse for being discovered 'in flagrante' with a young girl in a toilet cubicle. The gig itself was the singer's birthday so the punishment was perhaps a little harsh - especially since the show had been a stormer, made all the more difficult by the fact it was their first show in their home town. It was reviewed in glowing terms by Nigel Holtby of Record Mirror who asserted that The Mission had officially defeated The Sisters, even having the front to play The Sisters favourite '1969' and Patti Smith's 'Dancing Barefoot'. The humour and familiarity of Hussey's rapport with the audience proved that The Mission had once and for all scorched the over-serious element which had threatened to drag so many of their contemporaries into tedium. At the prestigious Town & Country show, the intro music of The Dambusters March had built the atmosphere up to a suitable crescendo, and Adams had to hit only one bass string to launch into 'Wasteland'. He hit the string, it broke and the whole gig had to be stopped and re-started, leaving the band to fumble their way through a mediocre performance. A couple of nights later Hinkler came on stage, smashed into the first chord of 'Tomorrow Never Knows' and promptly fell backwards into his amps knocking them all over and leaving destruction and flying equipment in his wake. The next night Brown was so drunk that his only recollection of the gig was sitting at his kit and thinking 'Why won't my hands work?' At the penultimate gig in Hussey's home town of Bristol, with the on-tour water pistol collection now requiring its own flight case, two 14 year old girls hitched themselves on to the band entourage - Hussey heard on the local radio that the police were looking for them and immediately took them back home, where their frantic parents generously told him they were surprised how nice he was considering the way he looked. With the by now dog-eared copies of 'Hammer of the Gods' still tucked faithfully under their arms, The Mission swept the UK up in a wave of reports about drugged and drunken debauchery. with the press usually highlighting this and nothing else. Hussey reportedly turned up at one interview at 4pm having already downed eight bottles of wine, walked into the room and said 'Have you got any drugs?' With headlines such as 'Venice In Peril' The Mission headed for Europe for the second time that year - the Continent had been warned.

Climbing into one bulging Transit van with fourteen other people, a full backline of gear and a rear door tied shut with a length of oily rope, The Mission headed for the opening date of their first headline European tour, playing thirteen gigs in total and supported by the band 3000, Revs whose singer Grape and bassist Steve doubled up as Mission roadies. The warm-up show had been at Croydon Underground where they had begun as they meant to carry on, with Hussey vanishing into the belly of the venue for hours with the pretty manageress. Once in Germany, Grape wondered through the streets draped in a Japanese national flag, informing everybody that he was in fact Emperor Shinto, despite appearances to the contrary. The band also attempted to make some cultural conversation as befitted their historic surroundings - one afternoon was spent in hot and detailed debate as to whether the omnipresent scooters were 'poofy' or not. There was even some romance, a tender moment which is best described by Hussey: "Our roadie Grape was knobbing some girl on a park bench...it was five o'clock in the morning and the sun was coming up..."[9]

This tour also saw several fans following the band all the way around the Continent, displaying a dedication and spirit which The Mission themselves found hard to believe. During the trek through Germany one of these followers, Ramone was stopped at a Border Patrol and searched vigorously. After finding nothing of any note, the Officer took a step back and surveyed the bedraggled traveller standing in front of him and muttered something in his direction. The unfortunate Ramone couldn't make out what he'd said and only managed to decipher a couple of words. Once he had been allowed to go The Mission enthusiast headed eagerly for the next show. On arriving and meeting up with a few friends who had also made the massive journey he retold his story for their benefits. One of them asked him what the officer had said and Ramone answered 'I think he said Eskimo'. With those words a whole new way of life was born.

Despite a few bad reviews in the European press, the band played a consistently blistering set and were received warmly across all of Europe. In many cases the continent was much more open to their unique sound as The Sisters of Mercy held much less favour in Europe than the fanatical worship seen in Britain. The Mission returned home tired but successful and Perrin remembers how he already recognised the ability The Mission appeared to have: "It was clear on that first tour that so many of the ingredients needed were already evident, the songs, the members themselves, it was apparent that it would develop into something special. They knew exactly how and when they wanted to do things, so all I had to do was put things in place so that it would happen."

The massive popularity of The Mission had been confirmed at the start of their European tour when they released their second single, 'Garden of Delight/Like a Hurricane', again on the independent label Chapter 22. The track shot straight to No.1 in the Indie charts, their second consecutive chart topper and again a first for any band, even though both Depeche Mode and The Smiths also had new tracks out. The track was vocally darker than 'Serpent's Kiss' but with this song The Mission began to establish their own unique variation on the gothic theme - already there was a pop leaning in their material that suggested that the gothic tag would not be justified much longer, and 'Garden of Delight' reinforced this suspicion. There were vocal comparisons with Siouxie and the Banshees which had been mentioned with the first single also, and there was further recognition in the press that The Mission were displaying chart potential already far greater than anything The Sisters had ever hinted at. Despite Record Mirror calling it "pompous and very, very predictable" the public reaction was very healthy and the release strengthened the band's growing following. When the single was released, 'Serpent's Kiss' re-entered the indie chart and at one stage they were at No.2 and No.3 respectively, even though The Wedding Present and The Soup Dragons all had releases out that week. The release also punctured the Gallop Top 50 this time at No.45, where it stayed for a month and confirmed that The Mission's very real chart potential was building, even though it had to sell without the help of a promotional video. Their incredible and meteoric progress thus far would not be lost for long on the major record companies. The Mission were taking control.

* * *

Just after the release of the 'Garden of Delight' double A-side, The Mission's enormous potential was confirmed when they signed a seven year, worldwide recording contract with Phonogram. With such independent success and widespread publicity it was inevitable that The Mission would soon be snapped up by the major labels who had until now been warned away by their restrictive contractual obligations to WEA. With that matter now settled the band were open to offers, and they were very much in control of their destiny, an unusual situation for a new band to be able to dictate terms with a major label. Hussey did not see signing to Phonogram as any form of compromise, as many 'indie fascists' do - he knew they had signed a very flexible deal which would allow them a great deal of artistic freedom and he felt Phonogram had no choice: "We were obviously doing something right - our first two indie singles had both been No.1, and the second one almost charted in the Top 40 which was almost unheard of at that time.

We were selling out the T&C. When we signed, our royalty was 14% which was very good for an alternative band. Even though we'd only made about £20 on that first British tour, they knew we were a touring band and that that helps to sell records. We got a million pound advance for 7 albums, which was pretty serious money." The money, although obviously a major factor, was not the main reason why The Mission chose Phonogram however. Perrin remembers the refreshing attitude Phonogram had towards the band compared to the limited vision of WEA: "The first meetings with Phonogram were very positive - we got the feeling that they perceived us as something that was a lot bigger than just selling a few records off the back of The Sisters of Mercy. It took from March until July to negotiate but we liked the people we met so we signed on July 7th 1986, in the foyer of The Elysee Hotel in Hamburg. We could also sign off the dole now - during Expedition 1 in the UK the band had to go back to Leeds to sign on, it was ridiculous. We had a host of record companies after us and we could dictate. They didn't offer us the most money but they seemed the best bet because for one they were a worldwide company. Chapter 22 came to us after the second single with a package to take us on - they probably could have done the job in Britain but we were looking for something bigger, and Phonogram's worldwide nature appealed very much, plus the fact that they saw us as more than just a Sisters spin-off band."

The A&R man who signed the band and beat hordes of other open cheque books was Charlie Eyre, previously with A&M Records and the man who had signed Paul Young, Simply Red (publishing), Musical Youth, Nik Kershaw, and would go on to sign All About Eve and Zodiac Mindwarp to various deals. After Perrin refused him free entry to The Electric Ballroom gig four months earlier, Eyre had eventually squeezed in the backdoor and immediately took to what he saw on the stage that night: "There was something about them. I didn't know the songs at all, but they all seemed to know what they were doing, they had an audience there, the lights were good, it was very moody, but not as dark or foreboding as The Sisters, who I wasn't really a fan of. They were different. And Wayne, to me, looked like a star." Eyre watched the band hawkishly through Expedition 1 and jumped at the chance to sign them once they were released by WEA, even though he had not seen them since that Ballroom show in January. He recalls how the early negotiations progressed: "They were all very suspicious of record companies. After hearing stories about The Sisters, about how Wayne and Craig were treated, I can understand that. Having been in it a bit longer Wayne was a bit more aware of what was right and what was wrong - he had an instinct about me I presume, and I certainly had one about him. We signed the deal in the Elysee Hotel, but I think that they were upset that I had no cheques with me. Tony had been hoping to put it straight into a bank in Germany!" His instinct about the band's maturity as a working unit was soon vindicated: "It's a strange relationship because I've never had one this close with a band before. I've had a close relationship with every band I work with but with The Mission it's something very special for me. There's nothing I wouldn't do for them. They don't generally regard me as record company. To me they're one of the great classic four piece bands. They love to play, you put them in a van and off they go, it's that old fashioned principle."

Playing small clubs, even headlining and having Independent Chart success is one thing. Playing the countries major venues and becoming regular chart contenders is another - many bands crumble under the pressure of a seven figure advance and all the expectations that such major deals unavoidably create. The Mission however took to the new environment like naturals, and casually brushed aside the mounting pressure. The results were immediate - they justified all the faith that Phonogram had shown in them when their third single 'Stay With Me' charted at No.40 in the Gallop listings, their first major label release and their debut Top 40 hit, going on the following week to climb another ten places to No.30. The track began with the now characteristic guitar work of Hinkler with Hussey's crooning of spinning moons in cities of rust, naked fires, glass and dust lifting once again in the chorus. Throughout Hinkler gave the song a quality and depth which perfectly fitted the framework laid down by the intricate but solid rythmn section. The track was promoted by another comical video that the band described as 'Carry On Goth that didn't quite work' but whose tongue-in-cheek goth irony was once again misinterpreted by many as serious. The B-side of 'Blood Brother' was Hussey's ode to Ian Astbury of The Cult with whom he was occasionally compared and about whom he once said "I don't want to be Ian Astbury, but I wouldn't mind fucking him."

So their decision to leave the hallowed ranks of independent labels was immediately justified. With their second single 'Garden of Delight' having charted at No.45, it was clear that Phonogram had provided that extra push that was needed to finally dent the Top 40 with 'Stay With Me'. Ironically though, The Mission were almost victims of the type of administrative blunder that only occurs with major record companies. When Perrin casually walked into a record shop during the week that 'Stay' was released, he was horrified to see that the vinyl inside The Mission's sleeve was in fact the new single by the eccentric funk band Was Not Was. The dilemma for him now was that if he walked back into the shop and told the proprietor, by the end of that working day the Phonogram machine would have leapt into action and whipped all the offending copies off the shelves, completely ending any chance the band would have of charting. After toying with the options for twenty minutes in the shop doorway, Perrin took a deep breath and headed home. So The Mission's first ever chart hit was in fact 'Robot Girl' by Was Not Was.

This hiccup did not dampen Perrin's and the band's delight when 'Stay' charted on the Sunday evening. "It was fantastic, a real buzz when it finally charted. I got a message from the promotions girl which just said 'No.40' on my radio pager. I didn't have a phone at this stage so I went down to the phone box and called the band." Hussey was similarly excited: "Listening to the charts when we first hit the Top 40 was great. Going in at No.40 was brilliant because we then had all night to go out and celebrate instead of having to wait around wasting drinking time for a high new entry. We went to this club in Leeds but they wouldn't let us in, and we were saying 'But you've got to let us in, we're in the Top 40' but they still wouldn't. Charting was a big thing though, because you have the pride to believe that your record is good enough to compete with what's out there."

The release was not all roses however - despite the success the single received some harsh criticism from the press again, with NME leading the way to a degree that was to become tediously predictable: "A limp little man and his turgid sidekicks...The Mission are in the charts and nobody I've spoken to seems to know why. My peers are unanimous as condemning them as awful and apparently even their record company Phonogram can't understand how their single 'Stay with Me' has ascended the charts." [10] Mat Snow was more direct: "I'd sooner cuddle up to a bag of chisels." [11] Also, in a trend that many followers felt would hamper many future releases by The Mission, there was widespread disappointment with the recorded version of 'Stay with Me' and many saw it as a very poor representation of the live show which was by now acquiring notable repute.

Most notably, the title of the single, 'The Mission III', which continued a trend started by 'Serpent's Kiss', further fuelled inferior comparisons with the imagery and style of perhaps The Mission's greatest influence at the time, Led Zeppelin, and inadvertently continued a debate about The Mission's retrogressive tendencies that raged for years to come. The accusations were clearly based in fact. The band's early artwork was packed with the runes and mythology found across much of Zeppelin's work, and the musical influence was always apparent. With Hinkler frequently using the double-necked style of guitar that Jimmy Page had first made popular, the comparisons inevitably arose, and when placed alongside one of the greatest bands of all time a fledgling group were bound to come out worse. The same venom which had caused Johnny Rotten to call Zeppelin 'drugged out arseholes' was now turned on The Mission. Against this, The Mission defended themselves by emphasising the tongue-in-cheek tone of everything they did - for example they admitted the runes and symbols meant nothing and were solely for aesthetic effect - the maidens on horseback, unicorns and castles which dominated their imagery were purely superficial. They openly admitted their reverence to Zeppelin and other '70's bands and never compared the two themselves. They emphasised that it was never meant to be serious, but even so the retrogressive insults continued unabated as the public and press decamped to either side of the fence over the issue, and the debate shadowed The Mission wherever they went for some time.

The video for 'Stay With Me', as mentioned, was intended to be a spoof of their growing goth tag and its filming serves as a fine example of the band's excellent ability to admit their mistakes and maintain an open and co-operative working relationship, but also as an example of the misconceptions being heaped on the band at this stage. In this instance they initially felt they could produce the video themselves, but this quickly proved to be an error, as Perrin explains: "We thought the 'Serpents Kiss' video was a success. In our naivete we said we could do 'Stay With Me' as well, but by now the stakes were a lot higher, up to £25,000 for the shoot. We used the same people as for 'Serpent's Kiss' but everybody was way out of their depth, so in the end we went back to Phonogram and said 'Sorry, it's crap,' and scrapped the whole thing." The final version unfortunately fuelled the goth label that was by now firmly tied around the band's neck: "They brought Tony Vanden Ende in; we were really concerned about the goth thing getting out of hand already, then he came in and said 'I've got this great idea with you all in coffins and there's loads of bats' and we were appalled! He convinced us that it would be so over-the-top that people would see it as intended, ie very tongue-in-cheek. Unfortunately people couldn't see past the bats and coffins and for most it just confirmed our goth status." Brown could not believe how people failed to see the humour in the video: "There's a bit where this bat flies over me head and you can see the string holding it as plain as daylight. There's another scene where Simon's sitting in a coffin playing a twelve string guitar - I mean, think about it, it's fuckin' hilarious." [12]

Misguided preconceptions aside, the summer of 1986 saw The Mission established as a formidable new force in British music. Within six months of completing their line-up they had toured Europe, scored an unprecedented two No.1 Indie hits and a Top 40 single, headlined their own tour of Europe as part of Expedition 1 which was massively supported despite only two single releases, and signed an extraordinarily independent deal with one of the world's most powerful record labels. By August 1986 The Mission were established as the new pretenders to the alternative music crown - even with the bad press they were receiving from many quarters they were developing a high profile love-hate relationship with the media, much of which centred around Wayne Hussey himself. On vinyl many had been disappointed by the output so far, so when the band retreated to Ridge Farm Studios in Surrey to record the debut album, the air of expectation was great. The band would not disappoint.

CHAPTER FOUR

"You could strike sparks anywhere. There was a fantastic universal sense that whatever we were doing was right, that we were winning...that sense of inevitable victory over the forces of Old and Evil. Our energy would simply prevail...we had all the momentum; we were riding the crest of a high and beautiful wave".

Hunter S. Thompson: Fear and Loathing in Las Vegas

AT the helm for the debut album, provisionally entitled 'God's Own Medicine', was Tim Palmer, a young engineer with whom Hussey had worked on the Dead Or Alive album, and a man who was noted for his direct, fast and productive approach to studio work. The band's incredibly strong sense of direction meant they were essentially looking for a co-producer on the project, someone who could contribute ideas but also accommodate their own definite direction. Palmer and the band were good friends and so he was an easy choice. The policy worked well - the album was completed in a mere five weeks. Brown explains the two key reasons why they were able to produce a finished record in such an incredibly short period: "The main reason was simple - we took an awful lot of speed. Apart from that though, the whole thing was typical of our attitude, because five weeks to us was a long time since we'd done the singles in a couple of days a piece for four tracks, previous to which we'd even done sixteen tracks in a day. Taking longer is not necessarily the key to a better record - there are things to learn from that, you have to learn to trust your own judgement and look at your own mistakes." Apart from their colossal amphetamine intake, the hasty production was also fuelled by the willingness of Phonogram to take a back seat, not a luxury that a debut band is usually afforded. In this case The Mission had proved they knew what they were doing prior to signing the deal. Nevertheless, speed or no speed, Perrin was still very surprised that they got the album out that year: " It was June when we signed to Phonogram and the album was out by October. We had a track record with our independent singles, so we went to Phonogram and said 'This is what we've done and this is what we want to do now, we don't want you to get involved. Just give us your backing and support and we can do it'. During the five weeks the record company had no contact with it whatsoever until it was being mixed - then Charlie Eyre came down, listened to it and said 'Great lads, but there is just one thing I'd like to change..'. We said 'Fuck off' so that was that. Simple really."

Hussey was very heavily involved in the production, which was partly why Charlie Eyre from Phonogram was confident enough of them to stay very much in the background. They had chosen a sensibly low budget and maintained their own direction by choosing Palmer who was ideal for the effective co-production that the band were looking for. This policy proved to have it's pitfalls however - the strain began to show, particularly on Hussey as the joint tasks of songwriter/lyricist and co-producer began to take their toll, and stories began to appear in the press that a rift was developing between him and the rest of the band. Although these rumours were grossly exaggerated, there was some truth in them, as Hussey explains: "I had a girlfriend who nobody liked and I'd stay with her all the time so there was some degree of alienation from that. But that wasn't the essence of the problem. Where it really stemmed from was the fact that I can't just turn off at the end of the day, I take it all home with me and that causes me to be isolated at times. You can learn to switch off but it is hard, especially when I'm so actively involved with the writing. It's in some people's nature to be like that, and that way you're more likely to hear things that aren't right, it does raise your standards." The strain increased and during the third week of recording he even considered quitting the band: "I got to the point of leaving because I wasn't happy with my performance and I felt I was letting the band down. The turning point came one night when I realised how much I loved the people who work with us, and how much a part of the band they are."[1]

However, many bands find recording a strain, and the main writer frequently finds himself isolated from the others just by the very nature of what he is doing, especially with lyricists who are openly personal as Hussey was. So why should he be under any more pressure than any other debut writer? To find the extra factor that weighed so heavily on his mind you have to look back to his Mormon upbringing and how his job brought him into conflict with his childhood background. The intensely personal nature of his writing produced lyrics that were at times almost too open to cope with, and in these speed-fuelled five weeks he found himself confronting all the guilt and conflict that had been bottled up inside him since he had left home. The manifestation of this came in this extreme creative self-doubt and his questioning of his very motivations for being in a band at all. In a fashion that would become typical of his approach to the press, Hussey had no qualms about publicly venting his fears and concerns at the time of the recording: "To me the album is an exorcism - everything that has built up in me over God knows how long. It's deeply personal and it messed me up for a couple of weeks while we were doing it. I just went a bit loopy and the rest of the group wouldn't talk to me. It just dawned on me that because the songs were written over such a long period of time I never realised how intense as a composite it was going to be." He continued: "The intensity of it all worried me and I wondered if I was baring too much. But I had to and I felt such a relief when the album was finished," and he added "Twenty odd years of frustration manifested itself in that, but at least it enabled me to get my religious hang-ups off my chest."[2] His paranoia even reached the stage where he was beginning to worry about the next album, because he felt all the tricks, riffs and ideas he had accumulated over the years had been used up on this record, and that his musical resources had effectively been drained dry. Ultimately, he managed to pull himself around and put events in perspective in admirable style: "The only thing I really worry about, and this is the God's honest truth, is what me mother thinks. She's my favourite person in the world...All this to me is temporary. It wasn't there a couple of years ago and it might not be in a couple more, but I know, God willing, she'll always be there."[3]

Having been written in an environment of speed use, 'God's Own Medicine' pursues a very undetermined course with Hussey acknowledging their riotous reputation by the spoken opening of 'I still believe in God but God no longer believes in me'. There was no central theme pulling the record together - instead the album visited the imagery and scenarios that had become associated with the gothic movement in full and unique detail, but with every ornate melodrama heavily tinged in self-deprecation. Overt references to speaking in tongues, cities of rust, fire, angels heaven sent and other worlds all decorated the gothic tag which was firmly hanging around The Mission's neck. Lyrically Hussey followed a highly characteristic course that would become the focus of The Mission's image over the next year, creating an identity that was unmistakably his:

"Heaven an Hell, I know them well,
But I haven't yet made my choice,
and

Fateful wind blows through this land,
Howls my name, heralds my fall".

The gothic aurals were omnipresent:

"The cut that bleeds, the kiss that stings,
The shooting up stars and desperate snows
That fall from shimmering skies,
So take my hand and lead me to the garden of delight".

With the opening track 'Wasteland' The Mission announced that they were capable of songs of epic status, with the thundering guitar landscapes filled with abundant hook lines and infectious melodies throughout. 'Severina' took them into pop-rock territory whilst the lush string version of their hugely successful single 'Garden Of Delight' provided a distraction from the intense guitar emphasis of the album. Adams and Brown displayed a co-operative rhythmic foundation that belied the band's young age, and worked most impressively on 'Sacrilege' and 'Dance On Glass'. Hussey ranged vocally from the shrieks of 'Bridges Burning' to the sentimental whispers of 'Garden', and showed himself fully capable of throwing off the accusations that he could not sing by pitching a classic treatment of the opener 'Wasteland' and the almost metal 'Sacrilege'. On the blistering introduction to this track Hinkler displayed his enormous talent for precise guitar riffing, which would come to characterise so much of The Mission's future work. 'God's Own Medicine' was a tremendous debut in as much as it unashamedly blazed an idiosyncratic path through the fickle musical fashions with a predominant pop sensibility which suggested that The Mission could fulfil their very serious commercial potential. The whole recording process had been quick and effective and this gave the record an accessibility and immediacy that was highly appealing - with 'God's Own Medicine' The Mission had announced their intentions in no uncertain terms. It was a remarkable debut.

* * *

The recording itself was broken only by an appearance at Reading Festival, on 22nd August 1986, on a bill including Doctor and the Medics, The March Violets, Balaam and the Angel and headlined by Killing Joke. The performance itself was memorable for them being joined onstage by Speedy Keene under his alter ego of Thunderclap Newman, and Hussey's drunken fall 20 feet into the crowd, after which he clambered back on stage and began hurling bunches of flowers to bemused on-lookers. The set blistered through to the now usual encore of 'Shelter from the Storm', with the ecstatic crowd filled with Eskimo's sporting their own T-shirts and the motto 'Rape and Pillage' (taken from the track 'Sacrilege'). The band, although blind drunk, remembered the show as a watershed in their career, despite being fairly low on the bill: "It was a turning point for us. We actually realised for the first time that we were quite popular. Even so, I vowed we wouldn't do Reading again until we were asked to headline..."[4] Their growing popularity was confirmed when they were invited to Radio 1 to record a Janice Long session which included 'Wishing Well', 'Shelter From The Storm', 'Tomorrow Never Knows' from The Beatles 'Revolver' album, and 'Wasteland'.

On 11th November, 1986 The Mission's much-awaited debut album, 'God's Own Medicine' was released, with the ten tracks packaged on vinyl in a gatefold sleeve with artwork again by Sandy Ball, with the now familiar but essentially meaningless Zeppelinesque runes and curious designs predominant. The public response was dramatic - 'God's Own Medicine' entered the album charts at No.14 and sold so well that it went silver in two weeks, and stayed in the chart for twenty weeks, going on to amass over 300,000 total worldwide sales. The album rapidly became accepted as the favourite of thousands who were increasingly becoming transfixed by the band's activity, and the demand for the forthcoming tour rapidly escalated. The Mission had confirmed their status as arguably the most powerful new force in British music.

Press reactions to the album were mixed. There were many detractors, as usual led by the NME who described the album in typically flowing language as "completely inane." Many people, including large numbers of the by now loyal die-hards followers were somewhat disappointed that the raw power of The Mission's fiery live show appeared to have been lost, and there was heavy criticism of the band's retrogressive tendencies and rejuvenation of music long since laid to rest by punk, as well as an uneasy reception of the overtly sexual lyrical content. However, against this was a huge element of support for the band's debut, with much acclaim for the quality of the songs and the individual character The Mission appeared to have already created. Some journalists were particularly generous, with Carol Clerk of the Melody Maker leading the way: "A remarkably entertaining LP. In my previous ignorance I'd think Mission and I'd think Goth, think dark and broody and boring, boring...the material is rivetting, colourful and extraordinarily varied...The Mission are at their most brilliant when they're at their most over-the-top."[5] Sounds further championed the cause: "If you badly wanted the first Mission album to be stupendous you won't be cheated. Rich with spicy passion dripping from every note, this record never once stumbles or falters, running on guitars of almost ridiculous clarity and relentless rhythm...I love to see the intellectual talking pop heads get wound up by hair and bangles and guitars, and with any luck 'God's Own Medicine' will make them sick with it's blatant disregard for fickle industry fashion...Not even one year old and The Mission prove that they mean to happen in an epic, quite spectacular fashion."[6]

Five years later Hussey would still see this release as unique and a document of how they operated and felt at that time: "I've always found that my lyrics are personal - looking back it is very much a speed and amphetamine album, and lyrically that is reflected by the number of tangents on there. In some senses there's no real central theme to any of those songs, even 'Wasteland', but against all that you have a great album. LP's are very short-lived affairs, they have no longevity, and that's sad. I think 'God's Own Medicine' was brilliant for a first album. For it's time it was a great album, partly because compared to what else was around it was like a real breath of fresh air. There's definitely a pop side to it which is probably down to our naivete at the time. There's a lot of little hooks all over that record, whether it be vocals or guitar or whatever, and it's probably the most instant album we've written. The innocence of saying 'Let's just slap it down' and doing just that in five weeks gives it that real freshness."

* * *

By the time The Mission came to launch into their world tour to promote 'God's Own Medicine', anticipation for the shows was immense. The plan of action was colossal, even by the band's own prolific standards - a world tour taking in fourteen countries and covering over 100 shows in just over six months, divided into World Crusades I and II. The opening leg in Britain kicked off early, the night before the first date, on a hotel roof in Nottingham, with Brown emulating his friends Metallica by winging into some air guitar, losing his balance and falling off on top of his precious Harley Davidson, causing £1400 worth of damage. In the process The Mission were banned from the most famous and hardened of rock and roll hotels, The Columbia, which had been the witness to the band living out their fantasy of following in the footsteps of The Doors, Led Zeppelin and The Rolling Stones. The first date was a fan club only gig at Nottingham's Rock City on 28th October, 1986 - unfortunately the early part of the tour was marred by a marked rise in violence at the gigs, with several nights being spoiled by clashes between fans eager to see their band and various local groups, frequently skinheads or rugby players turning up for a fight. The Liverpool University gig half way through the tour was particularly violent with knives being pulled and running battles in the streets, and similarly worrying scenes were repeated in Brighton and Cardiff resulting in the band having to leave the stage until order was restored. There was undoubtedly an element of the following who did nothing to placate the situation but in many instances there was a deliberate ploy by locals to cause trouble, and the aggressive attitude of many club bouncers who disliked the general roughness of Mission fans exacerbated the situation. The whole matter was not helped by press comments to the effect that The Eskimos were nothing more than "drink-addled beserkers, draining bars dry and carving a trail of destruction the length and breadth of the land"[7] and as the band toured an angry letter controversy once more raged in the Melody Maker letters page.

Nonetheless, The Mission continued regardless, and with their customary sick bucket placed carefully between the monitors, they produced their best shows ever. Many acknowledged the Manchester Ritz gig on 11th November as arguably the finest show the band had ever played - it was the first gig after 'God's Own Medicine' had been released and subsequently the show was a euphoric celebration for all concerned, fans and band alike - the bulging venue witnessed a frenzied reaction from The Eskimos, whose ranks had now been swelled by the likes of character such as Nightmare Man, Stoko, Rugby Loser and Ferret. Human pyramids had now become a permanent feature of Mission gigs, usually on cue with the rendition of 'Like a Hurricane' and showers of torn paper filled the air already dense with sweat and noise - the whole carnival atmosphere was completed by the fore-runners of The Eskimos, The Sausage Squad, hurling sausages at the band. Even by The Mission's own high standards, the gig was a classic: 'Blood Brother' was dedicated to The Eskimos and the encore of 'Shelter From the Storm' was augmented with chunks of The Doors 'Light My Fire', the Stones 'Satisfaction' and Midnight Rambler and Zeppelin's 'Rock and Roll', with Hussey raising the atmosphere to fever pitch by gently chanting 'Eskimo, Eskimo, Eskimo'. If there were any doubters that The Mission were a singularly exceptional live experience when the club opened that night, there were certainly none left when it closed.

The show rolled on until the UK leg returned to where it had started, at Nottingham's Rock City on the 26th November where the band were as well received as ever, summing up for the original Eskimo, Ramone, what was "undoubtedly the best month I've ever had in my whole life". Adams assumed the role of DJ and the band thanked those who had faithfully been to every show by giving them £120 for beer, only the night after having given them £80 for the same at Kilburn. The tour also saw the band allowing the travelling contingent in for soundchecks and whenever the guest list would not accommodate them their entrance fee would be paid for by the band. In one instance it also saw the employment of one fan, Ian, on the road crew, as he chipped in with catering on the second date of the tour and ended up staying. It was incidents such as these, alongside a series of incredible live shows, that confirmed The Mission's growing status as the so-called 'people's choice', and reinforced the intimate and exceptional relationship which they had carefully formed with their following.

Despite the ecstatic public reactions nationwide, there were still many in the press who refused to succumb to the irresistable rise of The Mission, such as Dominic Roskrow who described them thus: "Boring. Uninspired. Unoriginal. Repetitive. During The Mission's blissfully short set I searched for something nice to say about them...I settled for quaint. They're the sort of band who inspire people to stay in and watch the testcard or take up match-stick collecting...it all becomes a sea of insipid noise after a while."[8] Against this was a growing faction who were gradually being won over by the consistently brilliant live shows The Mission were producing on this tour, and for their own part the band retaliated to the criticisms typically by appearing on the front cover of Sounds magazine under the headline of 'We are absurd and ridiculous!'.

*   *   *

After two dates in Dublin and Belfast respectively, the band allowed themselves four weeks off over Christmas, punctuated only by a festival show in France, before launching into the gruelling European leg of World Crusade I, which would see them visit thirty venues in France, Germany, Belgium, Scandinavia, Holland, Switzerland and Italy. It would be an eventful month. They were sent on their way with an astonishing showing for such a young band in the Sounds Readers' Poll - they won Best Band, Best New Band, Best Live Act and Best Album. Hussey confirmed his growing love-hate relationship with the public by being voted fifth best sex object and eighth in the 'Worst Dickhead' category.

So riding on this considerable public endorsement of the band The Mission headed for Europe. At one of the first shows in Germany the band were disturbed to see most of the crowd consisting of Hell's Angels from the surrounding area, who had heard about the rumours of violence at Mission gigs, and had turned up in belligerent mood. Despite such a hostile audience the band blasted into the set, only to be continually barracked and heckled for the first three songs solid. The rougher elements of the crowd had heard about the sausage throwing antics of the early Eskimos, but in this case decided bottles would be much more entertaining, and showered the stage with flying glass. Dodging empty bottles with acrobatic skill, Hussey shouted out 'If you're going to throw bottles at least throw full ones!!' Immediately, somebody took him up on his request and hurled a full bottle straight at the singers head. Hussey ducked to his right, caught the flying missile, took a swig and threw it straight back to the Hells Angel who had thrown it in the first place. So impressed were the heavies that they invited themselves backstage and to the hotel to congratulate the Mission's lead man on his performance, where he spent two hours having his back slapped by massive tattooed arms.

Two nights later the band drank so many tequila slammers before the show that they found standing up a considerable problem and played most of the gig with Hussey, Adams and Hinkler all lying down. Headaches of a different kind were in order in Oslo when Hussey threw himself into the air during a particularly wild rendition of 'Severina' and promptly smashed his head through the low ceiling above the stage, before continuing the gig with blood dripping down onto his black shirt. Three dates from the end of the tour in Milan the singer's abused body could take no more and he collapsed on stage, only managing to maintain control of the hand which gripped the neck of his bottle of wine. He received no sympathy from the local police who piled backstage with sniffer dogs and batons, hoping his demise would lead them to a sizeable drugs bust. Slamming open the dressing room door they found only empty beer bottles, a half empty box of cigarettes and an open window out of which the band had escaped. Had they looked closer they would have seen the words The Mission written in cocaine on the table, half of which had already been snorted. The police rushed out of the venue and chased the band across town, where they were finally cornered on the way to the airport and unceremoniously strip searched. Undeterred, The Mission celebrated their 100th gig in Milan by indulging their new found enthusiasm for skateboards to the full in the Italian hills. After yet more drugs, they had tied their boards to the back of the tour bus, three at a time, and then the driver screeched down the winding roads, followed at breakneck speed by three members of The Mission, hair billowing out behind them and trusty bottles of Blue Nun under each arm, leaving amazed local on-lookers in their wake. Once more the police finally caught up with them but could find no law to cover the skateboarding offence, and so booked them on the premise of driving whilst under the influence of alcohol. The tour also had its share of strange gigs as well as strange hobbies - in one case the venue had the electrical earth for all the gear in the form of a pole in the ground, which would have incinerated any unfortunate that touched it. Another time at a gig near an airport, every time a plane landed the runway lights were put on and the band's PA went quiet from the powerdrop. Back at home the British press couldn't get enough of these stories - so well publicised were the bands escapades that they received the dubious accolade from The Times of performing 'old fashioned rock star heroics' and rumours even circulated that one well-known magazine was running a sweepstake as to which member of The Mission would die first, with Hussey easily leading the odds as favourite to become the next Jim Morrison. This all made for great copy - beneath the enormous intake of drugs and alcohol there was a growing weariness, but the band refused to slow down - indeed, any signs of stress in the band itself were rapidly pasted over with more drugs. The Mission rollercoaster stormed on regardless.

If the press had taken time out from calculating The Mission's expiry date, they would have seen a band making spectacular and unswerving progress. In January, just before the band had gone to Europe, the second single from the album, the band's fourth in all, was released. The track 'Wasteland' had the live favourite 'Shelter From The Storm' on the B-side, and it gave the band their highest chart position ever in the Top 40 at No.11. The video for the single was the first example that they were uncomfortable with this medium. A meeting was arranged with Tim Pope who would go on to achieve major acclaim for his work with The Cure. Unfortunately, Pope had lost his voice through illness so he brought his producer along with him to the meeting with The Mission to interpret his whispers. Ten minutes after he arrived The Mission stumbled in to the room with Perrin, all of them looking very much the worse for wear after a particularly busy night. The next half hour was spent with Pope vainly miming his ideas to Perrin, who did his level best to interpret the mumblings and grunts of the band, two of whom were asleep throughout. Pope did not take the project any further.

Fortunately this did not stop the band being invited onto the prestigious Channel 4 show The Tube, their first TV opportunity. The show was recorded before the charts for that week were compiled and Perrin is convinced that the chaotic and brilliant appearance that followed was a major reason for 'Wasteland's eventual high chart position. "When we did The Tube it coincided with the heaviest snow storms in Britain for decades, the M1 was closed, nobody could even get out of their house, let alone up the motorway. We had to get up to Newcastle - I'd flown in the day before but the airport was by now closed and we all thought the band would never make it. They set out in the old bus and I heard no word for hours and hours. I distinctly remember standing in the car park thinking they'd never get there and just as I'd resigned myself to a disaster the bus pulled into view - all The Tube staff were silenced in disbelief. There were 100 Eskimo's standing knee-deep in the snow outside but as none of the official audience had got anywhere near the studio they let all these fans in who basically took over the entire show and went absolutely wild, it was just incredible. I don't think The Tube had ever seen anything like it, our lot just went completely mad. Our midweek chart position had been mid-twenties and it looked like the record might go down, but The Tube went out on a Friday and come the chart on Sunday we'd gone up to No. 11. That was totally down to that incredible performance on The Tube - everybody watched the programme and we basically took it over. At that stage The Tube could make or break a band and this was our first major TV show so we were over the moon." The excitement of this show was later somewhat tempered by a debacle surrounding a missed Top of the Pops opportunity, although the band knew nothing of it at the time. With 'Wasteland' at No.11 the BBC invited them on to the show for their much-awaited Top of the Pops debut. Phonogram's representative's were so certain that the single would continue to climb the chart (even though they had not released a planned special format), that they politely informed the BBC that The Mission would not be available. As it turned out, the single went down the next week and so the band were deprived of their prestigious opportunity, and only found out what had happened a while later after a drunken record company executive's confession. They would have to wait for their Top of the Pops debut, but fortunately not for long.

With their previous releases The Mission had hinted at a pop sensibility that could take them into mainstream chart territory, and this had been confirmed by the enormous success of 'Wasteland'. However, this track had a grandiose, epic feel to it which distracted from the earlier pop offerings of singles such as 'Serpent's Kiss'. With their fifth single 'Severina', however, The Mission finally produced their best pop song thus far. Hussey was now displaying a vocal maturity beyond his experience and Adams' bass took a dominant role but still kept the track thundering on. Hinkler's guitar had now established its own style which was instantly recognisable, and the entire track was imbued with numerous and infectious melodies. Sounds magazine was impressed: "The romance, the beauty and the mystic charm. The Mission's kaleidoscope of intrigue spins wildly as we hear Wayne Hussey making for the charts. A sensual record."[9]

This accessibility was reflected when 'Severina' charted at No.25 and finally earned The Mission the much-vaunted Top of the Pops appearance which coincided with the start of the World Crusade II at

Sheffield City Hall on the 18th March, 1987, only five days after their chaotic European tour had finished. Despite all the prestige surrounding the show, the band found themselves a little disappointed, a feeling that has not been changed by subsequent appearances on the nation's premier music show. Brown was especially cynical of the whole affair: "It's an horrible day, you have a dressing room with no windows, no plugs points, it's like a prison cell. The play back's too quiet and they want you to do things that aren't really that natural to you, it's crap." Even so, the performance was well received and fuelled the groups growing stature in their home country; now that they had achieved national television exposure the sky was the limit.

* * *

World Crusade II did not start well. The same day they recorded Top of the Pops in Shepherd's Bush, The Mission were due to play the opening night of the eight date UK leg in Sheffield. They flew north and arrived late at the venue, losing the chance for a soundcheck and worsening the mood that had been already soured by the anticlimax at the TV show. The sound for the gig was never going to be good but Adams was in no mood for compromise, and half way through a clumsy set he kicked his amps over and stormed off stage. Not the most desirable of starts to a world tour. However, as the tour progressed the band took to the bigger venues and sold out crowds and by the time they arrived at the massive Brixton Academy they had turned it around into another triumphant outing, bolstered by the news that 'God's Own Medicine' had passed the 100,000 sales figure and thus earned them their first gold disc. Sounds were feverish in their praise: "Their big rock dream is coming closer every day, not with more speed, more bottles of wine, more limousine rides, but with their performance and their passion. The Mission had to happen, there was a huge gaping hole to be filled. 'Wasteland' thundered, 'Blood Brother' rampaged, and a thousand hands clawed the air when 'Garden of Delight' screwed its way out of the speakers. Enough of us love you for what you're doing for you to never need worry about those who'd like to stamp you into the ground. And as long as those people exist, we're always going to need you".

The support for the shows had been from the fledgling All About Eve, whose vocalist Julianne Regan had impressed Hussey at a gig in London the previous year enough for him to put their tape forward to various record company types with consequent success. This brief jaunt also saw the burgeoning ranks of the following now swamping the elite Eskimos and a degree of tension arose between the proud diehards who felt possessive about the band becoming public property, and the newcomers. Nevertheless, a second fan group called Cod's Crusaders were warmly welcomed on to the tour, alongside The Eskimos and The Missionaries.

This tour was also notable for the change in focus of the band's approach to interviews. Hussey in particular appeared in the press as reluctant to continue carrying the mantle of excess and debauchery that had been bestowed on them up until now. Previously The Mission had been unafraid to mention the drugs, the beer, and of course the women to a press hungry for such tales. By the time of this tour however, they appeared slightly more reserved with their comments, particularly amid concerns that it may adversely effect followers; Hussey only offered partial justification for his infamous binges, pointing to his strict childhood, which meant that while the other band members were all being booked for being drunk and disorderly at 16 and experimenting with drugs and chasing women, he was manacled to Church life until 18. He also expressed concerns about the strange world of music that they were becoming engrossed in: "Being in a group is ridiculous. You lose all perspective on things, locked away in a studio, or touring. And you're surrounded by people who want to take something from you..there are times when I feel really lonely, pissed off, and there are times when I feel like crying."[10] This was all a reaction to the meteoric rise the band had experienced and all that came with it. By now, the press had built Hussey up into a drug addled monster with an impossible substance tolerance; he could not have done the drugs they had said he'd done and still be alive. The bachannals had to take their toll, but nobody was interested in the down side of their indulgent lifestyle, this was a band that were on an inexorable rise upwards.

Despite this public mellowing by the band, the drugs and tour lifestyle were not reduced one iota. One member of the band was sent to hospital for 10 days to recover from various abuses, but discharged himself after only a day for fear of missing out on the fun, and Hussey, after telling Sounds that he couldn't possibly be as bad as he was made out, cheekily added: "Occasionally I will live up to what people expect me to be. None of us like to disappoint."[11] The tour was superb, the lifestyle indulgent and enjoyable, and the more the band did the more popular they seemed to become. With the success of the debut album in Britain and the subsequent sell out tour The Mission had arrived in emphatic fashion.

The human body had its limits however. Underneath all the glorious reviews, high record sales and packed out venues, there was a much darker side - physically the band were wrecked, and the unforgiving prospect of a mammoth 41 date tour of America lay in wait just around the corner.

CHAPTER FIVE

"You have to forget about what other people say, when you're supposed to die, or when you're supposed to be loving. You have to forget about all these things. You have to go out and be crazy. Craziness is like Heaven".

Jimi Hendrix

SINCE forming The Mission at the start of 1986 the rollercoaster ride they had begun had swept them from the Indie charts to the Top 20, from the law courts to gold records and from The Electric Ballroom in Camden to headline European tours, all in the space of an intense and whirlwind ten months. Along with them on the ride they had taken enormous amounts of drugs, women and alcohol but there was always that element of control, however small. The plan in the USA itself seemed ambitious but simple - cover 41 dates in ten weeks, take America for all it had and return home tired but triumphant. After all, they had always pulled through before so why should America be any different?

As was so often the case with major Mission tours they refused to wait to start the escapades. The night before their flight Tony Perrin packed them off into the hotel with instructions to get an early night, but when he arrived there at about 10pm from the office, the party was already in full swing. Hussey and the crew had dropped some acid and were running havoc all over the roof of the hotel; Perrin ran inside to see what else was happening and went straight to his room. He opened the door, took off his coat and went to get a glass of water. It was only whilst he was filling his glass that he noticed Jez smiling broadly at him from the balcony. Glad of the company away from the madness outside, he casually strolled over to talk to him, thinking he was obviously standing on the balcony ledge. When he got within five feet of the roadie he realised to his horror that he was actually hanging by his elbows, five stories up from the Bayswater Road, his courage strengthened by the acid he had just taken. Tim Bricheno from All About Eve came into the room and tried to help Perrin pull him in but the roadie was absolutely furious. When they eventually dragged him in he dived on Bricheno and started biting his shoe, cutting right through the leather into his foot.

Suitably prepared, and with their biggest crew yet on board, the band flew out to America. The large crew was their first mistake, one of many on this tour. "We took our whole production over, two artics, and we were playing clubs that you couldn't physically get all that gear in. You couldn't even get the trucks in the street, and we didn't use all our gear once. We just thought we'll go over there, America will fall to us like everywhere else has - at this point though it has to be said the band's drug use was fairly excessive. The first thing we did on landing was place an order for about five grammes worth of every narcotic substance we could think of before we'd even got out of the airport. Naivety on our part in our expectations exacerbated matters greatly aswell though." Once there, they met up with their agent Ian Copeland, brother of Stewart, whose band The Police owed much of their American success to the prolific gigging they had pursued with the help of Ian's FBI agency. The band instantly took to him and the feelings were mutual - however he was more than a little concerned when they told him that they did not want any days off on the tour, they wanted to play right through. He explained that in America you can't do that, much as it may work in the UK, and that if you did then there would be problems. The band however did not want to hear this, and feared that the momentum they had worked so hard to create would be lost if they paused for breath, so they put their heads down and ploughed on regardless, with Copeland's warnings largely ignored. In such a frame of mind the band set off, billed nationwide as The Mission UK since there was an American predecessor with that name even though nobody could seem to find the apparent gospel band. Convenient names, it seems were not The Mission's forte.

Starting in Toronto The Mission began their antics in earnest. After watching a sex video on the tour bus they had stopped at a truckstop and bungled a local hooker on, but were all too scared to do anything. At a later stop they were all systematically taken to the back of the coach by a hooker and treated to various services whilst the others queued behind. The tone for the whole tour was set at the New York Ritz club on 24th April 1987 when the band performed what Sounds magazine described as 'the best gig they had ever played'. The afternoon of the show Polygram had gone to great time and trouble to get the band a prestigious slot on one of the city's major radio shows, and the American record executives all crowded around the office radio to listen in, hoping the band would not say anything amiss. Everything went well, and the band did a great interview, whilst back at Polygram many sweaty brows were being dabbed. Just as the executives were about to turn off and heave a communal sigh of relief the band were asked to offer a question to the public for them to phone in the answer and win some Mission records. After a slight pause Hussey chipped in with his suggestion: 'Okay, which one of us has just dropped some acid?'

At the show that night the massed ranks of their American record company were afforded no more respect than the radio show. The show was incredible and the atmosphere afterwards was one of celebration, but The Mission were in no shape to engage in the normal rounds of smiling and shaking hands with executives - when Brown was complimented about his excellent drumming after the gig he replied: 'Good drumming? Nah. I'd done a lot of drugs and I couldn't control my foot.' He then turned to the most senior executive present at the show and said 'I'm really sorry, but I can't talk to you right now because I've just dropped some acid. Goodbye'.

The fierce celebrations continued unabated, with the crew taking the opportunity to sample the continent's special delights as much as the band. In the morning before a gig in New Mexico they went on a pilgrimage across the border to buy up crates of their favourite beer Corona. Two hours later the crew reappeared, wallets empty and shoulders laden down with crates of the stuff, trekking miles in the 110 degree heat. As they were nearly back to base, Hal the driver screamed past in a white convertible, grinning maniacally at them with his arm round a hooker and crates of beer piled high in the back, vanishing into the distance in a cloud of dust and cackling insanely. The beer was rapidly consumed and duly left them with severe hangovers, but this did not deter Nipper. The following morning, exhausted, he fell asleep in his breakfast, face down, and when he was pulled to safety he started gibbering in Spanish. The following day he rushed into the hotel room where the band were congregated, proudly displaying the 800 tablets of what was apparently speed, which he had managed to strike a bargain for that morning. After narrating how he secured the deal he greedily shovelled eight of the tablets down his throat. What he did not realise was that the tablets were actually mescaline. one of the most hallucinogenic drugs known to man. Later that day he walked into a notoriously dangerous truckers park in the middle of a desert in America whilst he was tripping, with red ribbon plaits in his hair and pink star sunglasses on his nose hugging everyone that he met, while the rest of the crew frantically scurried for cover. A couple of gigs later, Brown settled down for a well earned rest after a show: "I took some acid and fell asleep. The phone rang and it was Nipper. He was still tripping and he said 'Is it alright if I come down, these lot are really doing my head in up here.' I said 'Well, sure but I'm sure they're not annoying you on purpose.' He said 'Who? What are you on about?' I said 'Er, I've left the door on the latch, come down if you want' and he replied 'Come down where?' He never appeared."

The band were not to be left out of all this - for starters they insisted on the following rider for every show:

To Be Provided By The Venue:

5lt vodka,
3lt Bacardi,
5lt Baileys,
72 cans Red Stripe,
10lt Blue Nun,
5lt Italian red wine,
2 bottle Vermouth,
20lt sweet cider,
10lt dry cider,

1 large bottle Ribena,
400 Silk Cut cigarettes,
1 box of tissues,
One English newspaper,
4 Kinder Eggs,
A Bowl of Smarties (with all the brown ones removed),
12 Red Roses (De-thorned)

Every night the band were doing copious amounts of cocaine and speed with various chaotic results. At one particularly hard Hell's Angels club, Hussey and Hinkler took it upon themselves to act out gay sex in a cage which was set in the middle of the dance floor, surrounded by all the bikers; they were hopelessly tripping and completely unaware of their impending doom until Brown befriended a couple of hefty bikers with his knowledge of Harley Davidsons and got the two out by the skin of their teeth. Hinkler by now had engrossed himself in 'The Dice Man', a book by Luke Rhinehart about a psychiatrist who decides his every move by the roll of dice, whether it be stealing money or raping his neighbour. Hinkler was a little more conservative but equally adamant that the die had to be obeyed, as Hussey explains: "Simon started doing 'the dice life' at one stage. It's a great book but he really pissed Mick off once, which really takes some doing. Simon had a cheese sandwich and Mick asked for a bite and Simon said 'I'll just roll the dice' and it said no! Mick wasn't very pleased."

The frenzy continued in Philadelphia when the police were called to return two 15 year old girls who had vanished and turned up escorting the road crew on tour. In Boston, Hinkler dropped some acid right before going on stage and once that had taken effect he was shocked to see the keyboard apparently jumping up at him - that was manageable, but what he could not cope with was the fact that he thought Hussey appeared to be wearing a bright yellow zoot suit - he ended up constantly walking over to him during the set and pleading 'Take it off, take it off..' After playing a club in Pontiac the same night as U2 played the Silverdome, The Mission went on yet another drug binge, they were teetering on the edge and cracks began to show. Three weeks and fourteen dates into the tour and Hussey nearly lost control at Nashville. After travelling about 1000 miles to play a tiny bar, the band walked into the venue only to be told they could only park their two artics and two buses down a side alley half a mile away from the gig. The gig itself was a total waste of time with only disinterested locals taking advantage of the free bar. The singer had to be talked out of quitting.

The Mission were undeterred - by now they were basically a gang of friends let loose on America, with as much alcohol, drugs and women as they could wish for provided constantly. There was an intense camaraderie developing as the band went through all these chaotic events together, and gradually it became apparent that the band was thriving on this atmosphere of close friendship and an enviously child-like gang closeness. On this tour The Mission was a great band to be in. Even when the excess took its toll the band continued undeterred - after being chased out of town by the sheriff in New Orleans, more simulated sex displays, a gig in Dallas which was busted mid-set over drinking restrictions and Hussey being arrested for being with a girl under the age of 18, somebody cracked however. The driver. He was an infamously hardened drug head, famed for his colossal tolerance of every substance imaginable, a man who had basically seen it all and done it all. When there was no sign of any respite in the chaos he walked up to Brown, handed over all his drugs paraphernalia and said 'I'm out of here, I've had enough.'

Their agent, Ian Copeland was similarly astonished by the drug abuse and general debauchery that was going on, as Hussey recalls: "He served for years in Vietnam, but he was saying during this American tour we were doing more crazed stuff than people in Vietnam, which I must admit made me think a bit." It did not however, make him think that much - rather than calming down, the group escalated their drug use, alcohol consumption and other Paphian activities; by now it was an accepted element of their routine, as Hussey explains: "There's an element of living out your fantasy - you've read about it, other people have done it and now you have a chance to do it yourself. It was definitely a case of 'No snow, no show'. Sometimes we'd wait about an hour until the speed arrived. It's not fair on the audience but that was never a consideration at that point. I find it an intimidating experience going out in front of people. I just find I'm more able to deal with things going wrong or hecklers if I'm three sheets to the wind. It was massively excessive but I don't think it ever got to the stage where it was an addiction. It's difficult to say, but there was a long time when we did it every day, and various people outside of it, like Tony for example, were becoming very concerned. We always felt we had it under control, but that's the first thing that happens and then you can lose yourself. It just became part of our everyday existence - we didn't question it, we just did it. You're mid-twenty, all your birthdays have come at once, you're on tour with all these drugs, you can act as irresponsible as you want, be as rude and obnoxious as you want and they still come back for more. If there's a hotel room full of girls it can get very silly; you kind of feel the world's at your feet."

Addiction or not, in six days the band had spent the £8,000 earmarked for 'Miscellaneous' on drugs. As a result, bootleg tapes of their shows reveal many nights being played twice as fast as intended, with an hour and a half set sometimes lasting only forty minutes. In America, Polygram were reluctant to publicise their behaviour - the political and moral climate at the time was very much 'Just Say No', and thus their record company, perhaps understandably, could not be seen to condone such tales. Six months later Guns 'n' Roses and the Manchester scene made their livings out of it, but for the time being it would have to stay hushed up. At one stage there was a rumour that a memo had been sent around the record company warning people against the animal behaviour which the band had now become renowned for, which read as follows:

'The Mission are very nice people but under
no circumstances should they be given any illicit
substances. If they ask you for anything illegal
just smile and say 'Sorry''

The Mission did not forget the third of the holy trinity of music - their drugs and 'rock 'n' roll' lifestyle was colossal; all that was left was the sex, and there was plenty of that. Every show would see pretty (and not-so-pretty) black-clad girls filling the dressing room, with the lack of clothing being matched only by the abundance of drink and drugs. There was an element of the band which clearly attracted the girls, and it did so en masse. The front of the stage became a shrine for the many girls who followed the band in America, and the after-show entertainments never found the band short of female company. Hinkler compares this side of their tours to the notorious promiscuity of naval officers: "It got to the stage where we all had 'a girl in each port' sort of thing, you would see the same girls every time we went to a place. There was shitloads of womanising all the time. We were all drinking, drugging and womanising before The Mission but only on a dole-scumbag level, but now we had the money, the bigger scale, so that side of it was as bad as all the drink and drugs. Having said that, on one occasion I was with this girl in a room and it suddenly occurred that I wasn't into this one night stand shit. I put a towel on and went next door to Mick's room and I sat down on his bed and burst into tears saying 'I can't handle it anymore'." Once he had recovered from this temporary hitch, Hinkler, like the rest of the band continued womanising with reckless abandon.

*   *   *

This first American tour saw The Mission in a frenzy of drugs, drink and women which swept them inexorably onwards and upwards. It was almost as if the more they took the more they would succeed, because for all the discerning comments and furrowed brows, for many there was a perverse fascination in watching the band's chaotic behaviour. The press found reams of great copy in these tour tales and the public were either compelled or disgusted by the events, but certainly very aware of them. The live shows were relatively unaffected by the lifestyle, and with the band producing a majority of blinding gigs the frenzy offstage created a myth around them that avidly held people's attention. Hinkler feels that this hysteria of excess fuelled the fire that took The Mission so quickly to where they were: "There was a definite level where each person knew they could still produce the goods, after which they just became a drunkard and couldn't play a note. I think we knew our levels, and we benefited from being drunkards most of the time, because people seemed to like that about us, we were just a bunch of knock-about drunks having a laugh". It was the drugs however, that dominated The Mission's band culture, and Hinkler believes it was quintessential to their success: "It was the signature of everything we did. It put a stamp on our relationships, how we worked, what we were like. It effected everybody's character and totally ran the show, especially speed. Decisions were made at the drop of a hat on speed, and we'd just go out and do stuff. It was the fire of the band really, the fuel for the ride we were on, and with the drugs we just ploughed through everything. We were just pissheads together, and did all the things that being four pissheads on a big budget entails. When people applaud you for being a pisshead you tend to be a good one".

There was never any premeditated element in all these escapades however - the band behaved as they did because they wanted to, and on many occasions the consequences were detrimental to the group's welfare, not beneficial. It was never calculated - Perrin felt it was almost inescapable once he had joined the ride back in January 1986, and was swept up in all the activity: "It came along and it was exciting so you get on the ride and go with it, you don't look back to see how big it's got. It's such a rollercoaster ride that it's all you can do to keep your feet on the ground at all, because if you don't strive to keep that perspective you're in trouble. Everything had become so big so fast that the drug use was really no more than a natural extension of the rollercoaster ride that we'd been on. Maybe someone could have said 'Okay, let's put the brakes on and take stock, this is dangerous' but there's never been that degree of planning and it just isn't that simple to stand outside of something so incredibly intense."

* * *

Such stories make for good press and great profile - they do not however, precipitate the healthiest of lifestyles. As The Mission rollercoaster veered faster and faster, it was inevitably going to lose control and with it one of its passengers. On 15th May it happened - the ride came to a shuddering halt, and the passenger who proved to be the victim was Adams. All the crew and band had been equal participants in the chaos that had gone before, but there had been earlier signs that Adams was becoming disillusioned and losing control. After one gig he was all coked up and moaning about a wart he'd had on his ear since childhood. He stood up, went into the bathroom with his pen knife, squeezed the wart between two fingers and sliced it off. He came came back covered in blood, announced 'I've got the bastard', sat down and snorted another line of coke. Apart from such physical manifestations of this volatile edge he also expressed dissatisfaction with some of the politics of touring in the USA: "You're just something to put on while they get drunk; you play places where they have a beer advertisement and a band - the beer was half price and there was an English band on. Nobody was seeing us, why were we playing these places? I don't see any point in going back to Nashville for instance. I know three people liked us there, but they weren't from Nashville, they'd travelled. Nobody in Nashville wanted to see us. We turned up with an artic full of stuff and couldn't get any of it in. We were playing places as big as the bar of The Marquee, eight days on the trot - by day eight you just don't want to know." Having said that he had also rather worryingly expressed an attraction to the extremes America offered: "Everything's better over here - the drugs, you can drink all day if you want, you don't have really stroppy hotels with stupid rules. The extremes are quite open to you and they're a lot cheaper aswell as being much more extreme." It was this dangerous and explosive cocktail of disillusionment and excess that was to finally snap Adam's body and mind.

The scenario was the 22nd date of the tour in Los Angeles, the night after a show in Orange County to the south. The catalyst was a live radio broadcast for KRock FM, America's premier alternative radio station - what happened over the next twenty four hours nearly ripped the very heart out of The Mission. KRock FM had arranged two performances, one at 2pm and one at 8pm to feature in a forthcoming Dudley Moore film called 'Like Father Like Son', and had been plugging the event five times a day for weeks. Then at the last minute, with the band on their way to the venue in Los Angeles, the film company pulled out and effectively rendered the whole day pointless. Perrin, who was driving to the gig separately decided it would be best to cancel the show and let the physically and emotionally burned out band take a desperately needed break. KRock FM refused to cancel however, as Perrin explains: "KRock absolutely hit the roof. I was in the Hyatt on Sunset Boulevard, and I was getting major international grief in minutes. KRock were phoning Polygram in New York saying if this gig is pulled, don't just forget about The Mission's career with KRock, it'll be EVERY Polygram act. So Dick Asher, the President of Polygram USA phoned Phonogram UK and they called me at the hotel saying the band had got to do the gig, it had to happen. So I was faced with the prospect of having to persuade the band to do it - they did not arrive in the best frame of mind. By now they were completely fried and the crew were winding me up about how bad the band had got saying 'I wouldn't like to be in your shoes, they've flipped..' When the band bus pulled up into the car park the crew got up and legged it and pretended to be busy."

The band climbed off the bus at 6am, all of them wrecked, and when they heard of the events they immediately refused to play the gig. Hussey explains why they were so reluctant to fulfil their slot: "None of us wanted to do it, we were all fucked. Craig's always been the most violent, he was a bad drinker and the drug use didn't really help - he was already right on the edge. We'd finished this show in Orange County at about two in the morning, driven to LA, and checked in the hotel. We could only get a couple of hours kip at the most before the planned soundcheck at 9 the next morning, so we obviously did a througher, drugs, coke, liquid breakfast, Jack Daniels, the lot. We were all absolutely off our tits, but we were supposed to do these two shows in one day". Following an angry and protracted hour long discussion, Perrin convinced three of the band that it was in their best interests to play the gig, because of the difficult political repercussions of pulling the show. But Adams would not be persuaded and flatly refused to do the show. A vote was taken and he was outvoted three to one.

With the crisis temporarily avoided, Perrin knew that all was not well however, and was almost resigned to be a helpless by-stander in the events to follow. Having been forced to play the shows against his will, Adams set out to self-destruct. At 9 in the morning he arrived at soundcheck clutching a half empty bottle of Jack Daniels and made it perfectly clear that he fully intended to finish the rest off soon. As

Adams continued drinking, the first show came and went and was a relative success, despite Hinkler and the bass player dancing on stage in their underpants whilst on air. Immediately after this show the band could be found shouting at some kids in the car park for more drugs, and shortly afterwards the biggest drug deal of the tour went down in one of the backstage rooms. By now, however, the drugs and drink could not hide the immense tension that had bottled up in The Mission camp - when they returned from the dressing room, Perrin felt a sense of impending disaster: "I just remember trying to keep out of the band's way, hiding in the production office in the bowels of the venue, because it was out of control and I could see what was going to happen from the minute they walked in."

Retiring to the relative sanctity of their hotel, the band and crew tried to get some rest but nobody could sleep. The atmosphere was wrong, no-one knew how to cope with these new and destructive feelings. Perrin settled down on his bed for a brief nap, and was drifting into sleep when he was jolted awake by two police sirens screaming down Sunset Boulevard. He knew they were heading for the hotel and he knew something had gone terribly wrong. He jumped to the window and saw Adams standing in the middle of the Strip, no boots on, ranting and raving like a madman. In horror, Perrin watched helpless as the first police car spotted Adams apparently out of control and drove into him, knocking him flat. Perrin flew down the stairs and out on to the road - by the time he arrived there Adams was lying half under the police car, motionless. He was dragged off the tarmac and bundled into the second car. Perrin explains what had happened to precipitate this incident: "Craig couldn't find his room key, so he had ripped off his boots and hurled them at the hotel manager who'd bundled him out of the hotel where the police car had run him down. I'll never forget his face as he sat there handcuffed in the back of this car, it was the most terrible expression I've ever seen on any man. He just looked like a wild animal, his eyes were completely crazed."

It took all of Perrin's considerable diplomatic skills to get Adams bailed out of the police car and to persuade the hotel manager not to press charges. The gig that night was approaching and they could still make it. They had to. But the nightmare had only just begun. Far from calming down, Adams accelerated his drinking, consuming massive quantities up to an hour before the show. They were all sitting in the crew bus - the atmosphere was fraught with tension and conversation was strained. Some petty comment was made and Adams flew into a wild rage, screaming and ranting violently that he wanted his passport, he wanted it now and he wanted out of The Mission. When nobody moved he smashed his right hand into a window, breaking it badly and increasing his fury, and stormed off the bus. Within three hours he was on a plane back to Britain.

The chaos did not stop there - with Adams lost there was no respite, and the nightmare continued. They went back to the hotel where they were immediately escorted off the premises by an angry manager, and called their agent to cancel the evening's show. They later found out that David Bowie had been on the guest list, along with 200 fans from the show the night before since Hussey had offered them all a free ticket because he felt the band had played a bad gig. The political repercussions of all this were dreadful. The immediate emotional repercussions were worse. With the LA Times tracking Perrin down to his hotel to get the full story, and KRock FM running 'Mission Up-Dates' with the hourly News Bulletin, the band launched into a massive binge as the only way they could see to shut out the catastrophic events. It was not a good policy. The police were tipped off that Hussey was with an under-age girl - he was, but not the under-age girl the police were told about. So after all that had happened that day they were then raided at five o'clock in the morning by the local force. The police charged into the room and caught hold of Hussey, scaring the girl who started crying. Hussey moved to comfort her but the policeman flew at him and pinned his arms behind his back, face pushed hard against the wall. Pulling out a pair of handcuffs he slapped them around the singer's wrists and whispered into his ear 'You're going to get at least a year for this'. Meanwhile, the father who had tipped the police off had come to the hotel and found his daughter asleep in a car outside - after prolonged discussions Hussey was released but the whole entourage was immediately ejected from this hotel aswell. So Perrin found himself at 5 in the morning trying to flag down cabs to take him and the mountain of luggage to a new hotel, but it was too late. Word had spread around town and The Mission were not welcome anywhere.

With the band in shreds, Adams back in Leeds and the whole crew reeling from the catastrophic events of that day, the survival of The Mission was in serious doubt. Shortly afterwards when asked about the lifestyle that had precipitated Adam's breakdown Hussey said: "Many people we knew of didn't survive. That was a big thing that was frightening me, but I didn't really care. I think to a large extent we were on a death trip - we were just going to blow up or burn out....."

CHAPTER SIX

"'I am he who can play many games.' That is the essence of the happy child of four, and he never feels he loses.

'I am he who is x,y, and z, and x,y, and z only.' That is the essence of the unhappy adult".

Luke Rhinehart: The Dice Man

WITH the gig that night cancelled The Mission were left with less than twenty four hours to decided on their actions and head for Encinitas in southern California. The whole episode in LA had been fraught with intense emotion - when Adams had blazed around the tour bus asking for his passport home, the very existence of The Mission itself had been threatened, and the effect of this was traumatic. The rest of the band followed Perrin to the back of the bus where they all sat in confused silence and cried. Gradually they began to talk and confront the crisis - an hour later several key decisions had been made, the most important one being that The Mission would carry on, regardless.

The Los Angeles gig was remarkably the only date that was lost as a result of that eventful night in Los Angeles. Pete Turner, a balding mountain of a sound man, had played some bass before and now hastily took over, dwarfing the rest of the band. The following night in San Francisco they met up with a previous acquaintance called Surf who was himself a bass player and was now recruited to complete the line-up more effectively. Perrin had by now lined up a series of dates supporting The Psychedelic Furs and with these dates The Mission announced in no uncertain terms that their prolific touring attitude would continue unaffected. Incredibly, it also became apparent that their off-stage lifestyle would remain largely unaltered aswell. Indeed, the frenzy which had swept Adams into such a state increased if anything. As Hinkler remembers, instead of heeding the warning the band threw all caution to the wind and accelerated their excess: "In a funny way, and it's by no means a detrimental remark to Craig, but when he left it was the band's most rockin' period in some ways. He left us with several shows to do and we just went mental - we were doing ridiculous amounts of drugs so we just put it on the tour budget, you don't care when you're that fucked up. We got worse really, doing massive amounts of acid and coke, drinking Jack Daniels all the time, it just got unbelievable. It all seemed a part of the territory, and we couldn't care less. We looked absolutely terrible, no shirts on under grimy leather jackets, unshaven rock 'n' roll messes, but we kicked ass live I tell you. It was just like that first European tour with The Cult only worse. It was a culmination of way too many drugs and excess. It was a total burn-out. Certainly on my part it was a death wish almost, perhaps even more so after Craig left early, burn-out, die young."

The first gig with The Furs was in St. Louis but the band were still in Orange County, a trek across nearly two thirds of America, made worse by the fact that the truck they were driving had an automatic cut-out when it reached 55mph. As it turned out this was probably for the best, because it was decided that the cheapest way to get the equipment cross country was to give two roadies two thousand dollars each in cash and two big bags of cocaine. They forgot one crucial element - the two crew members would have to drive through Las Vegas to get to their destination. This horrible realisation only dawned on Perrin as they drove off and he waved forlornly at the disappearing exhaust fumes: "I was waving and smiling as they drove off thinking 'That's the last time I'll ever see them.' They weren't the quietest pair at the best of times but turning up in Vegas coked out of their heads with a thousand dollars in each of their pockets just didn't bear thinking about. They made it eventually, God knows how, but they didn't have a penny between them." The first sight The Psychedelic Furs had of

The Mission was when two roadies pulled up in a truck, both out of it on coke, with the bus cab showered in white dust. When Jez was asked his name he grinned inanely, pointed at Nipper and answered: 'I dunno, ask him.'"

Matters didn't improve once the band arrived. One gig saw Brown realising shortly before going onstage that there was no hope of his playing as he was blind drunk, and subsequently scurrying around all the bemused Furs crew and even their truck driver asking if they would fill in for him: "I was saying 'Go on, you can do it, you've heard us eight or nine times now, I bet you can do it.' Anyway, when we came onstage I walked across to my kit and I was staggering all over the place, really badly, no control whatsoever. I got onto the stool and I thought I'd made it, that was it, I'd made it. At that moment, just sitting down was my grandest moment. The next day I got some funny comments though - The Furs kept coming up and asking me if I fancied a drink." Two nights before The Mission had exacted sweet revenge on a record company executive, who became the unwitting bearer of all their anti-industry invective, as Hussey recalls: "We were chopping out some speed, which is a lot stronger over there than in the UK. He thought it was just coke so he said 'I'll have a line of that' so we gave him one. We met up with him a week later and he said 'You bastards, why didn't you tell me it was speed, I haven't slept for four days.'"

For The Psychedelic Furs, seeing this relatively new band blazing this trail of destruction and debauchery across the country was very frustrating because they had been placed under a strict 'No drink or drugs' policy after their own problems with this in the past. With such vast amounts of both being consumed with abandon by The Mission however, The Furs will-power cracked. Halfway through the dates The Mission were sitting in their dressing room doing a line of coke when one of The Furs slinked into the room and said 'Don't tell anybody will you?' and promptly joined in. Two minutes after he had left there was a furtive tap on the door and another member of The Furs sneaked in and did exactly the same, and so it continued until virtually all of the band and crew had crept into The Mission's dressing room, all thinking they were getting away with it in secret whilst everybody else was having to stay clean.

On arriving in New York The Mission went to a club where Hussey met up with a bootleg T-shirt seller from Birmingham who gave the singer £2000 as his share of some Mission sales. With the roll of notes shoved hastily into a back-pocket, Hussey rejoined the crew and headed for one of The Big Apple's many underground clubs: "We ended up in this really strange place. It was like a Vietnam Vets club, they searched you on the door for guns and knives and other stuff. We went in, all of us tripping, and it was full of the most bizarre bunch of people with stumps for arms and legs and mangled up faces. It was really heavy and because we were tripping it was all a bit crazy, surreal even". By chance Hussey met a girl in the club whom he had known from his band days back in Liverpool. After a few drinks she went back to the hotel and as they arrived Hussey remembered the wad in his pocket. Turning around to his old friend he hugged her and said 'Here you go, get a load of this, you can have it' handed her the £2000 and retired to bed. Fortunately the girl returned her surprise windfall the next morning, but had to remind Hussey where it had come from. The gig that night was no less eventful. After a great show at Radio City Hall, a Phonogram executive went to see the band and walked into the dressing room which Hussey and Hinkler were in the process of completely trashing. Hussey opened the window and hurled a bottle out into Rockefeller Plaza, where it smashed in front of the Plaza's private security who immediately headed for the venue. Whilst the two Mission men destroyed the room the executive prized the door open enough to tell the angry security that everything was absolutely fine, despite the sounds of smashing glass and furniture coming from inside. The pair were banned from the venue, even though they had to play the same club the next night aswell. As a result of the previous night's damage the duo were not allowed to soundcheck, but instead were escorted into the venue ten minutes before the show and escorted out immediately afterwards. All this was only a week after Adams body and mind had been shattered by just such a lifestyle. This was The Mission calmed down.

*   *   *

1 LEEDS, JANUARY 1986

2 COLUMBIA HOTEL, LONDON FEBRUARY 1986

3 ON TOUR WITH THE CULT, PARIS JANUARY 1986

4 PARIS, JANUARY 1986

5 'SOUNDS' PHOTO SESSION WITH MILES HUNT (THE WONDER STUFF)

6 BIRMINGHAM NEC, MARCH 1990

7 BIRMINGHAM NEC, MARCH 1990

8 WEMBLEY ARENA, MARCH 1990

9 NEW YORK RITZ, MAY 1990

10 NEW YORK RITZ, MAY 1990

11 AT HOME IN LEEDS, FEBRUARY 1990

12 RECORD COMPANY PHOTO SESSION, AUGUST 1988

13 HAMMERSMITH CLARENDON WITH JULIANNE REGAN (ALL ABOUT EVE)

14 'THE METAL GURUS', FULHAM GREYHOUND, DECEMBER 1989

15 READING FESTIVAL, AUGUST 1987

16 CARLISLE SANDS CENTRE, APRIL 1989

17 CARLISLE, APRIL 1989

18 HAMBURG CCH, MARCH 1990

22 LEEDS ELLAND ROAD WITH U2, JULY 1987

23 ELLAND ROAD, JULY 1987

19 LOS ANGELES PALLADIUM, MAY 1990

The Mission played the last American date of their World Crusade in Washington DC on 17th June, 1987. Ravaged and shattered but nevertheless triumphant they arrived home with only two weeks to prepare for what could be their biggest live show yet - on the bill to support U2 at Elland Road, a date complimented by another support of the Irish band in Edinburgh a month later, separated by six dates in Europe, after which they would have finally finished their collosal World Crusade.

This busy period was preceded by the release of a compilation album of their early Chapter 22 recordings by Phonogram. It consisted of nine tracks including a rare version of Patti Smith's 'Dancing Barefoot', two versions of Young's 'Like A Hurricane' which had become such a massive Mission live favourite, and extended mixes of 'Garden of Delight' and 'Crytstal Ocean' all of which were produced co-operatively by the band themselves. The track 'Wake' contained a final swipe at Eldritch in the words 'All your friends are dead and buried, they died laughing' and 'It's a taste of God's own medicine for you'. It provided an excellent summary of The Mission's career thus far and it is a reflection of The Mission's enormous domestic popularity that it charted at No.35 and went on to sell over 60,000 copies in the UK alone, despite many of the tracks having been previously released as B-sides. The release provoked this response from Ann Scanlon in Sounds: "It proves that from the very first chapter, The Mission had it all: the power, the mystery and the relentless hammer of the Goths."[1] One of the aims of 'The First Chapter' was to prevent the appearance of expensive imports of old material and it did just that. It could not, however, prevent the surfacing of two inferior and totally unofficial picture discs containing interviews of varying quality and interest, both of which the band condemned as rip offs. The band themselves released their first video compilation, 'Crusade' which consisted largely of excellent live footage form a show at Aylesbury Friars in 1986. With sales of this and the compilation album being brisk it was evident that The Mission now commanded a large and fanatical following.

The U2 dates saw a recuperated Adams eagerly rejoin the band, much to everyone's great relief. The gigs themselves were the first time that The Mission came across stadium rock at this level and it was to have a profound effect on them, would introduce them to the future producer of their next album and would alter the focus of how people perceived them from hereon. The bill other than U2 was impressive in itself with The Mission sandwiched between The Pretenders and The Fall. The Leeds show on the 1st July is remembered largely by the band for its drunkenness and celebrations; after meeting in a hotel bar the band's parents were introduced to each other for the first time, and headed for the venue leaving the group to remain firmly rooted to the bar drowning their nerves whilst their home town fans waited eagerly. Hussey remembers the gig itself as a highlight because "It was the most drunk we'd been in front of the most people up to that point!" The Edinburgh date on the 1st August was a similar story. With Brown so inebriated that his drumming was seriously affected, Adams kept walking over asking what on earth was going on to which Brown replied 'Er, um, I think there's a really weird echo.' Five minutes later Hussey announced to 40,000 people that the drummer was drunk and that effectively gave the game away. Afterwards Brown whispered to a roadie his secret, which he hadn't realised everybody in Edinburgh knew 'Don't say 'out right, but I was a bit pissed'. Despite their state at both shows, Bono took Hussey aside backstage and said he felt The Mission were going to be massive and invited Hussey to call in at his Irish home anytime he was over. The crowd and the press were similarly impressed: "The Mission regard rock 'n' roll as.a serious business. Not that The Mission are in any way daunted by the vulnerability of their position; they rock like demons. Today sees them on the crest of a wave they've been riding since the success of 'Stay with Me' last year. Nerve troubles can be excused. Meanwhile down in the crush, Mission fever is rife. 'Shelter from the Storm' is being transformed into an epic..."[2]

Sandwiched between these two U2 dates was a six show tour of Europe, the second time the World Crusade had taken them to the Continent. These dates included a festival in Lorelei sharing the bill with a hero of the band's, Iggy Pop, alongside Siouxie and the Banshees and Julian Cope. At the final date at The Heppen Stadium in Belgium they were supported by Sonic Youth and Nitzer Ebb and were greeted by a barrage of mud slung by a particularly aggressive audience. The press reception was not particularly warm either, as David Stubbs showed in his review: "I've never quite got the hang of The

Mission. Clearly they are not a calamitous band like the Eurythmics or Spear of Destiny. But as songs such as 'Wasteland' and 'Stay With Me' indicate they are not much of anything at all...when the dry ice lifts, all we're left with is more rock, more motor maintenance..they deserve their little pelting."[3] Despite some bad reviews Hussey remembers these dates fondly because he met his childhood hero Iggy Pop: "I'd always loved Iggy and saw him when I was a kid. I thought I've got to meet him and then one night I felt this tap on my shoulder and he said 'Hi I'm Jim, you're Wayne aren't you?'. One time I was in New York he invited me round for a drink. He's a lovely bloke, very approachable, despite this intense persona he has in performance". He continues: "It's like a light at the end of the tunnel...he was telling me about when he was sacked by his manager in England and he went back to LA and he actually lived on the streets for a while and was a real junkie, he lived as a bum for about a year, until Bowie came along and got him out of it. He's been through to the extremes and yet he's got so much peace of mind, it's so reassuring to know him". Such advice was sorely needed at this stage as the band were physically savaged by their world tour. On the 2nd August 1987, The Mission finally, wearily, but triumphantly completed their mammoth world crusade - it had been an incredible year and a half and The Mission had come through it all.

* * *

Back at base the band could now separate themselves enough from the whole episode in Los Angeles enough to begin to work out why it happened and come to terms with it. The healing process was obviously helped enormously when Adams rejoined the band at Elland Road, but each member of the band still had to go through events in his own mind and rationalise what had happened. Hussey was aware of how close the others had been to cracking: "Up until that American tour I never really saw this band existing very long. I thought 'It's happened, it's brilliant and as soon as it's not brilliant we'll finish it.' Then America happened and a lot of bad things happened. Craig was very negative, there were a lot of niggles. You could feel it building up and someone had to crack. Craig's a little more volatile that the rest of us."[4] He continued "It could have been any of us - we were all on the verge of cracking, it's just that Craig was more susceptible to it. Mick and I always manage to get through but we've been pretty close to cracking as well." "Craig cracked first but we were all out of it. The crew hated us, they'd set up for a gig and then dread the band coming, we were just arseholes, all the band". Even after Adams had left they apparently didn't see the dangers evident: "You don't think of it in those terms. It's a rollercoaster and you're on it and you just keep going. It kind of brought us to our senses a little, we toned down the drug use a bit for the rest of the tour, but we certainly didn't stop". He even admitted that as his face was being shoved into the hotel bedroom wall and the handcuffs being forcefully snapped around his wrists he contemplated a prison sentence with only one thought on his mind: 'At least if I go to jail I'll get some time to write new songs'.

Hussey also saw the positive side of the whole experience and acknowledged the important role that Adams played in the bands make-up: "America was positive in that it acted as a good balance. I was getting really paranoid about people looking at me in the street. Around the time of 'Severina' and 'Wasteland'.I was totally fucking self-deluded. I was going out on the street and thinking everyone was staring at me. But they weren't staring at me because I was Wayne Hussey, they were staring at me cos I was walking around with nail varnish, a skirt and a beard!"[5] He continued: "There was a time where me and Mick were walking around and there were these school girls following us. After a while they muscled up the courage to come over, went up to Mick, asked him for his autograph, and totally ignored me. They thought he was the guy out of Bros!"[6] The speed with which he had achieved his original goals, such as appearing on Top of the Pops and being on the cover of various magazines left Hussey susceptible to losing perspective, which is where Adams came in: "That first American tour was when it all became a lot more rock 'n' roll as opposed to a pop group. I liked being a pop star. The extremes were a positive thing. It was pop star tantrums, I'm prone to them unfortunately". "Craig in his own way is probably the biggest character in the band, the strength, he's my conscience. There's some things I can get away with, and others that Craig just won't let me get away with".

With hindsight Brown felt that their behaviour left them on an inevitable course for self-destruct. "It was a great laugh with really shitty bits, real extremes. It's like having an angel on your shoulder who looked after you, so the more off our tits we got and followed our instinct the better it was, it was all a totally integral part of the band. We were brilliant at it until it stopped and then it completely fucked us up, but looking back it had to fuck us up eventually. It's not realistic to pretend otherwise. We trusted ourselves to play the gigs in that state, but at one stage I got really self-conscious about being onstage at all because of the drug use. When Craig flipped we didn't really moderate, I didn't save any money that's a fact. It was an quite an experience, and once we'd got back together there was a real spirit between us that came out of that, and made us better prepared for the next time shit happened".

Perrin and Hinkler both felt that the American industry had exacerbated matters, although they acknowledge that the excess didn't help, and feel that this helped push Adams over the edge. Perrin particularly disliked the double standards apparent across the Atlantic: "In America it was very hypocritical because the 'Just Say No' environment was the thing. The record company people would purposefully come out with us because they'd heard we were having a good time, they'd egg the band on, take part aswell and then go back to the record company and say 'The Mission are a bunch of drug crazed maniacs'. So with the band in such a state it made life very difficult at times. Occasionally, you feel that the band think you have an ulterior motive for why you are doing things. My responsibility is providing them with as much information as possible about a decision they will have to make but ultimately they make the decision themselves. On that night in LA I knew before I went onto the bus that things were low but I had to try to make them see their long term interests. It was such an unrealistic situation, it was massively intense and they were all completely fried. You're in such close proximity to people and small things become major issues". He also feels that the record company handled the whole episode badly, and failed to see the benefits they could have taken from it: "I think the company over-reacted to that first tour, and failed to see that, if you want to be cynical about it, that they could have used it as a marketing tool. I was phoning them up and saying 'This is what we did last night' and they were saying 'Keep it quiet, you haven't told anybody have you?'."

Hinkler feels the press harping on about their antics created a dangerous situation whereby the band were encouraged and expected to be outrageous, after which people would go home and the band would be left to pick up the pieces and recover: "Let me tell you a home truth about those days. It was such a full-time, out of your head, day after day thing, that that's what got quoted in the press as being boastful, caused by being in that state. There's been a lot of shit written and a lot of overblown stories about the way we used to carry on. Things got said like 'I'm out of me head me' etc etc. Now we're back, we're not saying never again, we're just saying never everyday again".

Which just leaves Adams. After recuperating while the band finished the tour, he realised that he still wanted to be a part of The Mission, but also acknowledged that some things would have to change: "As soon as I got back to England I realised how much I missed the gigs, that was the real fun bit of it. At some point along the way that seemed to get forgotten". "When it first happened I didn't really care if it was finished or not. I just wasn't thinking about that, it just wasn't important at the time. I wanted to go home and go to sleep, I was fed up with all the record company bullshit and agency bullshit and gig bullshit". The irony was that alongside Hussey, Adams was the most experienced tourer in the band. The problem was that in The Sisters Of Mercy they had never been on the road for more than two weeks in America, usually because they had to return home to sign on the dole. With their mammoth trek across the States allowing no time off, against Copeland's advice, it inevitably took its toll. The industry joke that British bands would go to America to tour and would instead split up within a week was not all fantasy. It had happened before and it had nearly killed The Mission.

Once Adams had spent time with his friend and roadie Steve from 3000 Revs in Corfu, his approach to the whole tour environment altered somewhat - he was not going to suddenly stop, none of them had ever claimed that, but it would have to be on a different level: "I realised we couldn't do it anymore - it was fucking it up for everybody. We all discovered that it was a lot better not to go on completely out of your brain. We had to slow down. We had no choice, if we hadn't we'd have split up. It wouldn't have been through not liking each other or not liking the music, it would have been purely because of bad habits." The Mission did not split up however, and in many ways they emerged from the crisis in Los Angeles as a much stronger unit. Ultimately, America put The Mission off cocaine and MacDonalds, both of which they had too much.

*   *   *

Despite the Los Angeles incidents, the eighteen months since the band had been started had been a whirlwind of success and progress for The Mission. Their debut album had won them a gold disc and major acclaim as well as thousands of dedicated followers - all the doubts about their ability in the early days to throw off the shackles of The Sisters Of Mercy had been cast aside in a thundering ride which took them into the charts, on to the television, through headline world tours and on to scores of magazine front covers. Central to all of these achievements was the precious and unique nature of their relationships within the band - when Adams had flown home early, one member of the gang had been lost and it did not feel right without him. The warm and genuine respect they shared for each other grew from his troubles and emphasised that the band in a sense was secondary to their personal relationships - it is a tribute to band's inate ability to learn from their own very public mistakes that they came through America as a much more positive and closer group. By the end of their world travels and despite all the traumas, The Mission had gone from underdogs to headliners, and they showed no intention of letting up.

CHAPTER SEVEN

"Your ideas about friendship are formed when you're very young, and I don't think you make friends when you're very young...I think friendship is something which is proved. It's proved by what you do. It's proved by what other people do to you. It's a crucible, a test".

Pete Townshend

NESTLED in the Oxfordshire countryside, ten miles from Kidlington, is The Manor Recording Studio owned by Richard Branson, whose massive collection of bedrooms, games rooms, pool and saunas marks it as one of the countries most prestigious recording environments. After the incredible events of the last eighteen months, it was here that The Mission found themselves when work began on their much-awaited second album in August 1987. It would be a slow and lengthy process with the recording seeing The Mission stay at The Manor right through until Christmas - with the impressive studio facilities being charged out at £10,000 a week it was to be an expensive album. Mastering was completed at London's Townhouse studios with Mark Stent aka Spike, (who would go on to work with the KLF and Depeche Mode), and in all the whole, record took over seven months. The inspiration for the album came from the bands emotive and intense experiences in America, the excess, the lifestyle and the heat which was omnipresent - in addition there was a major change in Hussey's life which heavily affected the whole tone and lyrical content of the record as much as the volatile events of the previous tour - he now had a baby daughter called Hannah, who was born in October 1987, and whose mother he no longer regularly saw. In summary of the three central themes of the album, it was provisionally entitled

'Children on Heat in America', but this was later abbreviated to just 'Children'. The idea had come from one night at Ian Copeland's house, where the band were in his basement and noticed he had a drum kit with some guitars and various equipment. Brown and Hinkler started playing, were joined by Copeland himself, and then Copeland's young daughter started singing with them. All playing music, all children.

Initial work on the songs had very much been started whilst on the World Crusade, and the band had demoed some ideas in New York and Germany whilst Adams was recuperating in Corfu. Much to the amusement of their Led Zeppelin detractors, Hussey went to the Welsh Black mountains where, like Plant and Page before him, he planned to work the ideas through. The Black Mountains provided him with an isolated environment away from the hotel rooms which had become his home, in which to write new material. Despite nagging self-doubts, it was a very productive time and Hussey came away with songs of more depth and more content, and avoided the very linear, one-dimensional features of many songs that are conceived purely on the road. Even so, his own high standards and worries that they might become one album wonders were still very present and very real; with the start of the album approaching, his doubts and fears that had manifested themselves so deeply whilst recording 'God's Own Medicine' began to surface again. After the initial rush of excitement and enthusiasm of the first record they were now faced with the pressure that confronts and often destroys many bands when recording the successor to a hugely successful debut album. The Mission were not to be one of these bands.

At the helm was John Paul Jones, bass player from Led Zeppelin, arguably The Mission's single biggest influence at the time - how he came to be producer on the album is a story in itself. Frequently the producer of an album can be as fashionable a choice as the band on it, but in this instance The Mission were keen to avoid choosing the American flavour of the month name. Apart from the obvious appeal of working with a member of one of the biggest bands off all time, John Paul Jones studio work also interested the band - he had worked on arrangements for the likes of Donovan, Herman's Hermits, The Rolling Stones, Cat Stevens, John Pembourne, Stephen Grossman, as well as many classical pieces. Despite rumours of many others being in the race for the job, such as Bruce Fairbairn (Bon Jovi) and Pete Collins (Rush), Jones was always going to be the band's first choice. That is if he was interested.

His first sight of the band was at their drunken Elland road performance - he was not particularly impressed. The last time Jones had been to that venue he had been flown in by helicopter over the heads of thousands of ecstatic Led Zeppelin fans. He later told Hussey that after three songs of The Mission he thought about catching the bus home but resolved to stick it out. The initial contact had been made after Jones' management had let it be known that he was interested in stepping up his studio responsibilities to that of producer - many were sceptical of whether he could do anything after being in *the* rock band but he was adamant. The Mission were certainly not a band he had thought of, and when he read the mountains of press detailing their infamous tour escapades he consigned them very much to the back of his mind. Then he listened to 'God's Own Medicine' and was intrigued so he decided to go to Elland Road to decide for himself. After the show he was taken backstage to meet the band where bewildered on-lookers saw the bass player from the legendary Led Zeppelin talking to the singer from the Zep revivalists The Mission, who was saying 'Hello, this is my mother, my father, my brother...' So much to the disappointment of Tim Palmer who had worked on 'God's Own Medicine' Jones agreed to his first work with a gigging band since Led Zeppelin and chided himself for believing everything he had read in the press.

Over the next months The Manor would become home for the band who had spent so much of the last year and a half living out of a suitcase. It saw them retreat into an insular world of just the four of them, John Paul Jones and Spike, creating tensions with those outside of this clique. The spell at The Manor also saw Hussey again experiencing self-doubt and intense emotions during his writing, particularly as he musically articulated the guilt he was feeling for not living with Hannah's mother. When recording began though, the band were deeply ensconced in what they were doing, none more so than Hussey: "Working with John Paul Jones from Led Zeppelin...the best band in the world! When they were good they were the best, they had all the edges". And of Jones himself Hussey said at the time: "He's brilliant. Really unaffected but so aware of what Zeppelin achieved and what he was a part of...you won't hear a bad word against him. He thought we were awful when he saw us play at Elland Road, but even then he recognised that we were a band. He gets nostalgic at times, but he's a good guy, easy to work with, unaffected".

Jones worked in a very different manner from Tim Palmer - whereas with their first album there had been an attitude of getting songs recorded and down on tape quickly, Jones' background of meticulous and exact '70's production led the band to agonise for days over details that were minute but were seen as essential to the record's quality. Also, the material he was presented with was much more skeletal than previously so, largely because with any debut album the songs have been played live and evolved over a longer period of time. In this instance, many songs were very embryonic and were fashioned in the studio. This attention to detail did allow for some spontaneous live recording, with Jones himself contributing some keyboards. His aim for the record was simple: "Being in a band situation with musicians with guitars is so much a part of my production value, which is to get that band feeling on a record, rather than it feeling so fragmented."

With this philosophy in mind the recording began, and it soon became clear that there was a mellower side to The Mission emerging. Hussey was visibly changed - the birth of his daughter was the first time that he had been lifted out of the insular world of music and it affected him deeply. He banned drugs from the studio and appeared in various music papers announcing the virtues of fatherhood and his new puritanical streak: "A lot has happened to us in a short time. We've been learning, and my attitude's changed. A year ago I wanted to be a pop star, I still do but I won't play the game the same way". He went on: "Having the baby, having her here, it makes me realise that making records is a pretty meaningless thing. It means a lot to me, and the records mean a lot to a lot of people, but balance it against a four week old baby..." The man who had been told by Iggy Pop to 'calm down a bit' now appeared to have adopted a new philosophy to the indulgences of previous days: "The drugs didn't worry me until my daughter was born, then it kind of struck me that I want to live because, up to that point I couldn't have cared less to tell you the truth. It wasn't a suicidal thing, it was just that I enjoyed it, if it killed me, then fine."[1]

It was not just Hussey who had changed, although his was the most acute modification. Hinkler reiterated the new perspective which appeared to prevail by buying a house and enjoying decorating it throughout. Adams saw the days in The Manor and their mellowing out in somewhat lighter terms: "That's when we all started to get fat in these residential studios. You get up, read the paper, have a full Monty breakfast and maybe wander over to the studio."[2] Working with John Paul Jones also helped put their meteoric success in perspective, particularly one night when they were bragging about playing a big venue in America and Jones quietly said 'Well, I'm afraid we did seven nights each at Earls Court and Madison Square Gardens'.

This mellowing out seemed an ideal antidote to the wayward life they had led up until now, and acted as a check against their losing touch with events and becoming arrogant. But it was not that simple - there was a conflict. Against the fatherly arm of John Paul Jones warning them away from too much excess, and Hussey's new found puritanical streak, many of the band and crew were still using drugs behind people's backs. Also, as the album progressed the producer, mixer and band retreated into their own isolated world in the studio and shut out all comers. Even Perrin found himself isolated to some extent: "I thought at the time that it was far too insular to an unhealthy extent. They were locked up in this studio in Oxfordshire and they were very militant about what they were doing. That was the first time that I felt excluded because no-one outside of the band and John Paul Jones was allowed any say on the creative side". It was Charlie Eyre from Phonogram, who up until now had been very close to the band, who was most effected, as he explains: "On 'Children' I felt we needed someone who was going to take the whole attitude and sound of that album and make it sound 'world class'. I went down to The Manor and tried to persuade the band to get someone different from the engineer who was there to mix it. Briefly they went along with this, and then John Paul Jones said 'No, I don't want that to happen' and the band agreed. I knew that they were wrong, I was absolutely convinced. They were so involved in the record and Jones couldn't understand the relationship I had with the band, because in his days no record company ever went near a studio, it just never happened. He almost regarded me as the enemy. and he turned the band against me for a while. It got ugly. Jones was basically in charge of that album, Wayne took a back seat". At this stage at least this isolation was productive. Later on however, Eyre feels he let it get out of hand: "I made a mistake - I went down to the Townhouse where Mark Stent was mixing a couple of tracks. I walked in, the whole band were there with John Paul Jones. They played a couple of tracks which I didn't think were very good. I chickened out, I said 'Fine, carry on' and felt a complete wimp. They were so determined to do it their way". The only group who were not excluded were the band's parents for whose comfort the group surrendered their expensive rooms and spent the night all in one room accusing each other of farting.

*   *   *

Despite these reservations, once completed 'Children' gave the listener an inside look at the world of The Mission up to this stage - opening with shouts from the playground of Woodstock Primary School and a snippet of 'Serpent's Kiss', the album was a musical documentary of The Mission's career and lives up to this stage, and contained all the elements that the band had become so noted for. There were the pompous ballads, such as 'Breathe' and 'Heaven on Earth', which was a direct nod to the arrival of Hussey's daughter Hannah. There was a humourous side swipe at the band's retrogressive detractors in the blatant mockery of Zeppelin's 'Misty Mountain Hop' and 'Black Dog' with The Mission's own version entitled 'Black Mountain Mist'. The band's notorious tour escapades were not excluded, with Hussey chronicling Adams' problems in Los Angeles on World Crusade II in 'Hymn to America', and an infamous incident with a hooker was featured in the track 'Heat'. Aerosmith's classic 'Dream On' was also re-visited Mission style.

Lyrically, the record revealed more about Hussey himself than any Mission project thus far. Shortly after the recording he said: "'Children' is a very personal record lyrically. It was a catalogue of what was going on in my personal life - Hannah was just born and you can see the sense of guilt there about being an absent father. I was brought up to believe that if you have a kid you should be around to look after it, take the responsibility and get married. I didn't and it plays on your mind". It was during his ruminations about Hannah that Hussey was at his most subjective - he never attempted to hide his concern, nor his delight at Hannah's birth:

"I'm living in the hope, of a breath to be shared,
It's all I've ever wanted, It's all I've ever dared."

"You give me heaven and I'll promise you the earth,
Precious I want to be here for you.

The overall tone of the album was grandiose and bombastic, with Hinkler's instantly recognisable guitar motifs perfectly detailing the enormous sound The Mission had managed to cultivate. The rhythmic backbone of Brown and Adams established a solidity which prevented the music from losing direction when the tracks ran past the usual pop formula three minutes, with some tracks lasting up to nearly three times that. There were also the idiosyncratic gestures such as 'Shamera Kye' which saw the backwards guitar technique frequently used to such good effect replaced by a thirty second track consisting solely of Jez Webb's harmonica similarly recorded in reverse. Over the uniquely ornamental sound track, Hussey's vocals were both intimate and removed, travelling from personal lilts such as 'Heaven' and 'Breathe' through to thundering epics such as 'Kingdom Come', with Julianne Regan of All About Eve complimenting the texture on 'Black Mountain Mist' and 'Beyond The Pale'. The musical highlight however, was reserved for one track in particular, which soon became a pivot of the whole record and was so powerful that within months of release it had been acknowledged as a classic and generally recognised as The Mission's high point thus far. Originally based on the Eskimos themselves, it was an eight minute epic which built from it's acoustic introduction into a song of massive proportions, and was for many the first time that the band had successfully captured their huge live sound on record. That song was called 'Tower of Strength'. It was to be a benchmark of their success and quickly became a seminal record of massive influence. With this track as a central pin for the record, 'Children' took The Mission's sound from the irresistibly naive pop attraction of 'God's Own Medicine' to a massive rock monster of preposterous proportions.

All the concerns expressed about the record, although evident at the time, were mostly voiced after the band had left The Manor, and were the opinions of people not involved in the creative side of the new album. When interviewed about their hopes for the new record whilst still at the residential studio, the band were all very optimistic, particularly Hussey: "There's more substance to it, it's more powerful. I also think it's less instant - you could listen to 'God's Own Medicine' once or twice and really like it whereas there's things on this album that aren't designed for that at all". He was also proud enough of the lyrics to include a lyric sheet for the first time: "With the first album the lyrics were floating in the air, they weren't pointed. With 'Children' I can see it being massive. My belief is such that the songs are great and the band is great". Both sides clearly enjoyed the working relationship that had developed between them aswell, as Hussey recalls: "John Paul Jones would say something and you'd think 'I don't like that' but you'd think you couldn't tell him because of who he is. You'd tell him it was no good and tell him to do it again and then you're natural reaction would be 'Shit I've just told John Paul Jones to do it again!'". Jones himself was equally enthusiastic about those sessions and about the record: "It's utterly fantastic! They seem to like it - they don't throw things at me. It was a good working relationship, it was nice, having them all in the studio all playing at the same time, which surprised them I think. That was a nice feeling, it reminded me of the old days. I knew how they felt, it's one of those things, I can see things from their point of view and also they can't argue with me you see...well, they do a bit". Indeed, on one occasion when they were all doing speed and Jones was lecturing the band about their excess, Wayne promptly turned around to face the bass player from one of the biggest groups of all time and calmly said 'Shut up you old fart!!' So with the old fart put firmly in his place, The Mission prepared to reveal their new album to an expectant world.

* * *

The wait for The Mission's second album was punctuated by a prestigious headline slot at the Reading Festival, a confirmation that the band once described as "horrid men with shaggy long hair and inane lyrics"[3] had already established their own massive corner of the British music scene. Before the Reading show they had initially planned to release the track 'Heat' from the new album but this never materialised. To make sure they produced the goods at Reading they decided to play two warm up dates, one for the fan club only which took the form of an all day event at Nottingham's Rock City and then a slot supporting All About Eve at London's Marquee. Mick Mercer was at the London show and provided a full and extensive review of the evening: "Bugger me, it isn't as bad as I'd feared."[4]

These dates were ideal preparations for the band as they readied themselves for the highlight of their career in the UK so far - headlining at Reading's 25th anniversary festival, an accolade previously reserved for the likes of Thin Lizzy, Genesis and Meatloaf, and this year graced by bands such as Spear of Destiny, The Fall, The Icicle works, Fields of the Nephilim, The Godfathers and The Babysitters, with Status Quo and Alice Cooper headlining the two other nights. Again The Mission were appropriately artificially relaxed when they took to the stage but there performance was as memorable as any. The set opened with 'Wasteland' then went on to 'Like a Hurricane' which saw hundreds of pyramids sprouting up everywhere. Other highlights included 'Serpents Kiss', 'Sacrilege' and some of the new material such as 'Kingdom Come', 'Tower', 'Heat' and 'Child's Play'. With the police monitoring the Eskimos antics, the performance was a classic and was received with wild applause. The only negative side of the day was voiced by Hussey himself, who articulated the band's concern about their success affecting their ability to keep in touch with reality: "We live in fucking cloud cuckoo land, I haven't got a clue what goes on out there anymore. I don't know what's happening in the clubs or in the streets, I don't know. I used to go out a lot, go to the clubs, talk to people. At Reading, I'm in front of 25,000 people, arrive an hour before in a couple of limo's, ushered backstage, do the gig, back into the limo's. We were back in the hotel five minutes after we'd finished playing. The chances to talk to people get less".

Perhaps the most encouraging result of this show at Reading was that for maybe the first time the press saw The Mission in their true light - a preposterous band of enormous potential whose every move was heavily tainted with a wry smile and a large dash of humour. Roger Holland acknowledged this much neglected side of the band : "Amidst all the pomp and circumstance of the 'Dambusters March', an agile tongue pokes through a powdered cheek. Beneath the histrionics and hysteria, there lurks a genuine power. The Mish are awful, but they're awful in a big way."[5] Carol Clerk was even more convinced: "Never let it be said that The Mission don't have a sense of humour...it was their humour, their character, their sense of entertainment (alongside their variety and rock sensibility) which allowed them to get away with playing to the unconverted...in Eskimo-land the response was massive despite the problems of the nightlike dodgy sound. Dramatic and persuasive enough to rise above all the inconveniences, the band became all the more fascinating with the introduction of some new material...and the dance goes on..."[6]

* * *

From this appearance at Reading to the release of the first single from the new album in February, The Mission played only two low-key gigs, at Birmingham Powerhouse and Oxford Polytechnic, the latter being a benefit gig for the Mencap charity. In the meantime the album was being mastered and prepared for release, and a spell in London in the New Year saw some B-sides recorded. At the fan club shows and at Reading there had been an often bemused reaction to 'Tower Of Strength' because it was such a radical departure from the pop nature of 'God's Own Medicine', but this uncertainty did not last long. On 5th February, the expectant public heard its first recorded taste of the new album, when 'Tower Of Strength' was released as a single. It charted high, at No.12, despite the length of the track and was B-sided by 'Fabienne' and Aerosmith's 'Dream On'. The actual version that was released was very close to the original demo, suggesting that it was one song which did not lose its way in the lengthy studio deliberations of The Manor. It's reception was a key factor in building anticipation for the forthcoming album and effectively it had already become a central pivot for that record. The press reception was unreservedly enthusiastic; in giving the release the 'Single of the Week' Sounds magazine said: "This is one hell of a record. A huge, bursting soundscape that demands both ears be fully cocked as wave upon wave of big beautiful overblown noise washes against you, rising and rising til you're practically drowning in a sea of sweetest ecstasy. Then blackout...Utterly perfect."[7]

The quality which 'Tower' hinted at became apparent when the album 'Children' was released on February 29th 1988 and charted at No.2, only being kept off the top spot by the then ultra-fashionable Terence Trent D'Arby. Amongst widespread acclaim the record sold heavily, going gold in less than a week, as the public voted massively in favour of the new record. Despite the heavy press criticisms of recent times, The Mission had produced a record that was difficult to find fault with. There was a widespread welcoming of the more mature lyrical content and the more accomplished sound which separated 'Children' from its predecessor, as well as acknowledgments that The Mission had established their own corner of the music scene in which nobody else could compete. Robin Gibson was unreserved in his praise, and perhaps best summarises the warm press response to the record: "All the rock tradition they've plundered has gelled perfectly with their own vision to sound like nothing but The Mission - they're as instant and unique as a T Rex record. Children is a good, occasionally great album which powerfully surpasses their debut. John Paul Jones hasn't radically altered their thrust, just added some essential ballast and sprinkled the dream topping with subtle instrumental spices to speed their quest for the ultimate in monumental rock sound."[8]

Every record has its detractors and The Mission fully expected more than their share for 'Children'. The majority of the criticism understandably centred around renewed accusations of The Mission's retrogressive tendency - with John Paul Jones producing and with the band themselves making no attempt to hide their continued reverence of Led Zeppelin, the press response to 'Children' focussed largely around whether The Mission had succeeded in creating their own particular variation on this theme, or if they had suffocated in excessive references to the past and lost sight of the joke The Mission represented amongst dated rock romanticism. Ted Mico led the prosecution: "It's so easy to laugh at The Mission. The mere mention of 'Wasteland' is enough to send depressives into raging guffaws. They are a poor man's Sisters, a rich man's Cult, a blind man's Nephilim...At worst, the band are the seismic belch emitted after pop's banquet. It's no surprise that 'Children' happens to be buoyed around the Led Zeppelin myth - a legend only revered by those who can't remember just how excruciatingly tedious Page and Co. could be. Using relics to create new relics, The Mission have probably made the finest Led Zeppelin record Led Zeppelin never made, but one man's memory is another man's blind alley. It's time to detonate the ruins."[9]

With their stage show taking on grander proportions and their artwork featuring Roman coins and the continued use of runes and other such symbols The Mission were perceived by many as having lost themselves down the path of self-parody and musical plagiarism that earlier reservations about this tendency had warned them away from. However, as with the accusations that had surfaced around the time of 'God's Own Medicine', and whose scorn had found its focus with Hinkler's use of a double-necked guitar, the criticism repeated here essentially missed the whole point of The Mission. For a band entrenched in respect for '70's music such as Led Zeppelin and Bolan, the use of John Paul Jones and titles such as 'Black Mountain Mist' were so blatantly tongue-in-cheek and plagiarist that the humour was obviously apparent. Rather than steal ideas subtly or covertly, The Mission chose to do so openly and even publicise the fact. For those who took these influences seriously, the continued references to Zeppelin appeared dangerous, almost suicidal as the band were bound to compare badly; to The Mission the comparison was a combination of their respect for that band and a realisation that such pomposity had to be treated with a large dose of humour and comicality. City Limits magazine had been one of the few who had seen this humour earlier on, saying The mission were "shamelessly old wave, stunningly retrogressive. It's all coming back: crushed velvet, black hats with floppy brims, sitting cross-legged in concert halls, Tolkien, mirrors sewn into dowdy black frocks and the unshakeable stench of patchouli."[10] It was left to Mat Smith of Melody Maker, who was one of the few journalists who recognised this trait to perfectly sum up the entire retrogressive debate: "A flurry of long hair, a silhouetted Gibson double neck - the new world rising from the shambles of the old. If we are to believe that pop music should never look to its past for inspiration, then let's be thankful for genres. Let's forget, for a moment, about terminally dull indie-pop bands who don't want to grow old and enjoy instead the simple pleasures of a rock band who don't want to grow up. The Mission pick up where Led Zeppelin left off and add bits the Sisters missed out . A credible crystallisation of myth and mockery, hammer horror and hammer of the gods. As someone once said, it's not what you invent, but who you reinvent that counts. The Mission, by some feat of alchemical juggling, have dared to reinvent the gods."[11]

The band themselves had their own reservations about the recording, alongside some of those voiced by the press, but they were of a different kind, mostly concerned with the recording of the album itself. Obviously at the time of release they were extremely enthusiastic but soon they began to voice concerns, and Hussey soon found the record hard to listen to because it had been such an exorcism of difficult events: "Lyrically it's a desperate album. I didn't realise I was so unhappy at the time and that's why I find it really hard to listen to. But that was the state of our heads at the time". By the same token, Hussey recognises that the record stands up as a testament to their lives at that time, and despite reservations with the benefit of hindsight he acknowledges 'Children' as a valid album: "You spend five months making a record and you think you've done a good job. You can sit back and see the faults in all the albums we've made, but at the time it's very much a product of that time. Where your heads at, how you're feeling, the spirit of the band". He continues: "Children was the record we wanted to make at the time - we wanted to make that big bombastic record. We'd just come off the American tour, we were fried. Half of the lyrics to the album were confused. You're never totally happy but we definitely liked it".

The incredible tour of America the previous year had physically aged the band ten years; Hinkler felt that working with John Paul Jones also aged the band but mentally - he felt like a veteran of the industry despite the band only being two years old. In retrospect

Hussey now feels that by taking so long in the studio they may have lost the essence of what made The Mission so great at that point: "For that period it was too long - we were riding a wave from a year's tour and we were a great group, so maybe we should have recorded it almost live. Instead we messed around trying to make this big artistic statement, this big sounding record in every sense of the word and it didn't really come off. But we learnt a lot and the whole Zep thing was a great experience and after we got over the awe we held him in it was great". Adams was more enthusiastic about the production: "I like it, it sounds really unusual to me. The production is odd but I like the oddness...I listen to it more than the first album." Eyre from Phonogram realised that by not telling them his view on hearing the material at the Townhouse studios he was partly to blame for the reservations that were expressed: "I just wish Jones had taken a bit more counsel about what was going on in 1988 in contemporary music, because it was a whole different ball game. The band had to make that record at that time and they learnt from it". Brown feels correctly that all these reservations were with the benefit of hindsight, and it was too easy for an outsider to say they had taken too long: "We were encouraged to do that in many ways though. Spending so much time on the album was self-indulgent but the record company allowed us to be self-indulgent, especially considering the state we were in. Nobody said 'We're fucking up here' because we wanted to stay there for that time".

This is essentially the key - all reservations with hindsight are mostly unfair. The production, the manner of recording, the songs, all these factors are effected by the bands state at that time - the album 'Children' stands as a document of The Mission directly after their first world tour and how it affected their lives. Even though the band themselves expressed concerns whilst touring the album, the public reaction was unequivocally ecstatic. The facts are that it was a massive seller and for many people 'Children' became a classic album of the 1980's, and established The Mission as the biggest alternative act in Britain for years. The rollercoaster was back on track.

CHAPTER EIGHT

"I'm lucky. Somehow by doing what I want to do, I manage to give people what they don't want to hear and they still come back for more. I haven't been able to figure that one out yet..."

Neil Young

"I have admired you for years and have a complete collection of your press notices. Actually, I think of them as unfair reviews. As unfair as mine. They like to sling demeaning names, don't they?"

Yours,
An Avid Fan

Letter from serial killer Francis Dolarhyde to
Hannibal 'The Cannibal' Lecter.

THE world tour lined up for the promotion of the 'Children' album was ambitious even by The Mission's own prolific standards - in the next twelve months they would tour twenty-six countries and play a gig on average every three nights, including ground breaking shows in South America, a completion of the Led Zeppelin connection with dates with Robert Plant and a triumphant return to Britain and their first ever stadium tour. Their travels started inauspiciously enough with three low-key warm-up dates under the not-too subtle secret name of 'Wayne Craig Mick and Simon' beginning at Leeds Warehouse, then playing at Leicester and Norwich the following nights. After two days packing their massive stage set based on the children theme they set off for a brief North American tour during the second week of February, returning for the more substantial British leg of the 'Children' world tour.

With the rest of the band eagerly anticipating the gigs, Adams was similarly enthusiastic, but because of his problems in LA his zeal was somewhat tempered by a realisation that things had to change, and when he spoke of this shortly before the tour began, there was evidently some trepidation in his mind: "We had to calm things down, it was a no-option thing otherwise someone would have been seriously injured. Not anyone else, it would have been kept within the group. We couldn't have carried on like that. Maybe we've got older and wiser. It was dreadful, you made your own rules. Perhaps that's why I want to go on tour again, let's get out and break something. But not this time, I've mellowed out me, and I don't smoke half as many cigarettes. I think it's going to be a really sensible tour as tours go". Brown shared this attitude, particularly towards the live shows: "We all discovered that it was a lot better not to go on completely out of your brain. When you do it's complete panic for the first three songs. It was stopping us doing certain things, going on in absolute panic and paranoia - because I'm not doing these things anymore it's sort of more of a laugh. You were mixing it with other things which had become too important which was our own fault. It was becoming as important to find *that* as it was to do the gig, which got a bit stupid". No-one was suggesting that the band were suddenly cleaned up totally - the situations which had precipitated the drug and alcohol abuse would still be there, the treatment that was afforded a successful band would be more extravagant if anything, not less so. They were just prepared to accept their mistakes and heed them in the future.

The Mission launched into a twenty-six date UK tour, the highlight of which was a record week long residence at London's Astoria Theatre. Supported for the first half of the tour by Brown's old band Red Lorry Yellow Lorry and followed by hordes of Eskimos The Mission stormed through the dates - coming on to strains of 'Tadeusz', a self-penned neo-classical piece, the band blasted out a set which had many people marking them as one of the country's top live acts. Songs such as 'Tower' and 'Beyond The Pale' took on an epic status live which could never be matched even by the most proficient recording, and was ideally complimented by the more pop moments from the first album. Hussey was becoming a frontman of considerable style and the whole band gelled together perfectly after their months of hard touring. Despite their lofty status the band made it clear that this tour was a deliberate effort to remain close to their fans, who sacrificed so much to follow them around the barren motorways of the UK. Frequently early arrivals would be invited in to watch the soundcheck and food and drinks, as well as guest passes by the bundle, would be provided for those who needed it. In return the ranks of the Eskimos swelled rapidly, fuelled by the first publication of a fanzine by two of the founder members, Stoko and Ramone, which frequently lambasted the band itself or admitted to mischiefs such as when Nightmare Man defaced a crew member's car with an aerosol calling card.

It was to be the triumphant week at the Astoria however, that would overshadow the other dates on the tour. Now supported by All About Eve and Ghost Dance, and with John Paul Jones guesting on the encores, The Mission sold out every night and produced blistering shows of increasing electricity, culminating in an incredible Sunday night performance. Roy Wilkinson of Melody Maker was resident for the week and reviewed the events on the Friday night thus: "Earlier Wayne had acknowledged that 'Monday was a bit shit' - a confession easy to make from the tower of strength The Mission had by then created. In fact after Thursday's show one wondered what ultimate climax could come next. Not to worry though, there was plenty to come as.four simple rockers burn their name into rock's holiest annals."[1] Such was the impression that the band left that on completing the week they were sent a letter from the management of the venue thanking them for their performances. The motivation for these dates was largely to avoid what the band saw as the trappings of success, as Hussey explains: "On the last British tour I felt we were becoming detached. You need response, it's a reciprocal thing, you feed off it. The Bunnymen doing Wembley Arena, the idea of that is appalling. You've got too much responsibility to just accept it like that. That's why I like the idea of doing London Astoria for a week. Two nights at Wembley, four at Hammersmith, I fucking hate those places". He continued: "We're doing our best to make sure this tour is the best possible way to see a band".

Meanwhile, the off stage behaviour showed little signs of continuing where they had left off in America. Although they were ejected in just six hours from the hotel which allowed Led Zeppelin's motorbike-in-the-corridor routine, The Mission re-joined the rollercoaster ride very much at half speed. As security against the dangerous fringes of previous tours Hussey signed a pledge saying he would give up drink and illicit substances - the only snag was that they were all drunk at the time anyway and he sneaked in a clause saying 'I reserve the right to change my mind completely at any time, regardless of circumstance'. Adams was more concerned about his belief that he was jinxed and always got the worst hotel room: "I feel like a turd in a swimming pool. I always get the worst rooms! In this one place in Manchester there was only enough room for the bed, so you put your suitcase down and you couldn't get out! There's never enough room on the complaints form to complain, so I complain about that instead". What was perhaps more worrying was the growing level of violence at some gigs. There had developed an intense and often unseemly rivalry between Eskimos and the New Model Army fans, whose clogged feet would often cause serious harm to Mission fans. The musical interests took a back seat as band loyalties took on the mentality that had so troubled football in previous years. This rivalry had been intensified in April the previous year when the Eskimos had been featured on the front cover of the Melody Maker in their own right, and featured in a two page spread inside called 'The Dawn of the Ice Age'. This had enraged the New Model Army fans and ever since then tension between the two camps had been high. Several Mission followers who appeared in the press found themselves the victims of pre-planned physical assaults. Matters were not improved by the growing contingent of Hells Angels who tagged along just for the violence, most publically at Leicester where there were running street battles and vicious scuffles across the town.

The Mission continued undeterred. It was not until the release of the second single from 'Children', a track called 'Beyond the Pale' which only reached No.32, that the rollercoaster ride seemed to slow down. The track had provided the remarkable opening to 'Children' and represented The Mission's ability to capture an enormous musical atmosphere, with Hinkler's intricate guitar details anchored by a thunderous bass and drum line. Hussey's extensive melodies were complimented to great effect by the striking vocal talents of Julianne Regan of All About Eve, and the whole track built up to a massive crescendo with a memorably unusual mandolin solo. Despite the tremendous start the song had provided to the album, the single never achieved the success 'Tower' had enjoyed, as is so often the case for the second single from any band's album. For The Mission this represented the first public stalling of the ride they had taken in 1986, as Hussey explains: "We were on a roll and just kept going. It really went on until when we released that second single - that was really the first time we'd had a little downer with the music. When the album had gone in at No.2 it was all go up until then." Surprisingly this second new track was the final single taken from the by-now massively popular and widely acclaimed 'Children' album, although there was a DJ-only version of 'Kingdom Come' released in November 1988. The disappointment at the lower chart success of 'Beyond the Pale' did not last long. The dramatic responses they were getting from audiences nationwide were a recognition of the unique sound and approach The Mission had developed, an approach of which the band were very aware and were justifiably proud of, prompting the usually reserved Hinkler to say "I honestly believe that there's no-one doing what we're doing at the moment".

*   *   *

For the press who had squeezed so much mileage out of The Mission's round the clock intoxication, the absence of their usual tour antics presented them with a real frustration. Since the band no longer appeared willing to hurl themselves headlong into a self-induced physical and nervous breakdown for the sake of good copy, the press turned their acidic pens instead to personal slander. As The Mission played night after night to sold out houses nationwide, the less informative sections of the media targeted the band themselves, and Hussey in particular. The tone was set with 'Children' but the vicious treatment was a feature of The Mission's career that would stay with them constantly. As The Mission reached new heights of success, the press in general, and the NME in particular plumbed new depths of inanity. In April 1988 an article appeared in the NME which proved to be a forewarning of things to come as certain parties conducted a campaign of unprecedented personal, abusive and essentially childish criticism, with Barry Egan leading the way, finding nothing more worthwhile to say than that Hussey was "a congenitally deformed Dennis Norden who's been gene-spliced together with the child-catcher in Chitty Chitty Bang Bang", and classing the singer's name as an expletive by printing it as W***e H****y.[2] Relevance was quickly replaced by the more mindless careerist invective of journalists who ignored appropriate issues in favour of topics more reminiscent of the gutter press. Myrna Minkoff for example deemed the musicality of The Mission to be less important an issue than Hussey's virility: "He pops up in Smash Hits talking about fatherhood like an execrable pillock brain and case for castration. In 'Heaven on Earth' Wayne reveals himself to be the sort of dimbo who suddenly vows to fight for, to die for a woman simply because a teaspoonful of his stupid sperm has helped to cause her baby."[3] Hussey's physical appearance was also the focus of much scorn: "A white necklace hangs reluctantly about the neck that holds that undiscussably ugly head"[4] whilst the worst of the writers even stooped low enough to deem his new-born child fair game: "His jockstrap-encrusted brain has arrived in a new realm. For reasons best known to Himself, God had given unto Wayne Hussey a daughter."[5]

Even the valid and informed criticism of The Mission carried with it a venom and spite that reeked of pre-determined abuse. There was, quite rightly, much scepticism of the band's blatant retrogressive tendencies, which were freely acknowledged by The Mission, but unfortunately these critics chose to emphasise their point with disappointing vilification. One journalist chose to abdicate his informative responsibilities as a reviewer of 'Children' by saying only "I shall sell this tomorrow"[6] whilst another hack, although more forthcoming in detail, was equally dismissive of their new album: "'Tower of Strength' is a sketchy facsimile of 'Kasmir' or 'Friends' off Led Zep III, (and) 'Heat' stomps around the hemline of Heart and the borderline of Foreigner. In short the album is every Eskimo's wet dream and the Mission's visa from museum curator's to main exhibitors, (with) the usual guff about a quest for instinct and innocence...Wayne and his merry men plough safe pastures, the bands sphere of reference has not become so minuscule as to exclude the outside world completely. Like all great rock, The Mission are therefore free to create an insulated community, immune to the feckless whims of pop and standing for that great security blanket - constancy...the band are at their most effective when at their most meaningless. The only real mystery is how Wayne can sing this po-faced, pompous bilge with a straight face."[7] The most disappointing aspect of all their detractors was not so much the criticism itself but the abusive tone that the press increasingly adopted towards The Mission. Genuine reservations were lost amongst personal or irrelevant slander, whilst those with something of worth to say were allowed a steadily smaller voice.

Fortunately, there were many important issues raised by the handful of informed journalists who steered away from this pointless abuse. Much justifiable criticism was aimed squarely at Hussey in particular - at times he came across as arrogant, self-indulgent and irresponsible, and his habit of fabricating ludicrous stories in interviews antagonised many journalists - he told one fascinated reporter that he owned a pink cadillac convertible that he used solely for shopping at Sainsbury's, whilst another journalist scribbled in disbelief as Hussey informed him that he wanted to become pregnant and carry a child. Many accused Hussey of hypocrisy as he now appeared in the press at this stage as reluctant to perpetuate the drug-addled monster image he had acquired, largely at his own volition. His confidence in the band was frequently cited as conceit, and his and The Mission's social habits were the focus of much criticism.

On a musical level, the over-production of 'Children' was a serious accusation and added voice to those who justifiably felt that The Mission could be heading towards retrogressive self-parody in their overt and frequent references to their '70's heroes. There was a real danger that they would fail to assert their own identity by continually revering this period of rock music. Perhaps the most relevant question posed by the media at this stage was 'Could The Mission go on to be the next British stadium band, succeeding the likes of U2 and Simple Minds?' The band themselves had seen this level when they had supported Bono and Co. at those two dates in 1987, and to a certain extent this had already placed this seed of thought in their minds, as much as their public dislike of larger venues suggested otherwise. Evidently, lack of confidence would not be an obstacle in their path, as Hussey brashly claimed "We have the potential to be bigger than U2. This band is only two years old and we can do anything within the realms of possibility."[8] The danger when a band takes on board the mantle of 'the next biggest thing' is that the expectation frequently exceeds the actual product. The Mission wisely decided to distance themselves from a public debate about this apart from the occasional over-zealous outburst. Besides, there were still some shows which did not warrant such acclaim, and reviewers were right to point out their shortfalls, with one journalist calling them "weak, lumbering and shambolic, hollow theatre, plainly lacking in charisma and power; hardly the stuff of rock legends."[9]

Objective and constructive criticism however, was very much in the minority as The Mission became victims of some of the most virulent and consistently slanderous press treatment ever published. Unfortunately, as much as the band tried to pass off the severe criticism it inevitably affected them, but seemed to trouble Hinkler more than anyone else. His dissatisfaction of their treatment was very clear: "As far as I'm concerned, the NME can go boil their heads 'til Kingdom come, because I have totally no interest in them. Journalists can eat shit in hell, because they're scum. I hate it when someone spends a couple of days with us, sits in a bar with us and it's chat, chat, chat, joke, joke, joke, and they go away and don't say it. I'm going to disembowel them. It's NOT ON, what they do. I wouldn't be backwards in coming forwards in ripping their heads off. They're hiding behind the print, they are very cowardly. For what they said about Wayne they don't deserve a second chance. I could sit down and talk to them in a corner but they don't deserve that much effort. Just a good kicking".

It was becoming apparent that Hinkler was disillusioned by the press more so than the other members of the band, but in articulating his discontent he highlighted the many flaws in the music media. He tired of the interviews, the mindless questions and the distorted finished product. He would rather just play the music and leave all that to someone else. "I'm fed up with trying to be clever and smart and having me wits about me...I've long since decided to be tough and stupid. I've got fuck all to say really, mostly because I think anything I say doesn't make that much difference. And I can't be bothered to think of things to say. I'm in this band for one thing more than anything else, for rockin' out. Touring, having a lot of volume coming from me amps behind me. I get off on it, one of the few things I do get off on. The rest of the time I walk around in a daze really. You know, photo sessions, interviews, meeting foreign record company people. I just show my face - they talk a different language to me, a stupid language, a language of things that aren't essentially important. I really can't bring myself to speak like that and I end up answering with just flippant comments. I don't really want to do all that but I do want to keep rockin' out, it's purely selfish". At the same time Hinkler was clearly unhappy about the lack of interest many journalists showed in the group as a whole, preferring instead to concentrate on the singer, even though this had been an understandable trait of music papers since their very conception. During this tour his dissatisfaction was beginning to express itself inside the band, notably when he rather worryingly said in one interview "Mick knows me inside out, Craig knows me pretty well, Wayne's never really made an effort".

Despite these rumblings of discontent, the campaign against The Mission was essentially impotent. Indeed, it is possible that the derogatory features which filled so many pages had the exact opposite effect to that which had been desired. What this element of the press failed to see was that as The Mission became more and more successful, their puerile and careerist journalistic approach was exposed as increasingly questionable and irrelevant. Far from belittling The Mission, the virulent abuse which centred on Hussey in particular, created a mythology around him and perpetuated the dichotomous status afforded to pop stars throughout the years of being either loved or loathed. He rapidly became a very high profile media figure with half his audience wanting to be him and the remainder hating him. Either way, and partly as a result of these inane press criticisms, by the end of 1988 there was nobody interested in music in Britain who had not heard of Wayne Hussey and The Mission.

* * *

The only way they knew how to combat the severe criticism was to take to the road as only they knew how. On April 5th The Mission took their 'Children' tour to Bourges in France and began a European tour that would see them visit ten countries in less than twenty-five days, before flying out to America to commence an 11 date tour as headline band, and then joining Robert Plant's 'Now and Zen' album tour across the West coast in front of audiences of up to 25,000. Europe gave the band a tremendous welcome and the band completed the dates in high spirits, which bolstered them as they headed for the country which had chewed them up and spat them out the last time they had visited America.

This time Perrin had arranged American representation by former Police mangeress, Pamela Burton, because he never wanted to see a repeat of the Los Angeles incident, but also because there was real doubt as to whether The Mission would be taken seriously in America without US representation. She joined the camp at the end of 1987 and toured in February and on the Plant dates. After working on New York radio shows, she had set up Frontier Booking in 1979 with Ian Copeland as a partner, which lasted six years. She left to manage Simple Minds and briefly Iggy Pop, then took over with The Police, as well as working with Simply Red. Burton first saw The Mission on that fateful American tour of 1987, and was immediately attracted to what she saw - her observations give a fascinating insight into the band's state on that first tour: "I wasn't really interested until I heard the first line of 'God's Own Medicine' and then I spoke to Wayne and fell in love. I went to a show in LA and after finally working my way in I headed for the dressing room. First of all I had to part the sea of girls in lingerie and various states of undress with massive amounts of black hair. There were more fans in that dressing room than there were in the gig. I just introduced myself and everyone was staring at me in my suit and briefcase. The gig that night knocked me out but at this stage there was so much smoke on stage that I didn't see them until the third song. I missed rock 'n' roll, viscerally missed the spirit of sex, drugs and rock 'n' roll. When I saw them in that dressing room, people doing lines, drinking, Wayne was throwing up...it was hilarious and painful at the same time. For some reason, maybe because I didn't know them, the image of the whole thing didn't bother me. I thought it was fun, it was rock 'n' roll, this is what I grew up with. My work with The Police for all those years gave me the emotional stamina to believe that The Mission's music, particularly in America, is a process of education. When The Police first came out, the radio and the general public didn't know what it was, punk or reggae? It took four LP's to really make a significant impact. They started off like The Mission in tiny bars - one night Sting said to the minuscule audience 'I'm not going to introduce the band, why don't you introduce yourselves to each other?' At the end of my work with them they played Shea Stadium in front of 72,000 people. It took six years and so it gives me hope for The Mission".

She was now on board to keep the band in line aswell as to promote them across the Atlantic. As many before her had commented, the spirit of the extended family that was The Mission was often as striking as the music; despite their massive success The Mission were essentially still a gang of lads together: "If they weren't in a band together, then some equation, some selection of them would be doing something together. It is quite unique today, you don't get it. I probably didn't realise the extent of the band's esprit de corps until I did the four dates with them on this 'Children' tour in February, I was knocked out by it. When I see one of the roadies come into the dressing room and sit on Pete Turner's lap in the way that you would if you were a kid, like if your Dad was sitting in an armchair and you'd face him chest to chest and put your arms around his neck and he would comfort you - Ed, Nipper, they'll leap on to Pete's lap and he'll father them. When people say goodnight to each other they all kiss each other goodnight as well. When I first saw this, My God, such a wealth of emotion, I thought I've got to keep a perspective on this, this is not my family, this is business, but it's very difficult to maintain a business like attitude. Your facade will eventually break down and they want it to. I always assumed that artists wanted to know that their manager was capable and strong. In this band they want those qualities in you but they don't want them brought into the dressing room. They really delineate between us and them and once you're 'us' they're capital letters a mile high".

With Burton in place, and with a successful and relatively controlled first leg of their own headline tour of America behind them, The Mission began the Plant tour the following day. The first date, The Markus Amphitheatre in Milwaukee held a capacity of 21,000, a sign of things to come as they played thirteen dates of similar size to crowds who were themselves as eager Zeppelin fans as the support band. The reaction from the Plant fans was very mixed and somewhat erratic - most provocative was the band's re-work of Aerosmith's 'Dream On', which was a legendary track in America and ranked alongside the likes of songs such as 'Stairway to Heaven'- the cold response this number received was indicative of its sacred status. After several nights of decidedly luke warm applause after this song, Wayne voiced his opinion of their attitude: 'Thanks to those of you who listened, the rest of you can fuck off.'

Incidents were not in short supply either on their own dates or those with Plant. At Los Angeles the bouncers had been visibly attacking some of the crowd so Hussey stopped the gig and informed them that they were not needed, whereupon they eventually retired. In Phoenix the 80 year old Head of another major US record company mistook Hinkler's long hair for that of a young lady and subsequently spent the whole night touching him up, and propositioning and offering various strong drinks to the bewildered guitarist whilst the crew sniggered in the background. Both Adams and Brown thoroughly enjoyed the dates with Plant, as Adams explains: "They were brilliant. We'd calmed down. Mick and I had a really good time. I know Wayne and Simon weren't so keen - most of the audience had seen Zeppelin before and had probably never heard of us. Plant treated us really well, better than we expected. The crew were really good but when you're playing to the capacity of Reading every night everything has to be organised, there's no messing about". Brown was similarly enthusiastic: "When you play the Enormodome every night with Robert Plant you can't let it effect you. I liked the tour but Wayne and Simon didn't like the fact that people were still turning up when we were playing. I'd prefer to play to a big crowd that's still arriving than a tiny venue somewhere else. You can't let the size bother you because you'd fuck up if you thought about it too hard". As suggested Hussey was not so keen: "I didn't enjoy it really, he was great but I don't like playing second fiddle, not even to Robert Plant. That was very much my attitude at the time that we shouldn't be a support band. The worst part about it was actually playing the shows - on most nights we were in these purpose-built sheds and all our fans would seem miles away and it was really hard work to get it going. We had a tough time with a lot of the audiences but having said that I think it was educational and I'd do it again". The recreational side of the tour was enjoyed though, even if it was very much toned down from their previous American excursion. The first night they spent out with Plant and his crew, Nipper was thrown out of the club they were in after dribbling beer on an unsuspecting Steve from a balcony above. This time they were also prepared for any physical ailments, with Perrin bringing his 'poorly jumper' on tour for sweating out band illnesses, whilst he would go fishing in it, neither of which lent it a particularly pleasant aroma by the end of these dates.

This American tour also saw a marked increase in Hussey's stage activity - towards the end of the set he would abandon his guitar and wander around the stage, frequently seeking refuge in the lighting rig or balconies. At the New York Ritz with Iggy Pop in attendance, he was particularly mobile and climbed forty feet up to the second balcony, leaving an anxious Perrin biting his nails and worrying about insurance premiums. Once on top of the balcony Hussey stepped on the groin of a red-faced Steve Sutherland from the Melody Maker, before cutting his feet to ribbons as he stepped over the tables full of the drinks of bewildered record company executives. Such was his enjoyment that he failed to see one fan who went beyond the call of duty as he walked past by lifting up her shirt and flashing her rather large breasts at the singer who carried on oblivious to the side show.

The Mission played their own headline dates with an authority and poise that belied their young age as a band. One reviewer described the gig at Los Angeles Theatre thus: "Cool but intense, they conjured up a cauldron of sound but never lost their grip. You only had to watch Simon - head down, body jerking - to learn something about involvement...Mick giving it the force of a truck gone AWOL and Craig hurling his bass around as if it were balsa wood - The Mission were lost in their own lightning blur, the crowd coiled around their collective finger."[10] Other dates on the tour included the Filmore in San Francisco, whose boards had been graced by such legends as The Doors and Jimi Hendrix. It was not all roses though, especially at the penultimate gig at Portland's Starry Night Club, where the band played before a disinterested audience, sold only 6 T-shirts and caused a sell-out of the $2.50 ear-plugs behind the bar. They signed off the American leg of the world tour in great fashion though at the last night in Seattle, where 1400 people went wild for them, and afterwards saw Hussey forgetting the words whilst jamming along to Zeppelin's 'Rock 'n' Roll' with support band Balaam and the Angel. By the end of the dates, with shows such as these, The Mission were paid what was probably the greatest compliment in their eyes - Robert Plant said that of the thousands of bands vainly trying to copy Led Zeppelin, only The Mission had got it right because they had managed to re-capture the essential spirit of his band. Praise indeed.

* * *

Perhaps the most unusual feature of this world tour for 'Children' was The Mission's eight date tour of South America, which took them through Argentina, Uruguay, Brazil and finally Paraguay, where they were the first Western band ever to play in that country. The response was unconditionally fanatical, with sold out shows everywhere even though many were in cities ravaged by poverty and economic destitution. The logistics of the tour were interesting aswell, with the band frequently being informed that their album sales were minuscule, only to turn up at packed venues with several thousand fans all singing the words. Everybody involved warmed to these people, probably won over early by the sign at the airport saying 'Welcome Man With Hat'. Perrin was clearly taken by the whole experience: "It's different and it's very exciting. The dangers over there are far surpassed by the warmth of the welcoming you get from people down there. It's amazing that you go to Sao Paulo and see the awful way that people have to live, you don't expect them to be even aware of The Mission, it's not really a priority".

At their first stop, the Obras Sanitarias in Argentina they were relieved to find themselves asked more questions about Led Zeppelin than the Falklands war. In Uruguay, where 6,000 people crammed into a 2400 seater El Cilindro club in Montevideo the reception was ecstatic, with the language problem being eliminated by the reaction and the atmosphere as a whole, as was generally the case across the continent. On arriving in Rio in Brazil, Adams spent most of his time in the bathroom, his stomach having taken exception to the food. During the first show there, Hussey dragged a beautiful girl from the front row of the audience, danced with her, gave her flowers and then escorted her backstage. When he arrived in the dressing room, he was handed a piece of paper informing him that she was the daughter of the Head of the Brazilian record company who'd had a fit and said if Hussey laid a finger on his daughter The Mission would never sell another record in Brazil. After the show the band paid a visit to the Great Train Robber Ronnie Biggs who entertained them South American style and following a hectic night out, listened to their album and declared 'They're great! They sound just like the London Irish Fusiliers'.

Hussey found particular interest in the many red light areas of the continent: "It fascinates me, it's the sleazy side of life that I can find quite appealing. It appeals to something in me that is very base, a different kind of instinct. On the one hand you're appalled by it and on the other you're fascinated by it". Another night they went to a club called 'Help', two doors down from their hotel which sold beers for 30p each. Pete Turner, the mountainous sound man took full advantage of the generous prices and proceeded to get riotously drunk. Turner was a larger than life character who was ideal for coping with unruly crowds and argumentative promoters in a Peter Grant fashion that had worked so well for bands in the 1970's. What he had not bargained for however, was the attentions of a tiny Brazilian girl who took a fancy to him in this club and determined to corner him at whatever cost. As the band walked out of the hotel, they were treated to the comical sight of this enormous man running up the street, helplessly searching for somewhere to hide, closely followed by a tiny but adoring girl who clearly had designs on him, apparently undeterred by his cries of 'Bloody Hell, what's happening, help me.' When she finally cornered him she needed two beer crates to stand on just to try to kiss him. Still chuckling as they arrived at the bar the band were befriended by a group of burly American Marines, blind drunk, one of whom bucked up a tickle stomached Adams by slapping him heartily on the back and informing him 'Hey man I'm going to Afghanistan tomorrow, I've stolen this bottle of Bacardi, so drink this, shut up and enjoy yourself.'

Perhaps the most comical event of the tour was reserved for their appearance on a Brazilian TV show called 'Milkshake', which was recorded for posterity on the video of their South American jaunt, released a year later. In short, the whole show was chaotic - after being introduced by a Barbie Doll blonde presenter they proceeded to mime to the full length album version of 'Beyond the Pale' whilst maniac skateboard kids flew past the heads, and various frenzied youths spread havoc. When Hussey realised he would be stranded by the lengthy guitar solo on the full version, he went to make a phonecall in a British red phone box, returning to chat to Brown and then ordered a beer at the fake bar. Brown meanwhile had bored of the track, and left the kit to sit on a large Harley Davidson bike on stage, but unfortunately he lost his balance in the process and crashed to the floor. After the song had finished, nobody from the television company seemed to think anything unusual had happened, whereas the bemused band left the studio with Hussey out of shot saying 'What the fuck was all that about?'

After Brazil, and with Ronnie Biggs dubious compliment still ringing in their ears, they headed for a three night stay at the Projecto SP club, which was equally well received. Reactions throughout the tour of the continent had been incredible but nothing prepared the band for the reception they were afforded when they became the first Western rock band to play in Paraguay. In short they created a national frenzy. Having had to get Presidential permission to play there at all, they were detained for hours at Customs but eventually released. As they pushed open the doors to the airport arrivals, they were showered by hundreds of flowers from the hordes of waiting girls and besieged for twenty minutes. After having been extricated from the crowds by their own personal secret service bodyguards, the band were ushered into the only two limousines in the country, both of which belonged to the right-wing dictator who controlled Paraguay with an iron fist. They switched the radio on and found to their amazement that every station was playing The Mission. They headed for town and as they drove through the small busy streets people came out of their houses to wave and clap. All the streets had banners across them saying 'Welcome The Mission' and the air was full of confetti and paper.

Everywhere they went they were escorted by machine guns and armed guards, due largely to the fact that there were rumours of an imminent political coup (The fascist President would be overthrown two weeks after The Mission left Paraguay). At the pre-show press conference they were warned not to say anything about politics, so Hussey immediately stood up and launched into a detailed polemic about the state of the native economy. Adams was particularly intimidated by it all, and decided to stay firmly put in his hotel room. The band had been told they had sold twenty-six albums in the entire country, so they were understandably sceptical when they arrived at the venue already filled with 5,000 expectant people. Perrin admitted the heavy security caused him for the first and only time to be concerned about their actual physical safety. He need not have worried - the gig was a classic, despite the machine gun toting guards placing themselves on the audience side of the barriers, and wondering why nobody would stand within fifty feet of the stage. After Perrin had a quiet word they filed out and filed back in again, this time on the stage side of the fence. Hussey appeared completely unperturbed by the potential arms cache inside the gig: "Those kind of things you never consider really, you go out there and think 'I'm the front man, I'll do what I want'; you don't think of the repercussions, it's a complete licence to do what you want, because you can get away with it. At that gig if one of those guys had turned around and shot me they would have had a revolution on their hands right there and then".

The Mission returned home having broken even financially, despite the ravaged home economies, and having thoroughly enjoyed the whole South American jaunt. Hussey had his own particular reasons: "Just in terms of experience it was a great tour. I can't really remember how good the actual shows were, but the tour as a whole was great and coke's only eight quid a gramme. Quite often we couldn't leave the hotel because there were so many people outside, the reactions were incredible, they even have their own branches of the fan club, there's loads of affection, and they all knew the words to the songs even though they can't speak any English". All these events were recorded on a camcorder for the video 'The Mission - South America' which was released in September 1989. Channel 4 had originally lined up a four man crew to film the tour, in conjunction with a South American film crew. At the last minute, as the band sat in the airport waiting to fly out to Buenos Aires, Channel 4 got cold feet about the ability of the South American crews to complete the job and pulled out of the project. Perrin promptly stood up, walked into Duty Free, bought a camcorder, learnt how to operate it on the flight, and started to shoot the minute they landed. This footage is an excellent record of The Mission's tour, which was full of incident, drunkeness and even suggestions of religious accusations, which Hussey succinctly denied: "Quite often the image that has been portrayed has been one of four drug-taking, beer-drinking sexists from Yorkshire and we're not. Well, not any more than anyone else...We also get labelled as using religious imagery and being some kind of Satanist freaks. I've never lit a candle in my life, just burnt a few at both ends."[11]

* * *

Only a fortnight after coming back from their escapades in South America, The Mission found themselves in Tokyo for their first ever Japanese concert, which was followed by two shows in Osaka. The Japanese charts are flooded with mostly home bred bands and it is only certain bands, ironically such as Pete Burns' Dead or Alive, who have sold millions and can compete with indigenous acts. This was very much the case with The Mission - they were popular, but very much a cult phenomenon. The motivating factor behind these three dates was primarily to 'give them a shot', and that done the band could return home, with later excursions to smaller territories being less important once they had been there before. Before setting off on a six date Iberian tour, where they were received as well as ever, and recording a Liz Kershaw session for Radio 1, the band played a mini tour of the UK in Glasgow, Liverpool, Bristol and London, all to venues of no greater capacity than 500. Part of the reason for this was to return to the more intimate surroundings offered by such clubs, partly to put on a unique show for the fan club members who were the only people allowed in, and partly to warm up the band for the final leg of the world tour in Britain in November and December. With the fans crammed into the tiny venues and choosing the second of two sets that the band played each night, this tour was greatly enjoyed by all concerned, a real homecoming, and it confirmed the unique relationship that The Mission had managed to maintain with their audience. Grahame Bent was there to review the gig for Melody Maker and was enthralled: "There's an unnerving informality about this ritual - I mean this trip's way too homely to be in the slightest bit mystic. I mean did His Husseyness really stride past me in the foyer on his way to vote for his three fave Mish trax? Wow, I could really get to like this bloke...It's all done in the kind of carefree vibe that comes from playing for the one deliriously happy family."[12]

South America was unique and the fan club tour was thoroughly enjoyable, as were the brace of dates in Greece which acted as the tail end to the 'Children' tour. However, if there was to be a crowning moment in 1988 it was the band's stadium tour which began six days after they returned from Europe, and if there was to be a highlight of this tour itself, it was the band's show at Birmingham NEC on November 26th. Their first taste in larger venues came at Cornwall's St. Austell Coliseum but it was the following night in the Midlands that The Mission played what many referred to as their greatest gig, and all the band and crew were overwhelmed by the experience. It was a windy night in the Midlands when The Mission's coach pulled into the car park of the NEC, its progress slowed by the thousands of Mission fans heading for the arena - looking out from the coach across the sea of fans excitedly laughing and talking was a justification for all the previous two years hard work, and seeing their own popularity in such absolute terms made the disaster of Los Angeles and the heavy press criticism seem a million miles away. Once onstage, and with the Eskimos in heavy attendance, including two who had made the journey from Vienna, The Mission played to a filled house of 8,000 ecstatic fans, serving a monster set of both albums and managing to hold an intimate atmosphere despite the enormous size of the hall.

For the band however, it was not the set itself that was the real highlight - it was the whole intense experience, the atmosphere, the number of fans, the ecstatic response. It represented the culmination of everything they had worked for and all that they had aimed at in one fantastic night. Perrin was videoing the set for later use but found it increasingly difficult to concentrate. At one point an excited fan climbed on to the shoulders of his friend, an activity banned at the NEC and was promptly dragged to the floor by the security guards and pulled backstage. On seeing this Adams ripped off his bass and stormed backstage, undeterred by the effect it would have on the song they were half way through, and the 8,000 people watching, and was hastily followed by the rest of the band and most of the crew, where an angry confrontation took place between the band and the security. Eventually the fan was re-united with his friends and the security put in their place. Rather than disrupt the show these incredible events fired up the crowd to fever pitch - the atmosphere was by now electric and swelled when the band launched into a massive version of the epic 'Tower of Strength'. Half way through the song, as the second chorus kicked in, the massive lights were turned onto the audience who were ALL chanting the lyrics and thrusting their arms in the air. The band balked at this fantastic sight and Perrin dropped his camera, open jawed, amazed. In that single moment everything The Mission had been through in the hectic last two years was justified, all their ambitions and goals were represented in those 8,000 pairs of arms and the great wall of chanting. Needless to say the rest of the gig was a classic, and in some ways made the show at Wembley Arena, where security was ultra-tight, something of an anti-climax.

Four years later the incredible night in Birmingham would still hold sway as one of the best moments for all the band, and the whole tour itself is viewed with much emotion and pride. At the time a super-confident Hussey articulated what the rest of the band were feeling: "Unashamedly I'm convinced that we're one of the best, if not the best band in the world right now...you know in yourself whether you're good or not. This tour has been brilliant. It's the first I've ever done without doing any drugs, and I'm actually experiencing things I've never noticed before because I was in a bit of a daze. The drugs induced a lot of paranoia..but now we're rollin'". Such confidence had allowed the band to play venues the size of the NEC and Wembley

Arena, a risk which many bands would not have taken. It paid off and Hussey had no qualms about it when reminded of his earlier derogatory public comments about stadium shows: "You just get ideas above your station - you play Brixton and then think what's the next place. You see some bands play the big places and they don't pull it off and you think 'We could do that gig'. There's a lot of inverted snobbery in this country especially in the last few years about all this. One result of this attitude is that there's no real pop stars that spring to mind - we were one of the last groups that thought like that - Miles Hunt from The Wonder Stuff isn't a bad pop star at all but even he underplays. People like icons, they like to see you up there making a dick of yourself, half of them are there to love you and half of them are there to loathe you. Take Morrisey, I don't particularly like his stuff or The Smiths, but I think he's a great pop star, and it's essential to have those kind of people around. It's a British tendency over the last few years, and that's why there's a lack of British bands who've broken big recently. On the 'Children' tour we were delivering the goods live and we went for it".

This stadium tour confirmed the one feature of The Mission that separates them from so many other bands - their normality and down to earth nature never dents the mystique they hold for their audience. This explains how they could play a fan club tour, with the band themselves joining the back of the queue to vote for their favourite Mission songs, only a month before they stepped on to the stage at Birmingham in front of 8,000 people who saw them as virtual rock gods. The outrageous stories that surrounded The Mission's tour lifestyle revealed a mythical extravagance that for the vast majority was something that only rock stars were involved in. In complete contrast, as soon as the band stepped off the tour bus they were suddenly transformed from notorious and almost unreal rock 'n' roll monsters, back into a likeable gang of approachable lads who would gladly pull up on the motorway to give a lift to a rain-soaked fan hitching to their gig. In many ways, this closeness to their fans increases this mystique, because they are revered yet still apparently human, mysterious yet still normal. Visually The Mission had now created their own world of romantic imagery and particular fantasy, with visions of heaven and hell, misty mountains and lakes, maidens on horseback and devils, spreading across a great expanse of cosmic proportions; yet alongside this they had maintained an intimate and warm relationship with their following that was second to none, and which appeared to grow regardless of the band's massive status. The Mission represented a fascinating dichotomy: on the one hand, they were grandiose figures of idolatrous passion indulging in all the activities that rock heroes are supposed to, yet on the other they were four honest men who just happened to be in a band. The mixture was compelling.

* * *

A month after the tour had been completed this dual fascination was confirmed by one of the most successful showings ever by any one band in the Sounds and Melody Maker Readers Polls for 1988. The Mission whitewashed the competition, scooping all the major accolades in the Melody Maker awards including Best Band, Best Album (Children), Best Single (Tower of Strength), as well as second in Best Video (Tower) and Male Singer, with Hussey winning a dubious sixth in the Poseur of the Year award. What made this achievement all the more impressive, apart from the fact that it was mirrored by similar success in the Sounds Poll, was that U2 were second to The Mission in the categories, even though their 'Rattle and Hum' album had been a colossal worldwide success, thus proving Bono's own prediction at Elland Road that The Mission were heading for widespread acclaim. The band were overjoyed - they had all looked to these poll results in their formative years in bands, and remembered the furore when The Beatles had been displaced from the 1970 Poll by a group called Led Zeppelin. Their almost total absence from the NME polls did nothing to dampen their spirits, as Hussey explains: "I used to read all the polls as a kid so that was great. It took us a few days just to let it sink in. We didn't bother about the NME - I have a theory about the NME polls that we were deliberately written out. I know there was an editorial policy to write us out of the polls and give us bad press at that paper, across the board. They were never constructive either, just personal. They can do that, and I'm sure we're not alone in being picked out, but how else do you explain that in the Melody Maker and Sounds polls we swept the board and yet in the NME we had no representation whatsoever. That's very sad". Their success was particularly sweet as it made a complete mockery of the vicious press slander that had been such a feature of The Mission's career. The public had clearly been unaffected by the rantings of the press - the fickleness which had seen so much abuse hurled at The Mission was by now a tedious characteristic of the music press in general, and people were aware of this and ignored it - the tremendous Mission showing in the Polls of this year rendered the press comments largely impotent.

Such was the success of the 'Children' project that The Mission attracted thousands to their cause, with the total worldwide sales of 'Children' soon passing the 500,000 mark. At this stage many of the followers were predominantly the so-called goths - by now the band were generally acknowledged as 'the goth's goths' and that convenient media label appeared to have stuck, despite what the group themselves said to the contrary. The romantic imagery and flowery aurals gave the whole 'Children' project a flavour that perfectly fitted the aspirations of the hordes of goths who saw The Mission as the encapsulation of their entire lifestyle. Ironically, this peak for the band was seen by the handful of the original Eskimos as the end of an era, as they had finally lost the extreme intimacy that watching The Mission had once allowed them. Maybe this was a variation on the inverted snobbery that Hussey had talked of, maybe it was a form of elitism that penetrates band followings, but it is understandable when people have hitched thousands of miles and made untold sacrifices over two years that they might be disappointed when things change. The ultimate irony is that it was these die-hard fans who had forced The Mission to play bigger and bigger venues in the first instance, and thus they had inadvertently initiated the end of their own particular lifestyle. For the vast majority of Mission fans, however, the special relationship they had with the band was now as close as ever.

On a lighter note, the stadium tour did not stop the crew from continuing their own brand of professionalism, as Jez recalls: "When we turned up at these places like Wembley they were used to these American crews who were totally brilliant, and then we came along saying 'Yeah, I'll be back in a minute mate, I'm just off to get some more breakfast.' We got the job done though, and on a full stomach". In getting the job done, the 'Children' tour was universally triumphant and had The Mission quite rightly earmarked as one of the greatest live acts to emerge from Britain for years. It all worked, the album, the tours, the audiences, everything. All the bitter press acrimony and the more musical detractors seemed irrelevant when faced by 8,000 devoted fans in that two week celebration of everything that was so absurd, so preposterous and so magnificent about The Mission.

CHAPTER NINE

"People want art. They want showbiz. They want to see you rush off in your limousine".

Freddie Mercury.

BY The Mission's own hectic standards, 1989 was to be a quiet year. On a public level, their time was taken up by festivals in Europe and at home, two benefit shows, and a series of fan club dates, as well as witnessing the emergence of their alter egos The Metal Gurus. With this extra time available they were able to write and record their third album which would be released at the start of the following year - the first three months of 1989 were spent writing and demoing new material, with Hussey being admitted to hospital for two operations. Officially, the reason for his ailment was a stomach disorder, but the real damage had been caused by what he described as 'sexual deviance on the road'. He was somewhat cheered up for his recovery by the news that Robert Plant had been seen across America proudly sporting a Mission T-shirt.

On leaving hospital Hussey headed for the Welsh Black Mountains once again where he found a small derelict cottage which served as his home for the next few weeks and allowed him the isolation he needed to work on the new material more productively - the idea worked and Hussey wrote fifteen songs in three weeks. Initially the idea had been to take six months off after the gruelling 'Children' tour, but all of the band became restless within a month of separating and therefore found themselves meeting up and working the new ideas through. By May, progress had been so promising that work began in earnest on the new album, provisionally entitled 'Deliverance'. Publically, the plan was to keep a low profile until their various festival dates in the early summer. Then one evening whilst they were working in a studio on the new material, somebody noticed the television were showing pictures of an apparent football pitch invasion. Flippant comments were casually passed until it dawned on them that something was wrong, whereupon the band, like the rest of the country, watched helpless as the horror that became the Hillsborough football tragedy unfolded before their eyes. What was even more shocking was that it came so soon after the horrific Lockerbie airplane bombing. The same evening the band were approached to play a benefit gig for the disaster fund, which would coincide with a show they had agreed to do the night after on the 30th April for the Lockerbie victims fund.

The warm up for these two dates was at the inauspicious Champagne Bar in Horsham, a tiny venue situated between London and Brighton, which the band had made an annual occasion. Hussey explains their motives behind playing such a small gig: "Horsham's Champagne Bar was somewhere we always seemed to be in that neck of the woods in the summer, so we'd do a gig there. It was great because it had a tiny stage, a real tiny club. It was a case of we liked doing live gigs more than anything else - after the big tour for 'Children' we were very tight and it relieved the boredom of hours in the studio - small gigs are fun to do and it's the best form of rehearsal. We were booked into Nomis, this really expensive rehearsing studio but that's never as good as a gig, even at somewhere like Horsham's. We'd just turn up at Nomis, have some breakfast, turn a few things on, flash a few lights and look clever and then go home. One time though we actually rehearsed for more than five minutes and all the ladies in the cafe thought it was hilarious because we'd actually done some work. We knew the songs inside out so it seemed pointless - even for tours we wouldn't rehearse until the day before so it was all a bit much. Horsham's was an ideal way around this frustration".

The benefit shows themselves were tremendous. Paul Lester of Melody Maker was at the Liverpool Royal Court gig, where they appeared alongside Pete Wylie, and was absolutely enthralled: "An unreconstituted monster metal mash of Zep riffs and Stones licks for those too young to care about the originals...it's a huge and rhythmic affair, massively melodic and enormously mournful. And the crowd go wild...The Mission are still the most involving and multi-faceted adventure rock has to offer."[1] Halfway through The Mission's set the power suddenly went down and the large crowd was plunged into darkness - after a brief silence the Liverpool anthem 'You'll Never Walk Alone' began from the crowd completely spontaneously and soon became a rousing tribute to those who had lost their lives in the tragedy. For Hussey, who had been a little uneasy about the concept of the show, this gesture encapsulated why they were there: "You have to really examine your motives for doing these things, it's very sensitive, you have to be sure of yourself. It was a great gig, but when that happened it was so incredible, so emotional and everybody was in tears. They knew why we were there, it wasn't about the gig, it wasn't about the bands, it was about a show of support, a show of strength. At the same time though, you can't really derive any amount of satisfaction from it - I don't really know why you do it apart from just hoping that it will help in any small way. When you hand the money over, which is always a drop in the ocean to what is needed anyway, you almost feel like your conscience is cleared and it just isn't that easy. I just think it's a very difficult area, it's down to how individuals react. Take Geldof for example, he was brilliant, he went out and got the big names because he knew that was how to get the most money, but there were loads of re-releases before and after the event. Self-promotion is always evident, some people are into these things for all the wrong reasons".

May saw The Mission fly to Europe for a trio of festival dates with The Cure, who were by now a legendary outfit on the continent, sharing a bill alongside The Pixies and The Sugarcubes. The Mission were chosen as an ideal support band because they could attract a large crowd in their own right, and they shared many mutual fans. The shows were well received and the two lead singers found that they got on very well, despite Robert Smith's shyness: "It seemed like a great chance for a party. The first night we went out for a meal and me and Robert held hands and snogged at the table. We got on very well, he's very shy and quite hard to get to know. Later on their bass player was banging away on this piano and we were all drinking and singing. Me and Robert went outside drunk and were both sick then we hugged and fell over in the sick, really gross it was and I'm sure he won't thank me for remembering that. But I loved The Cure before those dates and

I have nothing but great respect for them after. I think they're one of the few groups who've kept all their integrity intact. I think you really do need someone at the helm to have the final say and both me and Robert do that - Mick is socially and politically more involved than I am, whereas I'll make decisions on the music more, but you have to have a decision maker. Maybe that's why we got on so well".

With so much success, playing venues such as the NEC and Wembley Arena, and with such massive record sales many bands would have finally let their close relationship with their fans wither and die. Not so The Mission. It is to their great credit that in 1989, the year after their biggest success worldwide, (which had seen them play in front of crowds of up to 30,000, off the back of a gold selling album and a massive headline world tour), their only tour as such was an eight date, fan club only jaunt around tiny 200 or 300 capacity venues in Scotland and the Highlands. The idea was primarily a way of breaking up the fatigue of studio work, but the chance to play in such small venues again after the arenas of the previous year was appealing to all of them. So they found themselves relegated to the cramped confines of a minibus once more, stopping off at basic bed and breakfasts on the way and having to buy their own alcohol for the first time in a long time. The Mission headed off for Dundee on 13th August, with Brown at the wheel, beaming widely as memories of his trucking days came flooding back. With most gigs the van would set off with the band plus a couple of crew members inside, but would invariably arrive at the venue jammed full of Eskimos, noses squashed against the windows, all in the name of The Mission.

Despite the hostile territory that Scotland offered hitch hikers and followers, the 101 so-called 'Season Tickets' for all the shows sold out in hours, and had to be restricted to that amount to prevent the tiny venues being besieged by hundreds of Mission fans all trying to squeeze into a tiny club already fit to burst. The weather did not help, with rain and wind beating the travelling faithful, even though it was the height of summer. More hurdles came in the form of the spartan local transport - for example the gig on the Isle of Skye was served by only one ferry per day so the rusty old vessel strained under the weight of 100 Eskimos and Missionaries, as well as band, crew and gear, whilst the local daily passengers looked on in sheer bewilderment at the masses of hair, leather and mascara and wondered what on earth had arrived in their peaceful little town. This bizarre ferry crossing would be the talk of the whole area for years to come. When they arrived at Stornaway, word had obviously got around, because the management of the venue politely told the band that the show would be stopped after the fifth fight.

Even so, the shows were blistering, with a band that had played to 25,000 every night with Robert Plant refusing to hold back with the 200 fortunates at each tiny club. For many Eskimos it revitalised their faith in the band which had been somewhat diluted by the escalating size of their shows, most notably at Wembley and the NEC the previous Christmas. Apart from being hugely enjoyable the gigs had three important effects. They honed the band's set for the forthcoming second headline appearance at Reading Festival, they rejuvenated the group's spirit and excitement which had been rather ragged after their intense studio work, and finally it acted as a showcase to the new material which had first been heard at the Fan Club dates in November of 1988. Tracks aired included 'Deliverance' and 'Gone to the Devil', 'The Grip of Disease' and 'Belief'. The tracks were clearly very embryonic but there was a depth in this new material that suggested the next album could be a considerable progression for The Mission. The song 'Deliverance' was already established as a live favourite for its thundering epic feel, and there was also a warm reception for a slower number the band were trying out called 'Butterfly On A Wheel'. The Mission also took the opportunity to revisit old favourites such as The Sex Pistols' 'Pretty Vacant' and The Stones' 'Gimme Shelter'. The tour saw Adams enjoying himself fully, and taking time out to try a spot of sight-seeing whereas before, in his own words "All that mattered was that the ale was good and the drugs were cheap." The only blot on this chaotic but immensely enjoyable landscape was when thieves broke into the bus and stole Hussey's briefcase, pens, paper clips, even blank paper. Three days later he received a phonecall from the local constabulary to the effect that his briefcase had been found, with all its contents taken except for the singer's lyric sheets.

On finishing these dates the band headed for Swanyard Studios in London to continue the album, before driving out to Berkshire for a prestigious second Reading headline slot. This year was something of a landmark for the festival, with the bill marking a deliberate new direction away from the heavy metal tendencies that had dominated previous years. This was due to the new promoters The Mean Fiddler Group, who had taken over after the festival's original prime mover Harold Pendelton, (who formerly owned the famous Marquee club in London) called them in to revitalise the event he had started way back in 1962. The Mission were at the vanguard of this new approach, alongside bands such as New Order, The Pogues, and The Wonder Stuff. Such was the renewed interest in the weekend that John Peel accepted the invitation to compere after having avoided the event for years before, like many other people who saw it as largely second rate compared to the superior American and European operations.

The Mission did not disappoint the sell-out crowd. Everett True was there for Melody Maker and loved it: "Campfires are glowing, lustrous in the night, a man naked and streaked with red runs past, human pyramids appear. I look to the stage and there glow four figures in blue and white and purple, reaching out, burning slowly, enveloping the whole site with their thin, gigantic sound and deep-throated intonation. The appeal of The Mission is very straightforward: it's a fix, a charge, a yearning for succour and the bright lights of home...The Mission fulfil a deep need inside all of us, the need for comfort, for warmth, for reassurance. They do this well, astonishingly well in fact, their music sweeping down from the stage, and enabling those who wish to lose themselves, to do so effortlessly, in nowhere. Everything is geared to finding that moment, that crescendo when the world stops right there, tears run down your face and you vow that this is the life...The Mission are perfect for this occasion."[2]

After this the band flew to Europe again for three more festivals, this time one each in Italy, Austria then Switzerland. This was really their year for festivals, and although such events often paid very well and exposed the band to massive crowds there were serious reservations about the enjoyment of them. Brown believes a successful festival appearance is all a matter of your frame of mind: "Festivals are strange, it's an attitude you have to adopt. The first time we played Reading was brilliant, we were riding a wave and didn't expect too much, but then when we headlined a year later, and we were really hyped up and they opened the curtains during the intro music so we're all sat there like idiots waiting for the tape to finish so we could start the set, a complete anti-climax. The simple fact is that, apart from the status side of it, bands do it for the money, not much else, whatever they might say". Hussey also dislikes the lack of control at such gigs, reflecting the bands perfectionist streak which they learnt to compromise when necessary: "I do enjoy them but there can be so many things that go wrong and are beyond your control. If you thought about how many people are actually in front of you you wouldn't be able to handle it at all; festivals are quite easy and enjoyable as long as you go into it with the right attitude, easy going, not to be precious about anything. It all depends on your attitude - if you can't hear yourself play, don't go mad, just get on with it".

As if to confirm their status as 'the people's band' The Mission broke up the mixing for the album by playing a Fan Club Convention show at Sheffield Polytechnic, where the lucky few could get to see their heroes for only £1, as well as the brilliant support line-up of The Wonder Stuff, Claytown Troupe, Rosetta Stone and Balaam and the Angel. After this date the band remained inactive for the rest of the year, amid rumours that there was a rival seventies band emerging under the name of The Metal Gurus, playing a set of 1970's covers only. The official history of the band was unclear, but a press release filled some of the gaps in the curious public's knowledge. The band consisted of Slink on guitar, Rick Spangle on bass, Lucky Mick on drums and a gentleman called Hipster Looney on vocals. Hipster and Rick were old friends who had lived next door to each other years back, and took a liking to Slink whilst discussing his passion as a semi-professional pigeon fancier over a pint in the local Tripe Throwers Arms. Slink ideally filled the shoes recently left by their disillusioned former guitarist Daft Eric Solo, and immediately gave up his job as postman. Lucky was a hod carrier by trade and only took up drums after a brief job modelling blouses for Freemans catalogues fell through. He was recruited as the last member of the Gurus, but only after tragedy had taken away their original drummer when he was killed in an accident with a bread van.

The Guru's career was short but dramatic. Although they would go on to release a Christmas single the following year with none other than the mighty Slade, their live career consisted of only two shows.

Hussey explains how it all came about: "The Wonder Stuff did the Sheffield fan club show for us then they had three nights at Aston Villa Leisure Centre and asked us to guest on one night. So rather than just go on and do the whole Mission thing we thought 'Let's do something different, let's dress up and do all our favourite '70's covers'. Then we went a step further and decided to have a warm up gig so we booked The Fulham Greyhound. We filmed the Stuffies gig and had a real laugh. About a year later we released the charity single 'Merry Christmas Everybody' with Noddy and Jim from Slade, with all proceeds going to Childline, but I think most of our audience didn't really know what was going on. At Fulham they all arrived expecting an hour and a half of Mission songs and there we were all dressed up in wigs, platforms, gold lame and singing 'Telegram Sam'. It was a great laugh for us though - these were the records we all bought as kids, I was in the Sweet and Slade fan club. It was whimsical, an obvious laugh".

Simon Williams of the NME was at the Fulham show, where they were supported by a young up and coming band called Ned's Atomic Dustbin, who were afforded the usual cold response that Mission support acts notoriously received. Williams revelled in the atmosphere: "The Metal Guru's look dazzling. Guitarist Simon models a Dave Hill top hat and chest-revealing crushed velvet number; Wayne is a silver sequinned roastabag, drummer Mick appears to have (p)lumped for lurex hot pants; and Craig, in blond wig, looks frighteningly like Sam Fox...a fantastic nightmare."[3] With these fun shows The Mission completed what was their quietest year to date for gigs, and waited, along with the thousands of anxious fans for the release of their third album.

* * *

All these events punctuated developments on the new album, and as the year passed by the record began to take shape. The album itself had evolved over a period of eighteen months - songs and ideas had begun to emerge whilst still on the 'Children' world tour, although serious writing had only really started towards the end of 1988. Whilst the band enjoyed a low key 1989 publically, the ideas that would make up their third album, to be finally called 'Carved In Sand', would see them in and out of various studios over the year. Producers short-listed for the recording included Kate Bush, Brian Eno and David Byrne, but it was Tim Palmer who had produced the debut 'God's Own Medicine' who was installed at the helm of Jacob's Studios in Surrey. This time recording would be far less intense than that on 'Children', which was primarily why Palmer was chosen. With the eighteen songs they had at their disposable, and with the memories of hours sweating over tracks at The Manor for the previous album, the band wanted to get the product finished much quicker. Palmer was known for his speedy work rate. In addition, since 'God's Own Medicine' he had gone on to work with Bowie, Texas, House of Love, and Plant's 'Now and Zen' LP which The Mission had supported. The policy worked - despite Brown being based in Leeds, the whole recording was completed in under three months.

The entire recording environment was a total contrast to that of the meticulous yet insular second album. Palmer himself was an active and contributing instrumentalist, and in one instance on the 12" mix for a song called 'Deliverance', the only spare guitarist was the studio's resident tape op boy, who was promptly armed with a plectrum and plugged in (the mix and samples for this release came to Hussey in his sleep and the whole record was completed in less than forty eight hours). There was no precious treatment of the tracks, a complete contrast to the previous project, with ideas being contributed and tried from all quarters. Also featured on the album was Tin Machine guitarist Reeves Gabrels, and the piano work of Guy Chambers. When the use of sitars was mentioned, the band decided to try the idea out - Palmer's management put them in touch with a 50 year old Indian gentleman called Baluji, whom Hussey and Jez Webb subsequently drove to pick up from the train station. It was not until they arrived and waved to him that they realised he was in fact completely blind. Once back in the studio he tuned his instrument, listened to the tracks twice and recorded his sections entirely by ear in one take.

Much of the recording can be seen on the hugely successful video 'Waves Upon The Sand' released in February 1990, and on this it is evident that the tone of the album was far removed from that on 'Children' - for example, click tracks were abandoned on many songs because the general feeling was that the choruses were becoming sterile as a result. Hussey later said that the best songs on that album were the ones that were completed in the shortest time, especially those that took only half an hour to write. He expressed no concern about accusations that he might be regurgitating chord structures and correctly cited the great chord re-cycler himself, Neil Young, as revered company. The whole philosophy was very much against the assumption that as a band gets bigger their albums necessarily become more complicated. Hussey preferred to keep his song writing simple, with only 'Sleeping Dogs Lie' stretching to fourteen chords. Hussey cited a similar approach to that used by Stevie Wonder when writing his music: "When I play guitar I always think of colours. It sounds a bizarre thing to say...but there's a lot of blues, greens, pastel colours, particularly in my guitar playing", and he went on to say "There's no reason why things should automatically be more complicated, it just doesn't have to be like that."[4]

As well as the nature of the recording being different, the actual material was very much more diverse. The subject matter was much broader, less specific than the triumvirate focus on children, heat and America found on the previous record. Also less prevelant was the highly personal focus of Hussey's lyrics, suggesting an end to the particular exorcisms of his own life that had so often caused him great stress on earlier recordings. Indeed, the central love song of the album, 'Butterfly on a Wheel' was supposedly about an ill-fated affair between Hinkler and All About Eve's vocalist Julianne Regan, with the image of love breaking the wings of a butterfly on a wheel being taken from an editorial published in The Times in 1967 by Editor William Rees Mogg on what he personally saw as the absurd harshness of imprisoning Mick Jagger on a minor drugs offence. The track 'Grapes of Wrath' took its imagery from John Steinbeck's classic '30's novel of same name, and the whole record was tinged with overt references to the Avalon legend, as well as what Hussey called "a celebration of women, a celebration of being in love, a celebration of coming to terms with who I am." The most striking and the biggest diversion from previous lyrical angles, however, was reserved for Hussey's reaction to a letter he had received from a female fan who was being abused by her father, and his treatment of this disturbing subject in the album opener 'Amelia'.

This provocative subject matter was not untouched before The Mission's track - notable contributions had been recorded by Suzanne Vega (Luka), The Men They Couldn't Hang (Daddy is Wrong), The Smiths (Reel around the Fountain), New Order (All Day Long) and even The Who (Family Business). What made this track unusual was the brand new direction it took for The Mission - after the unusual acoustic opening the track launched into an angry musical attack that is as shocking and brutal as the lyrical content. With Hussey playing the role of the abuser it was a courageously direct lyrical approach, whereby the immorality of the crime was not treated with evasive insinuation but left blatantly obvious:

> "Daddy says 'Come and sit on my knee'
> "Daddy says 'You're the only girl for me'
>
> Daddy comes in the dark of night,
> Daddy says 'Don't be scared, it'll be alright',
>
> Daddy says 'Don't tell Momma what I do to you',
> Daddy says 'If you do I'll beat you black and blue,
> Amelia, you make Daddy feel like a man,
> Amelia, Daddy loves you more than Mommy can'."

Such frank brutality was not a problem for Hussey: "It's an important issue, it's a sad issue, and there's not enough made of it;...it's sick and it's sad and I'm convinced it touches our lives far more than we're aware of."[5] The band were aware that this might cause controversy but felt that they could not shy away from the issue as so many do - Brown appeared in the press saying he was proud of Hussey for having written 'Amelia' and reinforced his singer's strong views: "Some people, some institutions think that as a subject it should remain unmentioned, swept under the carpet, whereas we think it should be talked about in the open and be accepted as a problem."[6]

Elsewhere, there were less direct lyrical approaches. There were references to galleons, angels, seas of love and heresy, all re-creating the gothic imagery which had been such a feature of Mission records up to this point. This gave the album an Arthurian tone, but marked The Mission finally throwing off the mystical Zeppelinesque comparisons - they had now created their own unique imagery and had established their own separate romantic identity. The focus on Hussey's personal experience was still there but the songs were quasi-conceptual, non-specific pieces, which when added to the portentous titles such as 'Hungry As The Hunter' and 'Paradise' gave the record a very individual sentimentality.

Musically the project saw The Mission produce an album of intense maturity. Hinkler's enormous guitar ability was predominant, with his inspiring work on tracks such as 'Belief' underpinning the record with a detailed and rich melodic quality, which earmarked this record as Hinkler's masterpiece. Perhaps his greatest effort was reserved for 'Deliverance' whose monumental sound relied largely upon his characteristic guitar style - the track provided an immense climax to the first side of the record in the same fashion that 'Tower of Strength' had done on 'Children'. With the rhythmic backbone never more solid, especially on the thundering 'Hungry As The Hunter', Hussey was free to extend his impressive vocal range. Over the course of the first side he ventured from the incensed spitting of 'Amelia' through the almost baritone treatment of 'Butterfly On A Wheel', finishing with the inspirational 'Deliverance'. The sitars fitted into place easily, resting most comfortably on 'Sea Of Love' and there was even a brilliantly simple gesture in the track 'Grapes Of Wrath' which featured only the same gentle keyboards that had leant such warmth to 'Butterfly'. With the variety on the first side shifting to a more acoustic approach on the second, the recording represented The Mission's most accomplished album thus far.

*   *   *

By the end of 1989 The Mission's album was complete and finished off with the new title of 'Carved in Sand', designed to reflect the transitory nature of life in that you can write in sand but it will soon be washed away. The recording had been both very efficient and enjoyable, and this confidence was reflected in the band's pre-release press comments: "We had to take a long time over 'Children' to get it out of our system but in retrospect we realise that wasn't a good way for us to work. I think this album is a reaction to that. For the first time it actually sounds like The Mission. We've carved out a little niche that when you hear it you know it's The Mission."[7] Hussey also said: "We played twenty-six different countries last year and everywhere we went we had brilliant reactions...the feeling we've got now is that the world is ready for The Mission. If the next record is half as good as we think it's going to be it's gonna blow worldwide..."

CHAPTER TEN

"Fans want to see people who can play: they respect certain values like professionalism, and they don't want to be treated like shit. They pay good money and they look forward to seeing some good music being played by decent musicians."

Bruce Dickinson of Iron Maiden

"If you're taking this seriously, you're a bigger fool than I am."

Prince

"Then we heard about this thing called the song, and we thought it would be nice to have a few of them."

Bono

WITH the release date of 'Carved in Sand' delayed until January 1990 because of priority being given by Phonogram to the new Tears For Fears album, The Mission released a single on New Year's Day 1990 as a taste of what was to come. The track was 'Butterfly on a Wheel' and was arguably their greatest moment on vinyl thus far, a very pretty and brilliantly simple song, but immensely effective. The newly bearded singer told the small Worthing and District Advertiser about the song and about how it reflected the new lyrical tone of the forthcoming album: "It's about the disintegration of a relationship, about being heavy-handed with someone who can't take it and doesn't deserve it...unlike the 'Children' album, which was me wallowing in my own despair, this is my observations of someone else's despair...We hope it's going to go in the charts but you never can tell."[1] He needn't have worried - 'Butterfly' charted in the Top 20 and went on to reach No.12, amongst wide acclaim: "The Mish have really outdone themselves this time dumping their goth mish mash for a truly wonderful song, swathed in iridescent melody."[2] The nation awaited the album release with even greater anticipation.

The delay also allowed The Mission to throw a unique album release party. Hussey asked the fan club, known as The Mission World Information Service, for the phone numbers of ten London based members. He promptly called them up at home and to their astonishment invited them down to the studio where their favourite band were mastering their new album. Once there, they were asked to write down their opinions of the record, aswell as the other tracks recorded. A great day was had by all, and many interesting comments were put forward, such as 'Did Bono write this one?'

'Carved in Sand' was released in the first week of February 1990 and entered the album charts at No.7, with sales so brisk that again, like 'Children', the record went gold within the first week of release. This time the press were forced to acknowledge the album's quality, with The Mission's famed personal detractors becoming few and far between. The general reaction was that the album held a variety and an emotional feel far greater than on previous records, largely attributed to Hussey's more skilled lyrical articulation of his feelings. Melody Maker led the applause and offered the most detailed and accurate appraisal:

"That The Mission have made it this far, intact, their wits about them, and smiling, is a triumph in itself. While they've long since proved their worth onstage in toilets and arenas alike the world over, The Mission's vinyl output had offered flashes of brilliance - half of their debut LP, bits of 'Children', nearly all the singles - matched by an equal amount of fair efforts and near misses. As well as being the work of a band that has developed a certain collective peace of mind since the fragmented semi-nightmare days of 'Children', 'Carved' also sees

Wayne growing smoothly into his songwriting shoes. The (opening) three songs are where The Mission are now coming from - all directions - and that is why 'Carved' is such a huge step forward. Growing up in public has made The Mission what they are...from all the nightclub mewling and puking, from all the press ranting and panting, has come an LP that tips the scales firmly in The Mission's favour."[3]

' Deliverance' was widely acknowledged as an automatic Mission classic anthem, and there was widespread approval for the provocative opening track 'Amelia'. Only Sounds magazine criticised the track because it "attacked the delicate subject matter of child abuse with a mallet"[4] and subsequently rang the NSPCC to get an official condemnation only to be told to their disappointment that the children's charity fully endorsed the song, its approach and its motivation. The only reservation with the track was that whilst it was as direct and shocking an opening as on any album, the new lyrical direction it hinted at was not fulfilled by subsequent tracks.

The reception for 'Carved' was largely one that The Mission had come of age, and produced and album that silenced the doubters, the detractors and the cynics who had consistently failed to understand the bands motivations - Hussey had once said when The Mission started that they were only looking to make one album - maybe this was that one complete album. To their credit, many former enemies admitted they were surprised. Southern Cross magazine admitted that they had written them off as doom and gloom merchants and said that this album had finally nailed these misguided preconceptions. "It isn't so introspective that you twist yourself inside out trying to find the meaning. It's now far more attractive and approachable... The Mish are learning to rock out with a sense of humour, and you know, it ain't half bad."[5] Andrew Vaughan was similarly positive about 'Carved': "It's easy to be cynical and accuse The Mission of tearing pages out of books written by the Bunnymen, Simple Minds, U2 or Led Zep, but everybody's got to start somewhere...their best, most imaginative album yet."[6]

The album was criticised in some quarters though, but at least this time the press offered objective and informed opinion. Many felt 'Amelia' was a healthy direction but suggested that there were too many formula numbers such as 'Deliverance' and that The Mission were teetering on the precipice of self-parody. Mat Smith of Melody Maker best articulated this valid concern: "At the moment they're in danger of becoming clones of themselves, disappearing into the goth black hole they worked so hard to escape. We need less Mish-by-numbers like 'Deliverance' and more songs like 'Amelia'...a chance for their true, largely unknown experimental side to shine through. Mass consumption may sound like a disease but it needn't be terminal."[7]

Ian Middleton summed up the feelings of those who felt the album was inconsistent in its quality when he said: "A strange mixed bag. Some songs are good, some are indifferent, a couple are frankly embarrassing and (there are) two thundering epics with the band firing on all cylinders."[8] Despite the widespread acclaim for 'Carved' it was interesting to see Sounds, a former bastion of Mission faithful, criticising the album heavily: "'Carved' catches The Mission on another wave of phenomenal ordinariness. Hung with all the usual accessories - junk shop mysticism, Sesame Street metaphor...Wayne Hussey's penchant for grass-roots human nature has lifted Goth out of the sordid, post-punk '80's and firmly planted it back in the flower power '60's. A well-worn in-bred hybrid of pomp rock and Avalon nursery rhyme...yer average Mish song has a tea and slippers familiarity to it."[9]

Even Charlie Eyre at their own record label expressed concern about the Arthurian focus of some of the songs, notably the 'hocus pocus, mumbo jumbo' coupling which attracted much ridicule in 'Into The Blue': "I personally get very uneasy about what I call the 'King Arthur' lyrics like 'Deliverance' - the chorus is brilliant, the verses make me cringe. That stuff has no relation to 1990 whatsoever. Wayne throws that stuff off the top of his head. It's laziness". Others said 'Into the Blue' was a re-run of 'Wasteland' and that side two was far inferior to the first side - all valid criticisms to a degree. At last The Mission were afforded an accurate appraisal by the press - even if the album had its weaknesses, it was an immediate and colossal success, and confirmed The Mission's massive status and success in Britain - the album also sold heavily worldwide as the band began to finally fulfil the potential they had threatened earlier in their careers. By the end of the world tour to promote the album they had sold over half a million copies of 'Carved' - the huge sales confirmed the positive public reception of the record, a reaction which rapidly began to translate into enormous ticket sales for the forthcoming tour, which by the time it had begun was already a sell-out. It seemed the sky was the limit.

* * *

The UK tour 'Deliverance' began at Leeds Polytechnic on 1st March and is generally regarded as their finest single tour to this point by band and fans alike. The stage show was a regal, panto-esque affair of rotating wheels, based centrally around the theme of a butterfly's wings on a wheel. Hussey's debauched theatricals and Hinkler's posturing arrogance perfectly fitted the colossal stage show which in many cases lasted up to two hours, taking the absurd pomposity of The Mission to greater heights of grandiloquence. Perhaps the most notable difference from previous shows however was the addition of a second guitarist, Wolfie. It was the first time that the intimate live unit of the four original members had been broken - the decision was taken to recruit an extra guitar to accommodate the rythmn role which Hussey was finding increasingly restrictive to his performance. Wolfie was well-known to all the band from his days with Adams in The Expelaires, after which he had joined Brown in Red Lorry Yellow Lorry. This was always a temporary appointment, and his duties were carefully assigned so as not to intrude on Hinker's highly characteristic and accomplished style. The decision worked well and as a result Wolfie stayed with the band for the majority of the 'Deliverance' tour.

The venues were huge, the crowds sold out, but the intimacy and skill with which the band played to these audiences never faltered. The band were tight, the whole operation was enjoyed by everybody and the crowds left the gigs enthralled, in both the UK and Europe. One of the key factors in this was their frontman. In Wayne Hussey The Mission now had a genuine pop star, for many probably the last great English rock romantic. With Wolfie on guitar, the stage was Hussey's own, and he used this new-found freedom to the full, and displayed all the trademarks of the great characters throughout the long and colourful history of rock. He loved the grandeur, pomposity and humour of The Mission with a passion, and was only completely at home when sharing the intimacy of the live performance with an audience he made no attempt to distance from himself. Away from the gig he continually provided the most provocative copy for the eager music press with his frank and open demeanour, and took the personal jibes which this made him vulnerable to with an admirable modesty, remaining positive about even the most vicious criticism. He had no resentment of the media or the music industry - on the contrary, he set out to accommodate what many see as the unsavoury side of the business. He also unashamedly indulged in the whole 'rock 'n' roll' lifestyle with a passion and reckless abandon only seen amongst a rare few. If someone treated him like a pop star he would be arrogant and controversial; if someone only wanted an autograph or a peck on the cheek he would duly oblige. The combination of all these factors created around Hussey an aura and myth that fuelled his own natural character such that for many he had already become an icon to follow and rever - he had everything, the arrogance and the modesty, the humour and the pomposity, the impossibility and the fallibility. In essence, he was either a star or an anti-hero, but never anything in between. On this tour, for the thousands of Mission followers, Wayne Hussey was the perfect pop star.

It is perhaps appropriate that the NME, long time critics of the band, should produce the most accurate and perceptive appraisal of The Mission's live set during this triumphant UK tour in February, with Roger Morton acknowledging the achievements of a band his paper had once called "a mixture of graveyard wailing and market research". He described the new Mission set thus: "Here we have triumph against the odds. The Mission have a way of dealing with the inherent silliness of their idolatrous, seance rock...it is not all pomp and serpent rants...they can be touchingly tender."[10] This ability to confront the silliness of rock with humour and insight was reflected in the live favourite Mr. Pleasant, which single-handedly defeated the accusations of one-dimensional rock tedium so frequently thrown at them, and prompted one reviewer from Record Mirror to call them 'The Clash of Goth'. After sixteen shows across the country, The Mission returned to Birmingham to finish the tour with a show at the

20 WITH JOHN PAUL JONES, MANOR STUDIOS, NOVEMBER 1987

21 WITH TIM PALMER, BMG MUSIC PARTY, DECEMBER 1987

24 PARIS ZENITH, JUNE 1990

25 PARIS ZENITH, JUNE 1990

26 READING FESTIVAL, AUGUST 1989

27 READING FESTIVAL, AUGUST 1989

28 READING FESTIVAL, AUGUST 1989

29 SAN FRANCISCO, WARFIELD THEATRE, MAY 1990

30 EDINBURGH MURRAYFIELD WITH U2, AUGUST 1987

31 EDINBURGH MURRAYFIELD, AUGUST 1987

32 EDINBURGH MURRAYFIELD, AUGUST 1987

33 RIO DE JANEIRO, SEPTEMBER 1988

34 HILLSBOROUGH BENEFIT, LIVERPOOL ROYAL COURT, APRIL 1989

35 ADAMS WITH PETE WYLIE AND MICK JONES, HILLSBOROUGH BENEFIT

36 HIPSTER, PERRIN AND NEIL PERRY, BACKSTAGE WITH 'THE GURUS', DECEMBER 1989

37 FINSBURY PARK, LONDON, JUNE 1991

38 MONTREAL METROPOLIS, HINKLER'S LAST SHOW, APRIL 1990

massive NEC, the night after playing Wembley Arena for the second time in their career. If the doubters about their suffocating retrogressive tendencies were still lingering they were blown away by this tour, never more so than at the traditionally difficult gig in the North West of the capital. Simon Price was there and excitedly suggested The Mission had reached almost semi-legendary status: "The Mission have done something that bands in their position just aren't supposed to do. They've done the impossible. They've got better. I've never seen Wembley Arena look so much like a carnival...Hussey and his men have reached an almost unparalleled grasp of the rock idiom. They probably see themselves as torchbearers, (perhaps the last) guardians of a dying heritage of crowd-pleasing rock entertainment. Who am I to say they're wrong?"[11] Peter Elliott was similarly enthusiastic: "1990 and hot damn - The Mish slay 9000 at the toughest gig in the capital. The Mission are an evolution, a great rock beast out of trash culture mythology; half geezer, half god...The Mish strike awe into faces red with cider. The Mish 1990 are a convincing rock leviathan, if a little unorthodox...live The Mission now have a power and a majesty..and in 'Butterfly On A Wheel' they now have a second classic song, after 'Tower of Strength.'"[12]

The epic status now afforded to the band was contrasted by their continued down-to-earth mentality, and was best illustrated in their ability to confront the ridiculousness of rock with a large dose of humour. A fine example of The Mission's attitude and their accomplished live talent came during this tour when they were asked to record a gig for the Channel Four programme Rock Steady at London's National Ballroom in Kilburn. In that one evening the whole essence of The Mission was crystallised into one chaotic hour where everything that could go wrong did so disastrously, and yet the band still came through laughing and with heads held high. The day's preparations for the filming had been tediously laboured and the band were not in the best of moods when they took to the stage at 9pm. Hussey launched into the acoustic opening of the disturbing 'Amelia' with his ferocious lyrical spitting immediately capturing the crowd's attention. As the rest of the band prepared to kick in, a TV crew member walked up to Hussey, and in front of 3000 bemused fans said 'Er, sorry but we weren't ready, could you start again?' Suitably annoyed the first twenty minutes of the set were a disaster culminating in 'Butterfly On A Wheel' being abandoned half way through. Once their initial anger had died down however, The Mission took to their task with a passion. With the proposed set list thrown into the crowd, the band decided to play whatever they wanted. Various cover versions were blasted out, including a rendition of 'Pretty Vacant' with a member of the audience taking the microphone. Meanwhile backstage, Perrin was fleeing from the programme producer who was running after him shouting 'You'll never record another TV show again!!' Back onstage Hussey was inciting the crowd to chant 'Rock Steady is shit' whilst the crew vainly tried to film the whole farce, and stopped in disbelief when the singer then announced that everyone could have their money back after the show. After another technical problem Hussey said 'I wanna love you but I'm getting pissed off, this is shit!' and launched himself into the first three rows of the crowd as if to disassociate himself from the spectacle. In the audience however, a strange thing had happened - The Mission had turned around a potential disaster into a celebration of the absurdity and inherent ridiculousness of their band; the worse the set became and the more that went wrong, the more the people loved it, and Hussey's refusal to let the TV intrusion spoil his enjoyment of the show infectiously fuelled everyone else's enthusiasm. When the final song had been played and Hussey walked off saying 'You let us get away with murder' the crowd were transfixed. It was a classic Mission gig. Rock Steady broadcast the gig anyway and wrote to The Mission to inform them that it was the best show of the series.

Aside from this the tour suggested a transformation towards stadium rock levels that could never have been imagined back in 1986 with the musical direction of 'God's Own Medicine', whose songs would not have stood up to such a test. Now The Mission were able to take in the biggest indoor arenas in Britain in their stride and negotiate the shows on their own terms, with the potential to be even bigger. Suddenly the rumblings of U2 which they had first seen at Elland Road three years ago, now seemed almost in reach. It was hard work though, particularly after the band had not surfaced in the UK for a regular Mission show for over a year, a fact not lost on Adams, who succinctly summarised events on the tour: "It were right hard, like t'first game o' the season when you've spent all summer on t'piss in

Ibiza."[13]

The celebratory nature of the tour was made all the more intense by their seventh consecutive Top 30 hit, when the monumental 'Deliverance' charted at No.27, just before the band had set off on the road. The track was already acknowledged as a thundering Mission epic and was already a huge live favourite - its success in the charts earned the band another Top of the Pops appearance which had now become widely anticipated by their fans for the bands drunken chaotic behaviour (and totally dreaded by the programme's producers). True to form The Mission caused utter mayhem at the BBC studios, based largely on the fact that Hinkler insisted on sticking his buttocks into the camera lens every time the cameraman zoomed in close for that famous Top of the Pops nostril shot. The band, like mischievous schoolboys, were kept behind long after everyone else had left to re-shoot several sequences. These British dates were also memorable for a legendary appearance by Hussey on the controversial James Whale Television Show. The singer was driven straight to the studio after a show in Sheffield and was already blind drunk before he was on air. When James Whale realised how inebriated Hussey was, he made a clever comment to which the singer replied 'You're a fucking pillock!!' and then turned to the amazed audience and repeated the obscenities. In the next 90 seconds, with the producer screaming down Whale's earpiece to get Hussey offstage, The Mission's front man managed to say 'fuck' twelve times, take his shoes off and hurl them at the camera and eventually get himself man-handled from the set. Wandering around the maze of corridors inside the television centre vainly trying to find a toilet, Hussey accidentally locked himself in the telephone switchboard room, where he personally took it upon himself to fend off the flood of calls complaining about a drunken pop star on the James Whale show with a barrage of yet more colourful expletives.

* * *

After this faultless British tour, and with BBC1 and Channel 4 suitably annoyed, The Mission set off for a eleven date tour around

Europe, covering Belgium, Denmark, Germany, Switzerland, Italy and France. On the whole tour they had made it clear that anybody bringing tape recorders into the shows would not have the gear confiscated. This idea, which on first hearing seems very unusual, was based on a policy Hussey had seen at a Grateful Dead concert around Christmas time the previous year. This massive American cult band had always sectioned off an area behind the mixing desk for people to record the show for themselves, primarily so that these personalised recordings would ultimately undermine the widespread and frequently lucrative trade in pirate bootlegs (which in The Mission's case saw some fans paying up to £30 for a single poor quality concert tape). Hussey recognised the role of bootlegs in a bands career and denied that such tapes affect record sales on the premise that the people who would pay £30 for a bootleg are the type of fan who would buy up every release anyway. The decision and the extensive press it achieved nevertheless infuriated their record company Phonogram, who immediately ordered the band to issue a statement the following week retracting their offer of free bootlegging. Even so the band had the last laugh by letting it be known quietly that those turning up with recording equipment would not be turned away.

Another policy which created press interest was their decision to employ their own security guards - the band had always had trouble with over-zealous security ever since the Eskimo pyramids and boisterous behaviour had become notorious, but in many cases they stood by helplessly as a member of the crowd was the victim of particularly rough treatment. The solution was to employ their own staff, who answered to the band not the venue, and they used video cameras to ensure their instructions were followed to the letter - a decision that reinforced their reputation for having great respect and fondness for their following and earned them a place in the hallowed gossip columns of that incisive topical journal, Playboy.

Support for the European and American legs of the tour was provided by The Wonder Stuff, by now themselves established as one of the UK's top alternative acts. The two groups had become close friends over the last months and hence this impressive live duo was established - their original meeting had not been so friendly, but it does provide an excellent example of The Mission's open attitude and willingness to accept well-founded criticism from informed quarters. Miles Hunt the lead singer with The Wonder Stuff had blasted The Mission in an article in the NME, culminating in this infamous assertion: 'The Mission? I wouldn't jack myself off over one of their records!!' Four weeks later Hunt was enjoying a quiet beer at the now-defunct Dingwall's Club in Camden when he turned from the bar and spotted Hussey entering the club. After meeting by accident in the toilet where Hunt had remained silent and resolved not to say a word to Hussey, he went back to supporting the bar. A tap on his shoulder five minutes later brought an offer of a drink from Hussey on the premise that 'You seem to have a lot to say for yourself' and Hunt reluctantly accepted.

Characteristically, Hussey made it clear that he agreed with some of what Hunt had said, particularly his objections to the corporate nature of the band around the time of the stadium tour for 'Children'. Hunt explains why he attacked The Mission in the first instance and why they subsequently got on so well: "I suppose it was because The Mission were always one step ahead of The Wonder Stuff - there was definitely a jealousy thing involved on my part. It was really the presentation of the band that I disliked, for example they used to format their records quite a lot and I was into none of that - at that time I would just go off about these things, I didn't really listen to their music a great deal, plus there was the fact that because Wayne was this big personality in the press I thought he was big enough to be knocked and I wouldn't have to worry about it. I picked my victim and he could take care of himself, which to me seemed thoroughly acceptable behaviour at the time. I think for Wayne it was just ironic that some Johhny-Come-Lately having a shout had articulated one of his concerns. We spent the rest of the night drinking from bar to bar and ended up in this hotel because his flat had no booze in".

It was during this first evening of many to come that Hunt realised he had fallen into the same trap of misconceptions that had caught many before him: "We got a cab to his flat and it was kind of weird sitting next to Wayne because it was like getting to know somebody whose face you are obviously very aware of. We were just firing questions off at each other - I asked him what he thought of The Smiths and Morrissey, who I liked at the time and he said 'I think they're shit, a load of bollocks'. The one thing I learnt on that night was that they had actually got a great sense of humour. With all this goth stuff I'd just seen it as very, very serious and pompous but that night made me realise otherwise, which is why they hated Morrissey at the time. Although their songs were serious and they were deadly serious about being in a band, they had this sense of humour which Wayne thought was obvious to people, very tongue-in-cheek. That was why Wayne hated Morrissey, because he sussed out before I did that he's a self-important prick. Wayne was saying things like 'How can I be serious when I was walking round in a girl's dress and make-up, with a beard and nail varnish, how much of a hint do you need?' and when I said I thought he was serious about all that stuff he just put his head in his hands and said 'Oh God, I give up!'".

Their unlikely friendship had resulted in The Wonder Stuff appearing at the Sheffield fan club convention in 1989, and the reciprocal offer of a support slot for The Metal Gurus when The Wonder Stuff played their own home town at Birmingham's Aston Villa Leisure Centre. These dates also saw the departure of The Wonder Stuff's bass player Bob Jones, and Hunt says Hussey was instrumental in nursing The Wonder Stuff through this difficult period because of his own personnel problems in various bands; just when the Birmingham band were on the verge of quitting, Hussey's infectious and positive enthusiasm played a key part in their revival, as Hunt explains: "Their European dates were coming up and Wayne phones me up and says 'Why don't you come on holiday with us?' meaning 'Would you like to support us around Europe?'. When it's put like that it's difficult to say no, even though I had just got married".

So this awesome pairing set off for the Muzik Zentrum club in Utrecht, where The Sisterhood had played their first ever gig outside of the UK back in 1986, and where this night's unsuspecting audience of 2000 were treated to two of the UK's top acts in the same evening. The after show value for money was equally notable. Hunt and Hussey were both blind drunk, and when The Mission's singer took a fancy to smashing the fire alarm glass in the hotel corridor at 4 in the morning, bemused guests who shook the sleep from their eyes saw one long haired drunk ranting on inanely and trying to smash the glass whilst another longhair was attempting to wrestle him away and onto the safety of the floor. One annoyed German resident who plucked up the nerve to ask the two rampaging singers to quieten things down was promptly and in no uncertain terms told to 'Go fuck off!!' After more utter mayhem a bewildered receptionist pushed Hussey into his room - by this time the two realised it was nearly 8 o'clock and headed for breakfast. They tumbled down the stairs and sat down at a table, which within seconds was surrounded by totally empty tables as the terrified residents ran for cover. Hussey armed himself with six boiled eggs and hurled them at two rather large Doberman Pincer dogs sitting obediently by their master and further incited canine revenge by barking loudly at them on all fours.

As it turned out the two friends did not have many more chances to wreak such havoc, as Hussey had taken to travelling separately on many occasions and Hunt was busy notching up enormous phone bills to his recently married lady back in Britain, and was pretty much keeping himself to himself. He does remember how The Mission used to wind The Wonder Stuff up though, notably the Stuffies newest member Paul: "They loved to sit in a drunken room and tell us we didn't know anything, 'You haven't been round Europe in a knackered Transit van, you haven't done this and that, you don't know you've been born, you've never lived' all very tongue-in-cheek. Paul used to take all this in and come to me the next day 'That bloody band think they know it all', it really wound him up".

Aside from showering unsuspecting dogs with various dairy products Wayne Hussey and The Mission went about slaughtering Europe with a series of blistering gigs. Andrew Collins of the NME was at the Dusseldorf Phillipshalle for a show which he rated as one of the greats: "The Mission might be a bunch of unspectacular beerboys in real life, but they're Gods the minute they touch the hallowed boards...they're about escapism, an hour-plus of grand, exaggerated gestures and cosmic relief. The Mission on stage are a 5,000 piece band. Parameters? Never heard of them. Wayne sings each song as if his life depended on it. The world's shrinking, The Mish are getting bigger." [14]

The sting of these European dates was lost somewhat when three dates had to be cancelled because Hinkler unfortunately contracted Scarletina, a highly infectious condition which the band could not risk contracting with the massive world tour lined up. This was all the more frustrating because Hussey had been playing through illnesses ever since having to cancel a gig in Newport earlier in the British tour. On a worrying note, Hunt from The Wonder Stuff noticed the return of serious drug use on these dates, something he had seen creeping in when he had first met the band. "Wayne was a shocking womaniser all the time but what struck me most when we were in Europe was that he put frightening amounts of funny powder away. One night we were up late, drinking to collapse and talking. At this stage I smoked loads of dope, but I noticed that for every fag I smoked he would chop a line of coke out. It was almost out of boredom, we'd be listening to some quiet record and talking, he'd chop a line out, snort it then chop another out. Over the two or three hours he was matching me easily cigarettes for lines of coke, eleven or twelve lines over a very short period. It was the same way that I would light a fag, he'd chop out a line, something to do. I didn't think it was a very safe way to live and I used to say that to him and he'd say 'It's alright'. I thought if you have a massive heart attack you can say 'Oh it's alright, it's just a massive heart attack.' He can take stuff to extremes".

The band were also drinking heavily again at this stage, with Hussey cultivating the ability to drink a bottle of wine, vomit it back up so that he could drink some more. One evening in a restaurant he would go out to be sick just as the other diners would use the bathroom, and would return and carry on the conversation apparently unaffected. Hunt had first seen this side of The Mission when he had visited them during recording for 'Carved in Sand': "They were a lot more chemically friendly, they always refer to 'God's Own Medicine' as their speed album, but around the time of 'Carved' they were into coke in a big way. It was all going on inside the studio, they'd get a CD box or album sleeve and chop out loads of lines and pass them round. Every time it would happen I would say 'No I'm alright cheers' and eventually Wayne would say 'Please leave him alone, he doesn't want any.' He would always jump to my defence, but they'd never hassle me about it, they just got on with. They'd never judge you by it, even though in those circles at the time it was more of a rarity not to do it. It was just like me buying somebody a pint".

* * *

Nevertheless, the shows in Britain and Europe were arguably the best the band had ever played, the reactions were universally superb and the world, it seemed was at The Mission's feet. On 20th April they flew out to Montreal to begin a massive North American tour. But all was not well. Shortly before the first show, Hussey and Hinkler had a blistering argument which seemed to bubble under for the whole day. The show itself seemed to be going well, until Hinkler let out his pent up anger and viciously kicked over his amplifiers half way through 'Tower of Strength'. When confronted by Hussey about it after the show, the two had to be separated to prevent them from coming to blows. The next day Hinkler could not be found anywhere and people began to worry. The following morning, crew member Steve Watson awoke to find the red message light on his hotel room phone flashing, and on realising that Hinkler had not stayed the night in the band hotel he rushed downstairs with dread beginning to creep into his stomach. The pretty receptionist politely handed him the message with a greeting and a smile. Watson read the message, his face went ghostly white and his mouth dropped:

> 'Mr. Hinkler sends his apologies but
> he will not be doing the rest of the tour'

CHAPTER ELEVEN

"At last the three companions turned away, and never again looking back they rode slowly homewards; and they spoke no word to one another until they came back to the Shire, but each had great comfort in his friends on the long grey road."

J.R.R.Tolkien: The Return Of The King
from The Lord of the Rings

LOSING a founder member of a band is a difficult and disruptive experience at any time - in the middle of a world tour with 82 dates still to play, and with so much of the band spirit having been placed on the four original members, Hinkler's sudden departure in Montreal was a massive blow to The Mission which would test their powers of survival to the limit. The first gig after Hinkler left was in Toronto's Massey Hall on the 24th April - with Wolfie already in place on rythmn guitar he was immediately promoted to lead after an intensive session of rehearsals in various hotel rooms during the day and in the soundcheck. The show that night was in front of 2,000 expectant fans who had all heard the rumours that this was The Mission's best show ever - the pressure on the band to perform was never greater and the strain showed. The band were tense and highly emotional but the show was excellent with the crowd greeting every song with wild applause. When the set arrived at 'Butterfly on a Wheel' Hussey picked up a lone acoustic guitar and, voice filled with emotion walked to the edge of the stage and said 'This is for our guitarist Simon, who left the band this morning'. That number and the encores were all warmly received by the audience and to uninformed observers the gig was a success. But any by-stander backstage would have seen all the band in tears, each alone with their own thoughts, emotionally drained by the disastrous events of the last twenty four hours. The only outsider who could console any of them was Ian Astbury from The Cult who had tentatively walked backstage to congratulate the band on their performance - as a fellow musician he knew exactly the enormity of their achievement to even play the show that night, let alone produce a great gig.

With Wolfie coping admirably on lead guitar for the time being The Mission resolved to finish the tour. With the urgency now removed somewhat, they began the process of coming to terms with Hinkler's departure, a process that would take them two full years to finally realise and in the meantime would indelibly effect everything that The Mission were involved in. Hinkler's unhappiness had been apparent before, most notably perhaps when he was sacked after that first Sisterhood tour way back in 1986, and with his various public announcements of distaste for the music press. However, it had not been an issue that was always gnawing away at band morale, constantly threatening to blow up in their faces. Quite the opposite in fact - as The Mission progressed through to their third album and all the success that this brought, they became renowned as a band with an extended family atmosphere of mutual respect and great friendship, which as Pamela Burton had noted, was incredibly striking to any outsider. Hinkler was very much an integral part of all of this, so what could have disturbed him so much that he left so abruptly?

It would be too easy and essentially inaccurate to dredge over events of the last four years and highlight certain incidents as omens of his impending departure; at the same time there were maybe certain characteristics that suggested that if anyone would become disillusioned (though not necessarily to the point of leaving), it could well be Hinkler. Charlie Eyre at Phonogram had expressed concerns about him previously: "Simon's a strange man. He's got this idea that no-one cares about him because he's the guitar player which is nonsense. Thereby he comes across as being rather aggressive and rather stupid. He's not, he's very articulate, bright, artistic and incredibly creative, musically and in other ways. Simon feels stifled and finds it difficult when Wayne keeps stressing how it's a band, four individuals not a dictatorship. Wayne certainly doesn't see him as an extra pair of hands, but that's not how Simon sees it. I'm very fond of Simon, but he's the odd one out. He's maybe got a chip on his shoulder which occasionally manifests itself in not very attractive ways. He does himself no favours".

For Hinkler it was also an intensely emotional experience, and one that would also take him some time to come to terms with. Three years after he left The Mission he views his days in the band with great fondness and has no regrets. To his credit Hinkler had never made a secret of the fact that he enjoyed being a guitarist, and only a guitarist, not a public figure available for interviews with newspapers, TV and radio stations twenty four hours a day. Such was his disillusionment with this admittedly unsavoury side of the business that on this world tour he actually refused to do the promotional work which is unavoidably incumbent in being in such a successful group - the others would do press in the day and Hinkler would often fly in on the night just for the gig. Taking it back even further, he also had to come into a circle of three friends at the start who already knew each other, and therefore in many ways he had the hardest task of all as the original outsider and felt this undermined his position at times - his sacking after the first European tour with The Cult in early 1986 left a legacy of insecurity which played on his mind, especially when the rigours of their extensive touring punished their weary bodies. At such times his feelings of isolation would start to re-surface: "There was definitely an element of being an outsider. Quite often I wouldn't feel a real part of the band, I was still the new boy playing guitar. I guess I carried that initial experience of being the last to join and then being sacked after the first tour right through to the end, although I don't think the rest of them felt that way". His subdued approach to interviews was a reflection of this nagging insecurity: "I would have been a lot more forthcoming in interviews if I'd have felt more a part of it. I was the quiet one if you like because I didn't want to go around shouting how proud I was of somebody else's work, it was always a case of blowing Wayne's trumpet. I didn't want to be a mouthpiece for Wayne, I found myself repeating his philosophy rather than mine. It's fair enough that the press are more interested in the singer than anyone else, so the good of the band was always put before anything else". However, all these factors are prevelant in many bands, at every level from garage outfits to stadium fillers. These reasons are still not enough, there had to be more.

The essential crux of the problem was a power struggle between Hussey and Hinkler which had manifested itself to differing degrees and at various stages in the band's career, but had become a debilitating obstacle by the time of the 'Deliverance' world tour. Whereas before the band had all, in their own words 'pissed in the same bucket', Hinkler's separation had grown steadily with his decreasing involvement in the press circus. This occasional isolation was a result of this power struggle, and was exacerbated in many cases by what the band felt was his negative attitude towards problem solving in the studio and in other musical areas. They felt arguments would flare with Hinkler about a problem that could have been solved through lengthy discussion. Unbeknown to Hussey, Hinkler had expressed reservations about his contributions during the recording of 'Children' at The Manor, so the problem had clearly been on the guitarist's mind for some time. He acknowledges the power struggle that finally demotivated him to the point of leaving was already troubling him on their second album: "It became very annoying that we couldn't have any more input. It was ironic that they set out with The Mission to avoid the whole Eldritch control syndrome that had run The Sisters. For that reason when we started the first step was to give joint credit for all the publishing. Having said that Wayne ended up doing everything himself, and it stank. He controlled everything, even all the imagery early on, all the gothic stuff, he controlled the lot. He would have everyone believe that it was four musketeers, and it was as far as the public were concerned, but you'd feel like a session musician at times. I'd done a lot of stuff before where I'd had input, but this was a first - it was also the first time that I was making any money out of it. On 'Children' I came up with eight ideas for songs, and I took them to Wayne and he said 'Yeah, they're great' and they were never seen again. It was always his stuff that got done. That pissed me off".

Despite Hussey never hiding the fact that he had a large say in the band's direction, Hinkler found that the idea of a democracy led by one voice became increasingly frustrating to his own musical aspirations, as he began to spend more time on other projects as an outlet for the ideas which found no home within the parameters of The Mission. During 'Carved' he had spent much time on his own working on the many ideas he had for film soundtracks, leaving Hussey to provide many of the guitar lines - by this stage Hinkler felt his proffered contributions would not be given fair consideration so he deliberately took a back seat on the project.

As a result of this, and earlier reservations, Hinkler found himself dissatisfied with the direction The Mission were taking musically: "'Children' for example should have been a really good, hard rock album. Rock lasts and we were at our best as a rock band. One of the great things about the four of us was that on a good night we could really kick ass, we were incredibly tight, very impressive to watch. One of the strongest things in our favour was that element of The Mission, we could do the business live. But Wayne wanted to be a pop star. With 'Children' the songwriting was at fault. We should have gone the rock path, we'd just done this American tour and we were burning, we should have rocked on that album, but as it was there's a lot of pedestrian stuff on there, too soft. We didn't feel like that, we were rockin'. At the time the big American rock bands like Metallica and Aerosmith were big news and we were all into that stuff but it wasn't really reflected on 'Children'. If he'd have thrown it wide open to the band we'd have done a lot better. We could have made a real good rock band- I'd never been a fan of pop music, for a lot of my youth it was on the other side of the fence from what I was into. The songs on 'Children' were written as pop songs in as much as the formula that was there. Also on the 'Carved' album I felt the acclaim was on reputation rather than on merit. That wasn't good after a while. Wayne was getting so much more self-indulgent with the music and there were some pretty poor efforts I felt, so by now I really felt like an outsider. I've always had a problem with Wayne's lyrics, right from the very start, I thought they were very shoddy, but musically I liked most of what we did".

For his part Hussey recognises this creative frustration that Hinkler felt, but at the same time did not feel that he was unduly tyrannical within the band structure: "It was an up and down relationship between us but you can't be that close to everyone you work with. I always felt I had to push him, he seemed to be lazy and lacking in motivation but if you did push him he was great. He wanted to contribute more - I found his stuff very good but hard to sing, which is quite often the case when a non-vocalist puts material forward. But he knew the situation when he joined, it was democratic but we wouldn't do anything I didn't want to do and I never tried to hide that fact. By the time of 'Carved' though, with all the film stuff he was working on, he seemed to be disinterested. He was always available straight away for guitar work, don't be mistaken, he was in no way obstructive to making the record, far from it. But when the other three of us went out on this promotional tour beforehand things started to build up. We inevitably ended up resenting having to do his share of the work. It had boiled over before Montreal - one night in Europe I was really worked up, we were all in a limo and he said something petty, I can't even remember what it was, and I just turned round and punched him. I was appalled at myself and immediately thought 'Why have I done that?' but it showed it was becoming a problem".

During the European tour prior to his departure, tension had escalated with petty arguments over basic tour arrangements worsening the atmosphere. Alongside this and the more serious creative tensions, were circumstances peculiar to a touring environment - Hinkler was socialising with people the rest of the band did not particularly like and bringing them on the tour bus. They all did this occasionally, and under normal circumstances would not dream of choosing his friends for him. A brief respite was found after his illness with Scarletina, when he went home to recuperate and the tension dissipated. However, after discussing the mounting problems whilst Hinkler was recuperating, the band climbed onto the tour bus in New York ready to head off for Montreal and there at the back of the bus before even the band themselves had arrived, was Hinkler and his crowd of friends. With one group at the front of the coach avoiding the group at the back the tension had immediately returned before even the first date of a lengthy tour.

Hinkler himself was physically very low because of his recent illness and also feels that the rest of the band did not really show much tolerance of his friends: "We'd already done a very big schedule, even by our own standards. We'd cancelled the last night of the European tour because I had this Scarletina. I was in the airport, lying on the floor thinking this band lifestyle was actually killing me because I didn't know I was actually ill, so I just thought the heavy schedule was destroying me. So after all this strain, I was faced with a whole new American tour, more hell, and I was already in bad shape. The prospect was not nice. On top of all that, I came offstage that night in Montreal and, like The Cult tour, I was sat down and talked to. Both Sue, my girlfriend and Steve, my mate were on the tour, but I'd invited them out and impressed on them to stay out of the way and offer to help whenever they could, and it wasn't as if they were the first people to come on the tour bus. So I was sat down by the band and told that my friends would not be welcome on the rest of the tour. I just flew off the handle at Wayne for the first time ever, because my friends were totally unobtrusive, quiet as mice - all of a sudden the band had decided that friends weren't allowed on anymore. I had it in mind that I was going to quit at the end of that tour anyway, because there were no concrete plans after we'd finished, so I was going to wait for a lull in the activity and then leave. Unfortunately, Wayne chose the wrong time to pick a fight and it pushed me over the edge".

Both sides clearly had grievances and the situation did not appear to be getting any healthier - it was all the more upsetting because of the closeness of The Mission's 'gang' atmosphere which up until now had been such a strong and envious feature of the band environment. Tension was escalating rapidly and by the time the band arrived at the venue for the night's show in Montreal the friendly atmosphere was fractured and very hostile. After demolishing his amps halfway through the show Hinkler stormed offstage without the rest of the band. He was extremely unhappy. The rest is history.

* * *

Throughout their career The Mission had always made it clear that they were survivors - the band determination to succeed had seen them through the corporate wars with Eldritch, through Adams problems in Los Angeles, through some of the most vicious press criticism ever published and through continual misconceptions about the band itself.

So the morning after Hinkler walked out and left the band stranded, and despite this devastating blow, the rest of The Mission made it crystal clear from the onset that they would not be calling it a day and never let doubts about folding the band even cross their minds. At the time Hussey said: "I feel bitter and hurt but I'm not prepared to give in" and went on to say "Basically I love Craig and Mick and I love the people we work with and it would be really sad to let an incident like this finish it."[1] With Wolfie in place on guitars, and a defiant determination not to let Hinkler see that he could finish the band, they headed off for the rest of the tour. With Hinkler crossing America in a hired car on his own personal tour, The Mission recruited Malcolm Treece of support band The Wonder Stuff to fill the spot left vacant by Wolfie's unexpected promotion. When the band reached Philadelphia, Treece's spell of two shows per night was ended momentarily when he was replaced by Greg, a long time fan and friend of The Mission. He was a guitar player himself, but even so must have been slightly unnerved by the proposition in the car park of the venue that maybe he would like to play guitar for his favourite band that night in front of 1500 people, amongst whom he had planned to be himself. With such stop gap measures The Mission completed the American leg of the tour, with almost no signs of the excess present on previous excursions, mainly because they knew they had a job in hand that was extremely difficult and could not afford to be distracted. They also knew they faced financial ruin if they did not fulfil their obligations to so many venues across the nation, so they grimly soldiered on. The focus and perseverance they showed in doing this was arguably as great an achievement as any of their gold discs hanging on their walls.

It is still more incredible that at this, the nadir of their careers with the band spirit ravaged by Hinkler's departure, The Mission still insisted on enjoying their touring - as a consequence of this admirable philosophy, and despite the extreme circumstances, the remainder of the tour had more than its share of typical Mission tour chaos. Perhaps most noteworthy was the apparent appearance of Robert Smith of The Cure for the encore of their show at the Los Angeles Palladium. Robert Smith, aka a heavily disguised Jez Webb, Mission roadie, caused a near riot when he appeared through the dry ice towards the end of the set. A few people had started to drift away at the end of a great gig when suddenly he appeared, clothed in fright wig, baggy jumper and over-size baseball boots, and the place went wild with hundreds of amazed fans rushing the stage all screaming incontrollably. After an incredibly Smith-like performance of 'In Between Days' Jez left the stage, leaving the security to cope with the rush backstage. Two girls ran up to The Mission's make-up lady and said 'How does Robert have his hair done?'. The make-up lady assumed everyone knew it was only Jez so she truthfully replied 'Oh, it's a wig'. After the devoted Cure girls had recovered from the shock they ran off screaming to their friends the hideous news about their idol. Another group spotted who they thought was Robert Smith walking casually into the dressing room and harangued the door man to let them in. After five minutes of hassling to see their idol, they fell silent as the door opened. To their great disappointment it was only some anonymous roadie - Jez, now changed back into his normal clothes, emerged and walked straight past the girls, who seeing their chance ran past him and into the dressing room. It had no windows and no other doors but incredibly Robert Smith was not in there, and the amazed girls left, remembering to add 'Miracle Disappearing Act' to their idol's many talents. The Mission climbed on to the tour bus and left Los Angeles, with people still debating whether it was in fact Robert Smith or not, an argument that raged for years to come.

At San Francisco the band played a blistering set, unaware that Hinkler and his friend were propping up the bar at the back - after the guitarist had been driving around America he decided he would like to see the band he had just left, but chose not to reveal himself, which was probably for the best at this stage as tensions were running high. At another gig, Hussey had seen a couple of bouncers hitting a girl in the audience and angrily ordered them out of the premises, refusing to continue playing until they had left. After discussing the matter with the manager of the venue, the embarrassed ranks of burly security guards slinked out of the arena, but waited backstage for the somewhat smaller Hussey, who had the dubious accolade of coming only fifth at that Butlins holiday camp 'Tarzan' competition when he was a five stone 8 year old. After finishing a generally boisterous gig which would see Hussey's future wife Kelly (whom he was yet to meet) stabbed in the leg, Hussey put his guitar down and headed for the backstage curtain with some trepidation, Sure enough, behind the cloth there were twelve huge bouncers waiting for him, arms crossed, legs bolted to the floor. The Head Guard, arms folded and face set, sauntered over to Hussey and peered down at the singer, who by now fully expected not to get away without at least a knife being pulled. With eyes fixed on each other, a full minute passed as the tension mounted until finally the bouncer made his move. He blew a big wet raspberry right in Hussey's face.

The band finished the tour in New York, but not before Hussey had visited Salt Lake City, home of his baptised religion the Mormons, a city which had been formed by Brigham Young in 1847, 24 years after the Prophet Joseph Smith had founded the Mormon faith. Brigham was later forced to flee amid allegations of having sixteen wives and practicing 'lewd and lascivious co-habitation' - perhaps harping back to the days when polygamy was the norm for the sect which would display such abstinence in later years, Hussey appeared on the local Utah Radio KJQN warning the night's audience: "This is a Mormon state, and tonight you're gonna see this Mormon in a right state."

The Mission limped home to the UK, having barely made it back at all and rightly being proud of pulling through such a difficult experience. Two days after landing back in Britain, they were somewhat cheered by their eighth Top 40 single, when 'Into The Blue' charted at No.35 and eventually reached three places higher. Several inferior comparisons to 'Wasteland' fuelled other accusations from some quarters that The Mission needed a new direction: "England lose to Uruguay. Some ex-lover of Madonna manages to sell pictures of her half-naked body to The Sun. Gorbachev comes under increasing pressure at home from Red Army hardliners. The Mission bring a new single out and it sounds like The Mission have since time immemorial. Life goes on; you can't alter it, you might aswell accept it."[2] The public, however, did not agree with this impatience - although it was less successful than the previous two singles taken from 'Carved', its chart position was a confirmation of The Mission's continued appeal in their home country, regardless of the difficult events of recent weeks, and with the video surfacing on Top of the Pops and The Chart Show, The Mission silenced the doubters who had queried their determination to persevere.

There was still no rest for the weary band - they had been asked to play The Pink Pop festival in Holland as the headline band in front of 60,000 people, as well as a festival in Italy and one in Finland. To accommodate the still vacant guitarist's spot Tim Bricheno from All About Eve, a close friend of the band, joined The Mission for these three festival dates and the European leg of the remaining tour, before resuming with his own successful band. Pink Pop went well, and the band were enthusiastically received by the massive audience, and the Italian TV interviews and shows all went well. But it was in Finland in Provinci, that the band basically went on a rampage and returned to the kind of riotous antics for which they had been so famed for in their early days. The restraint the band had displayed whilst completing the American tour without Hinkler was tremendous, but the emotional stress had to surface at some stage. That release came in Finland, a festival where drugs and alcohol were available everywhere and in enormous quantities, which to this band, ravaged by events over the last few months, was too much to resist - the effect of so much indulgence so openly available to a band who had forcibly restrained themselves was like letting a caged animal loose. It would be an unbelievable weekend.

The band's hotel was overlooking the festival site and once they had unpacked they opened the curtains and surveyed the area in front of them. It was already total debauchery, with almost everyone in view under one kind of influence or another, and people in various stages of undress aimlessly wandering around the site. At a camp site right under the window the drugs and beer flowed, and they could see the naked and stoned host swigging thirstily from a bottle of cider in one hand whilst he fried sausages in the other by holding them over the fire in the palm of his hand. It was then that the band made the decision that the only way to get the most out of this scenario was to lower themselves to the level of everyone else. They began their task in earnest.

The Stone Roses were on the bill alongside The Cramps so the atmosphere was very much one of anything goes. The Mission soon got hold of some acid which was immediately taken to calamitous effect. Within five minutes Hussey and the crew tried to storm the stage, their efforts becoming more desperate the more they were repelled, and when that failed they took to hurling logs and branches at the terrified security. Hussey was frog-marched back to his room as the main instigator in the chaos, where he was locked in and a colossal guard put outside his door to keep him there. But the festival promoters had made a fatal mistake. They had forgotten about the rest of the band. Undeterred by the loss of their Commander in Chief, The Mission continued their barrage, led incredibly by Tim Bricheno, who was normally very reserved and shy. He and Wolfie had got along like long-lost brothers and aided by the drugs proceeded to wreak utter havoc on the hotel. Both were also hopelessly drunk and ran around the hotel garden, ripping up every plant and throwing them all into the swimming pool, which rapidly began to resemble a swamp. Meanwhile, on the other side of the hotel Adams woke naked, out of his head and sweating profusely in the hotel sauna. He stumbled out and dripped his way to the pool area, where he began lecturing Wolfie and Bricheno about demolishing the plants and ruining the pool. In his state he decided the best way to emphasise his argument was to plunge into the swimming pool and to begin the laborious process of cleaning the pool. Just as he surfaced, and with a plant stuck to his head, a furious Hotel Manager came round the corner, and seeing Adams thrashing about in the water surrounded by hundreds of shredded plants, jumped to an obvious but misinformed conclusion. The unfortunate bassist was fished out and hurried after the irate manager who walked into reception to prepare the enormous bill for damages. Just then Soul II Soul entered the foyer to book in and were treated to the sight of The Mission's naked bass player, looking like some frenzied swamp monster dripping wet and covered from head to foot in limp greenery, pleading with the manager for leniency.

After convincing the manager that he would be on his best behaviour, Adams determined to be on his worst, and after dressing, headed for the backstage area. On realising he had lost his pass in amongst the pool full of plants he began trying to convince the two guards at backstage security of his identification. Seeing his arguments fall on deaf ears, Adams made a dash for it. With the bouncers rapidly closing in on him, he rushed into the promoters office where he hastily tried to explain his predicament. With the two bouncers now covering the door, the bassist found himself the source of much merriment as he vainly tried to get past the obvious language barrier to explain himself. As the laughter grew, Adams did the only thing he could think of in order to get their attention fully - he headbutted the promoter. Meanwhile, back out front, Hussey had escaped and was renewing his assaults on the stage, and was now hurling food and mud at the bewildered security. Back in the hotel, Adams was dumped unceremoniously in the bar to cool down and was supping a beer with Ivy from The Cramps and realised he needed the bathroom. Remembering the long walk to the toilet, and the state he was in, he excused himself to Ivy, unzipped his trousers and proceeded to urinate under the table.

CHAPTER TWELVE

"And I gave my heart to know wisdom, and to know madness and folly. I perceived that this also is vexation of spirit".

Ecclesiastes

Grimmet (noun): A small bush from which cartoon characters dangle over the edge of a cliff.

Douglas Adams & John Lloyd:
The Meaning of Liff

HAVING retired to a rehearsal studio to prepare for the forthcoming European and South American dates, The Mission were relaxing after the problems with Hinkler and their outrageous behaviour in Finland. Rehearsals were going well and there were signs that the atmosphere of friendship which had been shattered by the guitarist's departure was beginning to return. The phone rang, Hussey answered it and his face dropped. Then two more calls followed and within the space of one hour three original members of The Mission's unique road crew had left, and to rub salt into the wound, they had done so to join none other than The Sisters of Mercy. The Mission's extended family which had started the year in such fine fettle appeared to be irreparably and permanently shattered.

Knowing that the band were already reeling from the severe blow of losing Hinkler, it was astonishingly cruel for their close friends to leave the crew in such a fashion. There had been rumblings of discontent on the American tour, with Pete Turner expressing resentment about the amount of time The Wonder Stuff were staying on stage for. The band did not have a problem with this, the support band were friends of The Mission and they had been invited onto the tour - there were other minor grumbles but the essence of the split was that the three had been offered a lot of money to join Eldritch, bought out in effect. The music business can be a very lucrative trade but frequently road crews are left financially vulnerable whilst other non-playing members reap vast amounts, so there was little resentment about them wanting to do better for themselves and earn a higher wage. It was the way it was done, and the band they joined that particularly galled The Mission. This lack of thought by the crew members hurt the band badly. They felt betrayed and the atmosphere of despair deepened.

With the band in so much emotional turmoil many turned to their girlfriends for solace - for Hussey however, this had developed into yet another traumatic situation. During the American tour he was taken to one side by a friend and informed that his girlfriend had been seeing one of Hussey's own friend's behind his back, a situation exacerbated by the recent decline in what had been a year long relationship. Hussey explains how this came about: "The whole situation had been pretty dodgy for quite a while and she was screwing around with people behind my back, friends, people I knew. I was screwing other people also but it hurt so much because close friends were involved. Having said all that, I was a bit of a pig with my attitude in many ways so I guess I deserved it".

Almost everything that they had loved as a part of the unique Mission family had suddenly vanished and the unforgiving demands of their world tour allowed no time for consolidation. In addition to all these distressing personal problems, the band saw a proposed major UK festival in London fall through amidst bitter wranglings. The original idea for the so-called 'Day Of Conscience' was one which Malcolm Treece of The Wonder Stuff had casually mooted to emulate the massive Anti-Nazi League Rally in London in the summer of 1978, which featured The Clash, X-Ray Spex, Steel Pulse and The Tom Robinson Band. In an attempt to reverse the trend of charity gigs becoming band promotionals, the idea was to have many educational stalls by groups such as Greenpeace, CND and various Animal Rights factions, alongside the large bill of bands, and to concentrate on this humanitarian focus to the event. For Tony Perrin it was the single most important goal in 1990. However, with expected crowds of up to 150,000, the costs rapidly escalated and necessitated Perrin to scout for essential sponsors. With this development, tension arose between him and The Wonder Stuff's Miles Hunt who resented the hint of mercenary finances tainting the original idealistic flavour of the event, and after public differences in the press The Wonder Stuff pulled out of the show. The situation deteriorated when Lambeth Council, ironically a renowned militant body, bowed to residential pressure and refused to issue an entertainments licence for the proposed site of Clapham Common. With the alternative sites not coming up to strict safety standards the event was effectively killed.

Hussey knew the complications of the idea, and reflected on its failure: "I thought the whole thing was unfortunate and the attitude that you could do a free gig of that size was essentially naive. It would have cost a fortune and no-one would put that up for nothing. I wanted to get as big names as possible up there because we might not even have to play and we could still have a great day. You need people like Morrisey and Plant to pull the crowds. We tried to carry on after the Stuffies pulled out but it didn't happen. In many ways the only way you can subvert is from within, so we could have had all these stalls from Greenpeace and the like with no political alignment. We wanted to do something that people would remember and bring traffic around the park to a stand still. There was a bit of bitching in the press about it but there was no real fall out".

The Wonder Stuff's Hunt now realises that he may have been overly optimistic about the costs of such a day, and to his credit readily admits his naivete: "I just wanted it to be very simple, I was very idealistic about it all at the time, so when they started mentioning sponsorship and stuff I just wasn't interested. Now I know what's involved I know you could never pull a free stunt like that without somebody coughing up. There was also a lot of disagreement about the bill. I wanted people to see a warm, slightly comic feel, rather than people going into the park and furrowing their brows. I was never comfortable with the 'Day of Conscience' tag either, I'd rather it had been called 'Good Egg Day'."

This controversy was to be typical of the year for The Mission - the massive response to an outdoor gig featuring The Mission ironically created problems which added to the turbulent events they had already experienced. 1990 was to be a year of extremes for The Mission. Publically they enjoyed their greatest success worldwide to date and record sales flourished; privately it was a very traumatic period with the band emotionally shattered and in danger of splintering into bitter and resentful self-induced destruction. So having lost a founder member, some of their crew and in Hussey's case his girlfriend, matters were exacerbated by the public rows over the failed 'Day of Conscience'. The whole camp, so admired for its community spirit and its friendships was in tatters as people began to argue and tempers flared. Speculation in the press was rife about the future of the band and had been so since Hinkler walked out with headlines such as 'The Mission - We'll Never Splish (Hic)' not helping matters. It was a scenario that would have destroyed many bands - it nearly did exactly that to The Mission, and they tried vainly to force the stress to the back of their minds by continuing the tour regardless and pasting over the cracks with more and more drugs and drink. At first it seemed a brave decision, but by December it became apparent that it only denied them valuable time which needed to be spent coming to terms with their losses, and also left them in an environment which was dangerously abundant in all these various indulgences.

* * *

The respite from the world tour was brief - after honing Wolfie's new role at RAK and Riverside rehearsal studios, The Mission flew out to South America on the 23rd of August, for a seven date tour of Mexico, including two shows in Mexico City, the first by a rock band for ten years. Supported by the superb Power of Dreams on all dates, The Mission played to sold out crowds every night and seemed unaffected by the recent departures. At a Phonogram dinner after one show the Master of Ceremonies took it upon himself to re-enact the 'slaughtering of the ox' scene from the film Apocalypse Now on a suckling pig, much to the guests disgust and the band's amusement. On the second night Hussey took a hearty swig from a flask proffered by one of the audience and ten minutes later had to flee from the stage to vomit the dubious drink back up. His annoyance was somewhat atoned for by the sight of beer drinking donkeys on the beach the following day, and the astonishing flash floods which caught the band out in the open whilst taking a rare tourist trip to the pyramids of the Aztecs. Mexico was enjoyed, despite recent events, but the pollution and poverty obviously left its mark on the band's memories: "Mexico City was bizarre - the poverty and smog was terrible. Really dirty, horrible. It really fucked my throat up. You'd be in some really flash hotel and one block down from that there'd be sixty people sleeping under a flyover, complete extremes."

With Mexico finished they dragged their weary bodies to the airport to catch a plane to New Zealand for the first date of an eight date Australasian tour that began in Auckland. The South American Customs were not finished however, and impounded all their backline gear for several days, forcing the band to borrow equipment from local groups in New Zealand, which resulted in what Adams described as 'the worst gig we've done since Alice in Wonderland'. After more problems saw two gigs cancelled, they took out their frustrations by playing a football match against the New Zealand national squad, albeit one consisting largely of waiters, butchers and car mechanics, and won comfortably, with Hussey re-living his childhood fantasies by scoring a hat-trick. After only one day off, they flew out to Osaka for the opening date of a three show stop over in Japan, which went well and confirmed their cult status in that country. With these dates behind them the band turned into the home straight of their eventful world tour, having the luxury of a week off before the final legs in America, Europe and finally Britain.

Not content with filling the gossip columns when they were playing, The Mission managed to hold the attention of the national press during the week away from touring. At the start of October when they were rehearsing, Hussey was sitting in a pub enjoying a quiet drink when a large and angry local walked up to him and said 'Are you still sleeping with other people's girlfriends?' Many papers reported that he was subsequently thumped in the stomach, beaten up and a beer glass smashed over his head. The less dramatic truth was that the offended party simply bad-mouthed the singer and emptied his full glass of beer over a stationary Hussey's head. It did not seem to be Hussey's year.

Before embarking on the last stretch of their 'Deliverance World Tour' The Mission recruited another guitarist on rythmn in the shape of Paul 'Etch' Etchell, who was a friend of the band and former guitarist with the band Ghost Dance, and joined up despite being asked to play keyboards with Leeds based band Loose. Although neither he nor Wolfie were seen as permanent replacements, they gave The Mission the feel of a complete line-up for the first time since Hinkler left. Whilst Hussey was washing the Newcastle beer out of his hair, Etch rehearsed with the band in a studio in Ossett, West Yorkshire. Suitably ready they flew out for a two day festival instigated by The Cult's Ian Astbury called The Gathering of the Tribes, in Monterrey, California on the 6th and 7th October. Originally inspired by the idea behind the ill-fated 'Day of Conscience', The Mission were somewhat less involved in this project, certainly from the point of what the gigs were in aid of, as Hussey explains: "Ian took our idea and did it over there, and there's nothing wrong with that because the end justifies the means. It wasn't a revolutionary event - I was off me head, one gig was good, one wasn't. I did an interview with MTV and told them my main motivation was to get a free trip to America which was not really what they wanted to hear but at least it was honest. My motivations weren't really aligned as they might have been, and my private life was very indulgent at the time".

Five days later when they began their second European tour of the year, this self-indulgent lifestyle would once again take over with the emotional cracks which had started on that night in Montreal starting to split wide open again. The sizeable tour began in Nice and finished twenty-eight dates and six hectic weeks later in Dusseldorf. The loss of control that had begun to show during the summer by now was running rampant through The Mission camp, as they sought to blot out the hideous memories of events and personnel losses with drugs and drink. The shows were surprisingly good, given the extreme circumstances, but underneath it all The Mission were crumbling, a band in agony. On the 8th December the NME put The Mission on the front cover with the headline 'Czech Pint Charlies: The Mission: Britain's Stupidest

Band'. The article inside, entitled 'Chunder Acheivers' catalogues their European tour and tells stories of physical abuse, excessive drug and alcohol abuse, profuse and bloodied vomiting, nasal bleeding and generally debauched behaviour (in typical NME style it didn't admit that as the band were vomiting yet again so was their correspondent). The article was a frightening insight into the The Mission's ravaged and desperate state of mind at this stage. Amongst all the laddish stories and beer drinking games, there was an underlying fear and confusion, a total lack of comprehension about what had happened to them in the last eight months. There were still plenty of signs of the humour and easy attitude of The Mission, with comments such as Brown saying "There's nothing like sitting in the shithouse with a pile of trucking magazines if you want a bit of peace." The reporter described them as "the drink-fuelled, drug-addled, bloated, long-haired footy fan, scum-load of Western decadence that is The Mission World Tour". Behind this facade however, there was an anxious and muddled aura about the band, none more so than Hussey himself. After the beers had been sunk and all the jokes told, he was in a desperate mood. He admitted to having recurring and vicious nightmares where he would kill various people, and was quoted as saying "I'm just oblivious to a lot of what goes on. It's not deliberate. It's just 'What's going on?'" More worryingly he also said: "We lost Simon, we lost some of the crew and I split up with my girlfriend. All these people were integral to our lives and we've had no time to, kind of, grieve their departure...The last few days I've been having really vicious dreams. The last one me and Wolfie murdered three of the crew, holding guns to their heads and shooting them...I woke up in a sweat thinking 'This just isn't me. What's going on?...Why am I doing this?'"[1] The Mission were disintegrating before the public's very eyes.

Against this backdrop, the fact that they played to 10,000 screaming Czech fans in an enormous ice rink and from a gig point of view blazed a brilliant path across Europe seemed almost secondary. In addition, that week they had enjoyed their ninth Top 40 hit with a new track called 'Hands Across The Ocean', which had not made it on to the final listing for 'Carved', reaching No.28. The song was arguably The Mission's brightest pop moment thus far, heavily laden with rich melodies and hook lines, perfectly complimenting Hussey's ever-more mobile vocal expression. The video was featured on both Top of the Pops and The Chart Show and the track also received a warm press reception, as this review from Sounds shows: "Wild man that he is, Hussey seems to have been anointed with rather more musical talent than many of his peers. With such blood brothers as The Cult running short of real tunes and Jaz Coleman tinkering with his symphonies, Wayne is emerging as something of a pop brain."[2] The extremes continued.

This continued public success failed however, to lift the gloom that was clouding over The Mission camp. The band were imploding on their own personal traumas, but the transient nature of their lifestyle was not finished and they now began to realise that the longer this continued the less control they would have. They still had an eight date tour of the UK left to complete before they could finally rest their weary bodies and minds. Starting in Glasgow The Mission still managed to produce remarkably vibrant sets. The second date of the tour was the first of two nights at Leeds Coliseum - Dave Simpson of Melody Maker was there and was mightily impressed by the band's resilience: "It's testament to the band's enduring belief in themselves and their music that after so long exposed to the rigours of touring they can still lash out 'Amelia' like it was written the day before. The remarkable intensity the Mission project live is quite at odds with their jokey public image". Wolfie and Etch's inclusion on guitars left Hussey more of a focus of the band than ever, since he was now "free to concentrate on his (impressive) vocal pyrotechnics."[3] Despite expressing concerns about their tendency towards cliche, in many camps they received strong praise, and the quality of the shows was not lost on the exuberant crowds either, despite Hussey walking on stage at Leeds and saying 'So the NME reckons we're the stupidest band in Britain...so what does that make you lot then??'

True to form though, The Mission had their share of detractors - many re-voiced fears that they had become impotent self-parody, and criticised the several acoustic numbers and occasional mistakes, accusing the band of going through the motions just for the sake of it. To a degree this was the case - backstage The Mission were in desperate shape and were constantly bickering and arguing amongst themselves. Unfortunately the personal tone of the criticism remained, as this review from the final night at Brixton Academy shows: "I never realised the Mission were so utterly dreadful until I saw them in the flesh tonight...there were absolutely no redeeming features. If you're gonna pretend to be Led Zeppelin at least have the good grace to be musically competent...in the cold light of day, Wayne Hussey is the perennial sideman who got ideas above his station...give it up, pack it in, go rear sheep. You're just occupying space and wasting our precious time, you have no idea what it's all about."[4]

On 26th November The Metal Gurus released the single 'Merry Christmas Everybody', recorded with Slade's Noddy Holder and Jim Lea. Recording the single had been a dream come true for the band - Slade were their childhood heroes and working with them was an incredible opportunity. The best moment was reserved for one night when they were rehearsing the track and Holder and Lea came to meet them. They were just starting a version of Slade's 'Goodbye T' Jane', so Holder walked up to the microphone and sang the entire number, whilst The Mission grinned widely at each other and watched in awe as one of their great heroes played along with them. Unfortunately, once released, the record not a great seller, largely because The Mission's fans didn't really know what to make of the track. Hinkler was collaborating fully still on the Gurus project and when he appeared for the encore of 'Tower Of Strength', 'Like a Hurricane' and 'Merry Christmas Everybody' at Leeds Coliseum at the end of the tour, it fuelled the many rumours that he was re-joining the band. Much to the fans disappointment, this was never going to be the case - the two camps were now socially good friends again, renewing the strong relationships that had developed during his time in The Mission but that was as far as it went - The Metal Gurus were now a joint project between Hinkler and The Mission, but the low sales of their single saw them take early retirement and with them went any chance of Hinkler's return. The band played the last date of their third world tour on Wednesday the 12th of December at London's Brixton Academy. 'Carved In Sand' was still selling very heavily and had been widely acknowledged as a Mission classic. Against that, when they walked offstage at Brixton to more bickering and arguments, many feared that they had just seen the last Mission gig ever.

CHAPTER THIRTEEN

"I did not have the time or mind to take in the significance of that 'goodbye', nor recognise it then as a clear indication of his knowledge of what the end was going to be for him".

Laurens Van Der Post: The Seed and the Sower

"Give me a mandolin and I'll give you rock 'n' roll".

Keith Moon of The Who

THE new year brought a new home for Hussey as he moved into Wapley Barn in the remote Herefordshire countryside, whilst Brown and Adams retired home to Leeds and London respectively. Personal relations had never been more strained and the 'Deliverance' world tour had nearly destroyed The Mission. At this early stage the future was very simple - nobody intended to make another Mission record. After the trauma of the last twelve months it would only be a fool who voluntarily rejoin the whole band circus again. Hussey considered an acoustic tour of the USA and even thought of taking up guitar with All About Eve, to replace Tim Bricheno who had left to join The Sisters of Mercy. They all had no intention of rushing back into a studio and out into the rigorous touring environment that had so ruptured everything in their lives the year before. The start of 1991 was a time for reflecting on the emotional chaos of the year before, and although nobody dared voice the question, the thought on everybody's mind was 'Why continue something so destructive?

Settling into the isolation of his barn in Herefordshire Hussey finally had the distance to realise the mistake the band had made by grimly resolving to continue the 'Deliverance' tour regardless: "When Simon left it was a real shock. We'd been together for five years at that point and you just don't leave a bunch of mates in the shit like he did. The very last thing on my mind was to finish it. In retrospect we should have finished that American tour and come home to recuperate. But we went on to do Mexico, Australia, New Zealand, Japan, and all the rest of it, and in many ways it worked because 'Carved' sold so well. It would have lost us a fortune if we'd pulled out of that tour and we'd have been liable for it; that was part of it and the other side was we didn't want Simon to think he could just walk out and it would all finish. At the time we felt really betrayed, but it was probably better for him to have left then than to make the eight weeks a misery, but carrying on as we did just gradually destroyed us". He also reaffirmed earlier suspicions that the core of the problem was essentially a power struggle between him and Hinkler: "With all the stuff he said about disliking the press - I just think that was an excuse. He wanted more of a say in what was going on. It was more of a resentment - it's basically my group, it's always been my baby. As far as a democracy can work it's been pretty democratic, with all of us wanting the same thing. But I think there definitely came a point on that last tour when we all wanted different things and we didn't know what the collective aim was anymore".

All the members of the band and crew that were left from that original and unique incarnation soon recognised that The Mission as such could never be the same, and if it was to carry on it had to be something equally good, but different. Only now, away from the hectic schedules of touring and the intense environment that brings, could any of the band attempt to come to terms with what had happened. It would be a long, slow process. For the time being the band articulated the effect the various departures had on the indomitable Mission community spirit. Hussey knew it directly caused the dreadful substance abuse that became paramount at the end of 1990, and resulted in each member of the band hating even being in the same room as the others: "We were sick of each other. We all thought about calling it a day. Craig and I were fighting a lot on that tour. Simon's leaving had such a large effect on us emotionally and we weren't prepared to acknowledge that. We were on tour so we just kept going but that meant that we'd dealt with it practically but never confronted it emotionally. When we did we realised why we'd been so unhappy as a group. In the meantime, the tour continued and it was awful, very low. We'd done the drugs and stuff before, like on the first American tour in 1987 which was very exciting until Craig cracked in LA. Then we were young, it was what we wanted to do, and I never really considered that I was doing any damage to myself - it was great being a singer in a new band with every indulgence catered for. But the time of the 'Deliverance' tour it was all much more destructive, sinister if you like - I had very little self-esteem and we were all getting lower and lower. I was doing all these drugs and drinking very heavily so that I'd feel anaesthetize to all the shit that was happening. I missed that element of being in a gang - when Simon left all of a sudden it became a job whereas before we were all together. We used to believe collectively that we were the best group in the world - we also realised we were the shittest group in the world because you can't have the highs without the lows, you'll always have bum nights. But during that last tour in America that camaraderie died. I travelled separately, it was a case of on that tour we were all very unhappy so we just kept out of each others way, we daren't confront the problem".

The most dangerous and threatening element of any drug use is when it becomes an essential emotional crutch - on the 'Deliverance' tour the drugs had assumed just such a dominant, negative and ultimately destructive role in the band, whereas before the band had seen their use as more of a social indulgence. Hussey recognises this and feels they were fortunate to come out of the 'Carved' tour in one piece: "I'd stopped doing speed and playing, but I was still getting drunk every night and I'd do speed or coke on days off. It had started before the tour. 'Carved' was a cocaine album - we were down in the country and I was doing at least a gramme of coke a day. Miles Hunt came down a few times and I was doing all these drugs and drink, and he told me afterwards that he was really worried because he'd never seen anybody do so much stuff. It was bound to affect the album, affect your judgement, affect the tour. I think we are pretty fortunate, we've come out of this thing relatively unscathed, there's a lot that don't.

Many go on to smack - I did and I liked it, but it was so dangerous, that's when I knew I had to stop. We've always done the drugs but on that tour it became more and more of a hindrance because as you get older your body is not able to function on it so well. Also, from a practical point of view, the songs became more difficult to sing and when you're in that state the first thing that goes is your throat, so it began to determine which songs we could and couldn't play, which isn't very fair".

Hussey spoke for all the band when he articulated these reflections - for Mick Brown the tensions of 1990 made him feel insecure in a band which up until that point had been a complete and secure unit: "It was fucking horrible for the rest of the year - it was a big blow to us all, suddenly realising that you might not be able to achieve what you wanted, it was like that angel on your shoulder, which always seemed to pull us through in the past had just disappeared. There was a massive variety of feelings around that time, there was some serious trouble being caused and with Simon we'd had conversations along these lines before, trying to get him to see solutions rather than problems. He didn't really make much effort to see the solutions, or get involved. These things happen though, and it's all too easy to spot them with hindsight". As Hinkler's manager back in his pre-Mission days with Artery, Tony Perrin faced perhaps the greatest personal loss of all, and he felt it: "It was a body blow. It was the first fracture of the original gang, we were as tight as any outfit could get, as an extended family it was rock solid, so it was a real shock".

* * *

Alongside the reflections of what had been lost, there was a frustration at the opportunities that had been missed during the 'Carved' project. There had been rumblings of discontent about the 'Carved' track listing soon after release of the 'Carved in Sand' album, and the crux of the matter was simple. Many people, including The Mission, felt there was a possibility that with their third album the band who had always displayed an ability to cross international borders with their own unique brand of music, could just take the next step onto the world stage, and become Britain's next stadium filling band alongside the ranks of U2 and Simple Minds. It was never an overt policy - far from it - but the possibility was there and was quietly acknowledged. The reasons why this didn't happen are numerous and are all open to argument. What is clear is that the band felt they didn't help matters with their final choice from the eighteen songs they had originally recorded for 'Carved in Sand'.

The public manifestation of this frustration was the release in October 1990 of 'Grains of Sand', a compilation of the unreleased tracks held over from the 'Carved' sessions. The record contained twelve tracks of a variety not previously seen on Mission albums, and displayed the full range of the band's extensive talents. The lively strumming of the jaunty opener 'Hand Across The Ocean' startles the listener who was expecting a sub-standard B-side compilation - although some were indeed B-sides the release was far from inferior. There were the powerful Eastern tones of 'The Grip of Disease', ideally contrasting the camped up version of The Kinks 'Mr. Pleasant' which was the first time The Mission had allowed themselves an overtly hilarious departure from their normally more subtle humour. There were the epic pieces which people had come to expect from The Mission such as 'Divided We Fall' and 'Grip' but that was not all. There was an orchestral offering in 'Sweet Smile of a Mystery' and an acoustic only track in 'Love'. The piano treatment of 'Kingdom Come' and 'Bird of Passage' revealed Hussey's vocal talent to the full and the acoustic versions of 'Butterfly on a Wheel' and 'Tower of Strength', although not as powerful as the originals, were an interesting variation. Hussey's lyrics were also spread across a much wider range than previous records. In 'Grip' he used the flowery language he had made his own trademark:

"A palace and a throne and a kingdom of my own,
Knights in armour and courtesans,
Maids in waiting with blood on their hands,

However, in the track 'Mercenary' he took a much more blatant approach to the angst and betrayal he felt at the crew members leaving

The Mission:
"You're a sycophantic, bull-shitting, cock-sucking, arse-licking mercenary,
Mind-numbing, money-grabbing, mother-fucking, scum-of-the-earth mercenary,
Cringing, grovelling chicken shit, you pissing waste of time,
You crawling whining hypocrite, you fucking piece of slime.

You can take the money and run, but there's nowhere you can hide,
You arsehole mercenary.

He approached the erotic theme of oral sex in 'Heaven Sends You' with a similar directness:

"I'll kiss you on your breast, I'll drink your milk,
I'll run my tongue between your legs,
I'll kiss you, kiss you, kiss you on your sex,
And take you in my mouth,
And I'll kiss you until heaven sends you".

'Grains of Sand' proved that The Mission had such a catalogue of material around the time of 'Carved' that they could easily release a compilation such as this that would comfortably compete with the original album itself. It was evident from the textures and variety on 'Grains' that the band had a depth and range that they had not previously been given full credit for, and this record went some way to correcting this anomaly.

Many reviewers were sceptical of such a compilation release, suggesting the band were ripping off their loyal fans by releasing a record of tracks not previously deemed good enough to grace 'Carved in Sand'. This was myopically missing the whole point of the release - generally it received very good press for a mid-price album. The NME, although reserved overall, felt it was a reasonable album and applauded the comical version of The Kinks 'Mr. Pleasant' which had been first aired at The Hillsborough Benefit Gig. Raw magazine, which in the past had been particularly vicious towards The Mission was more enthusiastic, pointing out that it would indeed stop expensive imports, and labelling it a veritable bargain. As was often the case, it was left to Mat Smith, the one journalist who seemed to understand The Mission from day one, to evaluate the release in its proper context. He pointed out the sleeve notes on 'Grains' suggested the disappointment about 'Carved' and hinted this record was almost an admission by Phonogram that they had been wrong:

> The songs featured on this album were for the most part recorded during the 'Carved in Sand' sessions, May to August 1989. For one reason or another they were not chosen amongst the ten tracks eventually included on that album. Much debate ensued before the final tracklisting was settled upon and still some since. This collection is an opportunity for you to formulate your own opinions.

For Mat Smith this was evidence of his suspicions: "Here was a band firing on all cylinders, but literally blinded by all the different music they'd come up with. In the face of artistic confusion, in stepped the powers-that-be to stamp 'Carved' with a marketable identity which basically meant that anything new and unusual went out of the window. From then on, the role of 'Carved' as a cross-over LP was effectively sabotaged...In the light of much of 'Grains', the skeletal hand on the LP sleeve shouldn't be seen as anything other than the Mish clawing their way back from a premature burial at the hands of others."[1]

'Grains of Sand' sold well, charting at twenty-eight but effectively the chance had been lost. The track listing on 'Carved' had stopped that album being for The Mission what 'The Joshua Tree' had been for U2. Hussey explains why there had been so much debate about the choice on 'Carved': "We recorded eighteen songs and tried to choose the track listing democratically, but in retrospect it didn't work. I should have just said 'I want this on, this and I don't want this..'. There were too many people outside of the band who influenced the final decision. We tried to please too many people and ended up without the best choice of the songs we had. Side 1 of 'Carved' is great, it's got all the elements of a great record, all the variety, but Side 2 dips very badly, and that cost us."

"We sell records, we don't sell vast amounts, but what we do is sell records everywhere, worldwide. That's why at this point we were poised to crack it, but with 'Carved' we fucked up. The lyrical content was pretty flimsy, all that magic, legend and myth, although that was what I was interested in. Every album I write is a period of time and the songs are how you feel and show your interests, but those lyrics had no relation to what was happening in 1990". Even so, despite the band's own reservations, many people disagreed. and believed 'Carved' had been capable of raising The Mission to this elite world stage, among them such reputable sources as Q magazine, CD Review and The Guardian, who said "'Carved in Sand' marks The Mission's inexorable rise to stadium status with it's combination of colossal rock riffs ...they may not be U2, but what they lack in commitment they more than make up for in volume."[2]

There was a very real danger that by approaching this next rung, if they failed they could be lost forever in the no-mans land middle ground between stadium filling millionaires and cult outfits such as Fields of the Nephilim, enjoying the benefits of neither, and with the public left unsure as to their true identity. Having cleared the indie fence which the majority of bands never get past (to be fair many never try or want to), and unhindered by the colloquialisms so peculiar and restrictive to many British bands, The Mission were now facing the fence marked 'Global'. Many willed them to jump straight over and achieve that status, particularly those camps disillusioned with the thudding clump of mega-rock and what they saw as the posturing arrogance of U2 and Simple Minds. On the other hand, some parties felt The Mission could never hack it in the big league, as Robert Sandall of Q magazine suggests in no uncertain terms: "'Carved in Sand' remains rooted in the same old minor league posturing, and echoes of the Bunnymen and re-treads of Led Zeppelin which inspired their earlier efforts. Indeed, strip away the songs' ingenious wrappings...and you're left with a shadowy one-size-fits-all drone...The Mission have got a lot of ground to make up before they challenge the likes of U2 and Simple Minds up on the world stage."[3]

Another element in the jigsaw was The Mission's own reluctance to take the next step, largely because of the effect it might have on their treasured band environment. They thrived on audience contact, both during shows and at the numerous, highly popular Fan Club gigs they still arranged despite their massive status. If they became a stadium outfit there would be less time for these things, and the rigours and public exposure on the world stage would make such features practically impossible - fan club gigs would probably end and projects like The Metal Gurus, from which they had all gained an enormous amount of enjoyment, would have to be shelved. So perhaps The Mission were denied their shot at this chance by their inherent preference for the down-to-earth side of being in a band. By being so approachable and friendly they automatically forfeited the right in many people's eyes to be taken seriously. The singer of a band playing to 120,000 people finds himself in an unrealistic position and in many senses he has to adopt an unrealistic lifestyle to accommodate that. In 1990, The Mission were not prepared to do this.

This reluctance by the band to assume all the trappings of a global band was displayed around the time of 'Carved' in several ways. The Mission operation had become a massive international outfit, with many decisions being made on the band's behalf without their knowing any details at all. Their frustration at this loss of control led them to sack many of the people involved in this complex web of delegation, especially across in America. Hussey explains why: "There were decisions being made on our behalf that we didn't know about until six months later and which we simply wouldn't have made. The whole thing about delegation just got out of control. I think that the more people that are involved the more ideas there are complicating our direction. Plus, even if they don't think so, these people have vested interests and the fact is that the more money we generate the more money they make. In that situation, quite often the last people they think about is the band, what it will do to the band emotionally and physically to pursue such an intense schedule. It's not a nastiness, but they see it as an opportunity, a chance and we frequently aren't considered in the equation".

At one point on 'Carved' this projected status went as far as for them to be assigned a wardrobe girl, whose first action was to give them a £10,000 cheque with instructions to buy some new clothes. The band were never happy with this idea and it was soon scrapped: "In terms of the what you look like you have to feel comfortable. If you go out on stage in £5,000 worth of clothes you look like it aswell. We just looked like clothes horses and were totally uncomfortable". Hussey was also unsure about the major press commitments such worldwide status would bring - in the past there had been no better interviewee than Hussey, who was always polite, informative and enthusiastic. However, on the six week promotional-only tour of America before 'Carved' was released, even his patience was stretched: "It drove me nuts. It gets to you when you're asked 'What's 'Amelia' about?' for the tenth time that day. You end up feeling like you're telling lies because you've said it so often, and then you progress to telling actual lies just to entertain yourself". This frustration would only get worse if they took the next step up the ladder.

Perhaps the final element of The Mission's failure to take to the world stage during this period was their apolitical nature as a band. At this time U2 led the way in politicising stadium shows, and it became clear that if The Mission were to progress, it would be unnatural for them to do so along these lines. As singer and mouth piece Hussey showed a creditable restraint from espousing his views on various subjects: "You can only be involved in issues if you genuinely are - I would feel a charlatan otherwise. There's a very thin line and if you don't feel comfortable about your motives then you shouldn't do it. We've never had a political agenda because as a social group we all have very different political ideas. When we started it would have been grossly unfair for me to write about things I believed because it is automatically assumed that I'm speaking for the rest of the band which I patently wasn't. It was a very deliberate and conscious decision not to write politics into our material for that reason. It's never come between us in any way, we are apolitical if you like but we all agree on very general humanitarian issues. It's alright to do this stuff once or twice but if you have to do it all year it becomes quite calculated. I wrote 'Amelia' with good intentions but after a while singing it live I lost all the intensity and feeling - you've got to lose the meaning somewhere along the line. Plus, I believe there are bigger and better people out there to deal with all that".

With the luxury of time and distance from the horrors of 1990, The Mission now realised that they had in fact missed a rare opportunity to open up a global following, partly due to external factors such as the tracklisting on 'Carved' and partly due to their own inherent reluctance to accept certain criteria incumbent in that status. Having said that, this had not stopped other bands in the past - The Black Crowes had managed it, so had ZZ Top and both were equally apolitical and strictly individual in their approach - the only snag was it had taken them both ten years on the road to get there. At the start of 1991, after a massively successful year publically, the calamitous series of events that had savaged The Mission on tour meant that they had no intention of touring ever again. In such circumstances it is all the more remarkable that The Mission were now firmly established as one of the country's premier acts - 'Carved In Sand' had gone on to sell over one million copies worldwide, an extraordinary achievement for any band. So despite their own personal ruminations, all these reservations and reflections were largely lost on a fascinated public, who awaited their next release with baited breath.

CHAPTER FOURTEEN

"If you do what you always do you'll get what you always get".

Leon Sadler.

*"I think we ought to forget our own identity and the costumes
and just do our own thing".*

Tom Wolfe: The Electric Kool Aid Acid Test

AT the start of 1991, and for the first time since they started the band back in Leeds in 1985, The Mission had time to themselves, and they were able to relax and take stock. Time was spent with family and friends and the band were allowed to finally re-enter some variation on normal life, and began to reflect on what they had achieved rather than what they had not. It was a very relaxing and therapeutic time. By the middle of the year, Hussey would be married, having bought an isolated converted barn, and finally passed his driving test - all very placid stuff for the man who had been earmarked to become the next Jim Morrison. Brown had sold the flat he owned in London which he rarely used and bought a house with his girlfriend back in his native town of Leeds. Adams, after initially retiring back to Chiswick in London, moved south later in the year to Brighton after his girlfriend became pregnant. Tony Perrin had also married and now had a baby daughter, with a new house also in Herefordshire. Fairly soon, a new attitude began to emerge from this altered environment, and a greater sense of control prevailed, as Hussey explained at the time: "I feel a lot stronger than I did two, three years ago. I still have self-doubts, you always do, that's all part of the whole creative process. My dependence on drugs and drink has completely gone now, I do those things for leisure, for fun, whereas up until 1991 it was very much a part of it all". That part, as has been seen, spiralled increasingly out of control and Hussey admits that the excess of the 'Deliverance' tour scared him. When he found himself being kept awake for days and driven mad by taking purified crystalline amphetamine, known as ice, he realised that the time had come to ease up: "I still like that altered state and I think you definitely see things in a different light, a different perspective and things work on different levels. But it's a dangerous area to talk about because you cannot be seen to advocate it on any level or else you could be condemning a lot of people to addiction. Many people aren't as able emotionally to deal with drug use as others. It has to be controlled. There's some things I wouldn't do again but having said that I don't regret anything, although there's large parts of my life that are just a blur, I've little or no memory of it, particularly shows. I can't remember venues at all..."

The first few months of the year were very much for recovering - but still the nagging question remained unanswered as to whether there would be another Mission record at all. All three went through phases where they saw no valid reason to continue, and the argument against carrying on was indeed a strong one. The last year had brought such stress, physical abuse and emotional friction for everybody, and the thought of launching into another mammoth tour appealed to nobody, particularly now that their personal circumstances had all changed. Sitting in a remote barn surrounded by the picturesque Herefordshire countryside seemed a million miles away from the crises of 1990. What possible attraction could there be in living in each others pockets for eight months and dredging their bodies through the rigours of touring yet again? But it was not that simple. When Hussey had been 12 his Dad had shut him in the shed to play his guitar - twenty years later the shed was just a little bigger, and the stakes somewhat higher, but the motivation was essentially the same. So after only six weeks of the projected six months off, Hussey found himself in the Barn, toying with some very interesting ideas for songs, and material began to spring to mind that he was increasingly anxious to try out. The problem was Brown and Adams were hundreds of miles from the isolated barn he was living in and he couldn't be sure that they would be interested, so he told himself to leave it at that. But the ideas would not go away, and coupled with some material that had evolved during the 'Deliverance' world tour, Hussey became very excited and his enthusiasm slowly but surely began to return. By now he had a small studio of his own and so during February he began to put some tracks down, and called the two other members to casually ask what they thought. Adams and Brown drove to Herefordshire and listened to the new material - pretty soon it became clear that it was very substantial indeed, and glances were shared with smiles as the band realised they were on to something new. So by the second month of their first vacation they found themselves beginning to work on a new project - no conscious decision had been made and their return was not even discussed - ultimately their love for the band and their great friendships had made the decision for them.

* * *

Prior to these developments with the new material however, The Mission had experienced serious problems with their record label, Phonogram. Although the independence the label had allowed in the band's formative years had enabled them to fully develop their unique sound, unshackled by the confines of commercialisation, the relationship had been a tense one for some time, and combined with all the other distractions around the time of 'Carved' the atmosphere had become particularly strained. With The Mission touring so much abroad, they had excellent working relationships with their overseas companies, but ironically at home this was not the case. Solving these difficulties was part of the reason why 1991 was such a quiet year for one of the industry's most prolific outfits. Towards the end of 1990 there had been a series of disagreements which for the band represented a worrying trend in Phonogram's attitude to The Mission. They were concerned that their approach was holding the band back overseas - for example, Phonogram would not provide financial support for

The Mission's Australasian leg of the 'Deliverance' tour, and the band instead chose to self-finance the trip with some success. This was one of the many incidents which caused the band, by 1991, to want to leave the Phonogram label - they knew from their days on WEA that a disinterested label was too much of a millstone around any band's neck. Tony Perrin, who had the difficult task of deciphering record company policy for the band, perhaps best explains where the problems arose: "We felt that the attitude of the UK label was holding us back overseas, where we were being taken much more seriously - they were always disappointed that we never sold more than 150,000 LP's in the UK but we felt for our genre of music that was an achievement, and that we could make up for this by our sales overseas. This was always the case, even with bands like The Cure".

There was also a degree of dissatisfaction with the way the industry as a whole operated around the time of 'Carved' and this disagreement was one of many that frustrated Perrin and the band: "The politics can be exciting and it can be frustrating, but as a manager it's my bread and butter. I particularly didn't like seeing people within the same company working against one of their own bands because that will benefit a certain A&R man's career - I'd seen things done which actively undermined bands' careers but benefited an executive's. Things like that are totally destructive and would not be tolerated in any other multi-national business. Also, quite frequently there is no international responsibility or co-operation and that's just not acceptable. Often we felt we had to succeed inspite of the record company, and that's the philosophy behind why we've done so many gigs. Admittedly, it is a creative business and it's difficult to quantify at times, but unfortunately there are a lot of people who have got a free ride and have got on without actually achieving anything. That's the nature of the beast - there has to be a balance between the commerce and the art. It's still a very maverick business and that conflict will always be there, the fact is that the core is subjective and creative but at the same time there is a product that needs selling. But around this time, we just felt that we were producing the goods live and on vinyl, but our record company wasn't conducting the business side of things as they might have done".

So The Mission held talks with various other companies and fairly soon were presented with an opportunity to move to another label within the Polygram group of companies. A senior Polygram executive, who had heard of The Mission's disillusionment, had already let it be known that he would smooth the way for the move. Perrin takes up the story: "I arranged a meeting with our label and took in our lawyer John Kennedy, who had freed The Stone Roses from their contract with Silvertone, and told them we wanted out. They turned round and asked us what would it take to keep us on the label. By this stage we were convinced that our relationship with Phonogram was as good as dead, so we decided the only way we'd stay was if we could have total control of the next LP, with absolutely no record company input whatsoever. Amazingly they agreed fairly quickly - this was a pretty unique offer for a band of our status, so with this amount of control on offer, we went for it and so work began on the album under those premises".

* * *

Actual recording work on The Mission's fourth album, provisionally entitled 'Shades of Green' began at the start of June, 1991, and marked the start of a period of enormous change and experimentation by the band, who up until this stage had worked within very definite parameters. With Brown now based in Leeds, he would drive down to Herefordshire with his car full of tapes of club music which he'd been listening to at home. Adams would sometimes go with him to these clubs, and with Hussey also becoming attracted to the burgeoning dance scene, the original Mission parameters of largely '70's music began to be replaced by a much broader sphere of influence. Part of the attraction for the band was the irreverent approach of many dance bands to their material and also to the sacred batch of songs deemed too 'classic' to cover, which reflected a less precious approach currently being cultivated inside The Mission camp. This deviation from the methods which had brought so much success was largely a reaction to the musical constraints of that success, and to finally nail the gross generalisations about the band which had led to their records being flippantly reviewed in one paper as 'Standard goth fare.' With this new focus in mind, Mark Saunders, who had re-mixed 'Into The Blue', was approached to produce the record, after Hussey had decided against assuming the role himself. Saunders had worked with The Cure on their 'Mixed Up' LP, aswell as Ian McCulloch, Neneh Cherry, Erasure and The Farm. Initially, the band had demoed some very early ideas with Andy Partridge from XTC, but this had not worked out - when asked if this was due to artistic differences, or some other musical nuance, Hussey said "We scrapped all the stuff we did with Andy - it was shite."[1]

After taking the position, Saunders asked his engineer Joe Gibb to become involved in the project. Gibb remembers why they were attracted to working with The Mission in the first instance, a band he previously knew very little about: "I was working with Mark and I'd just finished the Ian McCulloch LP 'Mysterio'. Mark said The Mission had sent him a tape and asked me what I thought of them. I'd never really listened to them much, I'd always had them down as just a rock noise, and more noise than rock. This tape was all pretty rough demos, but programmed in a very naive way which I found very appealing, very refreshing, and not at all what I expected". With Saunders and Gibb now on board, The Mission exercised their new independence from Phonogram by deciding to record the entire album at Wapley Barn in Herefordshire. So before Gibb had even met the band he found himself walking around the multifarious music shops in London and buying up various extortionately expensive pieces of equipment - within a week he had purchased enough for an entire studio. The central purchase was a Yamaha DMR8, which was the latest sixteen track desk technology, so new in fact that Gibb was one of the few people in the country who could operate it. It was already clear that the new record would be nothing like any project The Mission had attempted before.

Working at the Barn with their own equipment was very productive - the beauty of this arrangement was simple: with the record company taking a back seat, the band could record the album away from the pressures of a £3,000 a day studio, full of interfering record executive types, which would very probably have resulted in them churning out a standard rock album, almost to order. Since they now owned the gear themselves, the only costs were those of renting the barn, which were minuscule by comparison - in addition, Saunders worked with equipment that was very far removed from the lengthy processes that had seen them take up to six months just recording on previous albums. The Mission's open acceptance of this new technology was absolutely central to the success of this approach, one which would have been frustrated by their earlier attitudes, which by their own admission, had been essentially Luddite. Hussey felt it was time that the band looked past their former parameters and methods, and ventured into what was for them virgin territory: "There's a lot of snobbery about it, and people shy away from it because it's technology, but you still have to be creative with it. There are evils inherent with the technology and you can become too mathematical, but there is a marriage there that I don't think has really been achieved yet - there are very few bands who seem to mix guitars and the technology to great effect, although it can very easily go too far the other way though, and that runs the very real risk of being inhuman, too clinical. We were very excited by this new gear - at the same time I feel people will always respond to the human element because that's what we are - I used to be of the opinion that if you couldn't sit down and play a song on an acoustic guitar then it wasn't worth doing, but that's too extreme, too conservative by far. I'm still ten years behind everybody else as far as technology's concerned but we're very excited about it all; I do think that you need the base, a song has to be behind it all, or a feeling or a groove that is essentially human, and then you work from there".

The set-up in the Barn was unusual to say the least - the living room became the vocal booth, one bedroom acted as the control room and the bathroom proved to be perfect for acoustic tracks. Progress was speedy, with a healthy friction developing between Hussey and Saunders, whose very different backgrounds synthesised together to great effect - it was a tension which remained controlled, and never threatened to erupt into conflict as it had done way back in The Sisters days. With Hussey being the only band member based in Herefordshire, the project very soon became dominated more than usual by his direction, and there was even a suggestion that this could possibly evolve into a solo project. Such thoughts were dismissed though, largely because Brown and Adams were still contributing on the record: "They were both involved, it was still a collective effort. The drums are all programmed and much of the bass is sequenced, but I still needed their say so on what went on, I still looked for, sought and needed their approval". This increased input by Hussey himself was matched by a new musical freedom created by Hinkler's departure. When he had first started putting down some of the tracks in his bedroom (much of which would find its way onto the finished album) Hussey noticed that the restrictive shackles that Hinkler's presence in the band had sometimes created now appeared to have gone: "All of a sudden you weren't working within the parameters of a band and I didn't have to write songs with fitting a guitar in mind. When Simon was in the band we did do things without his guitar on, like 'Amelia' but he didn't like it. He didn't see that in some cases it was easier for me to bang it down than take hours explaining it. Craig and Mick certainly never minded, they've never been precious about it - they adopted the attitude that whoever it takes to make a song sound good you should go with them, it doesn't matter who is and isn't playing". A few weeks into the recording Hussey was highly optimistic of the new working environment and the progress being made: "It's good working with Mark. He really stretches me. He comes from a completely different field of music than I do, stuff with sequencers and he's not that well versed with working with guitars...it's a good balance between sequencers and real music."[2]

Aswell as heralding a new studio approach, this album also saw an influx of guest musicians on The Mission's record, which previously had been limited to occasional contributions by Tim Palmer and the odd lucky studio tea boy. Hussey's old friend Miles Hunt from The Wonder Stuff co-wrote a track called 'Who Will Love Me Tomorrow' and there were sizeable instrumental contributions from Anthony Thistlewaite from The Waterboys, Martin Alcock, formerly of Jethro Tull and Fairport Convention, Ric Sanders, also from Fairport Convention and Abdel Aboud, personal violin player to none other than King Hussein of Jordan. Jaz Coleman of Killing Joke also contributed string arrangements on the record. With such a wealth of talent, there was bound to be a variety and flavour to this album that was previously not the case on Mission records. Hussey explains why he opened the doors to these new musicians: "I'd been writing in the same environment for so long it was becoming too safe, too sterile, so it was good to work with new people. The variety that gives the record is ideal - many records are one dimensional and people seem to listen to that, whereas I've always liked records like a lot of The Beatles stuff that would have this great variety of sound to listen to across the whole record."

Thematically, the album saw a return to the singer's earlier approach, with the record being focussed more than ever on Hussey's personal experiences, with the traumatic events of the 'Deliverance' world tour being drawn upon heavily for inspiration. The themes developed were very much in an emotional vein, and largely focussed around four central impulses: love, hate, jealousy and violence. Lyrically however, there was a marked new direction, a distinct departure from the flowery gothic articulation he had previously been noted for. In writing 'Like A Child Again', this new approach produced a classic pop song and a focal point of the album, with Hussey leaving no room for insinuation regarding his feelings for his new wife:

"I'm not trapped anymore,
Between Madonna and the whore,
When I'm with you.

You make me happy, and I hope you feel the same,
You make me feel just like a child again".

At the same time he articulated his disappointments at the friends who had let him down so badly, in the the infectious 'Trail Of Scarlet':

"You gave yourself away for the sake of a thrill
And for the price of my conceit you were a steal,
I'm so devastated,
I'm so very very let down".

Hussey made no secret of why he was looking to this more direct lyrical avenue: "On earlier records I mostly wrote the lyrics on speed, and when you're on speed it's easy to lose discipline and lose sight of the central theme". He continued "I had to move on. I wanted the songs to be more direct, to get away from that flowery gothic language - because I couldn't articulate feelings very well I tended to use language to disguise the fact."

Since they had enjoyed time off for recuperation and reflection before they commenced the new record, they were able to distance themselves from events and avoid the songs being drenched in morose and depressing observations. The subject matter remained very intense, but the overall impression left by the record was very upbeat. Hinkler's departure, Hussey's split from his girlfriend, and the drug abuse on tour all featured heavily, as well as other elements such as the book 'Helter Skelter' by Charles Manson. The track 'Even You May Shine' records a week in California when Hussey was reading the psychopath's biography whilst taking vast amounts of the drug ice. In this state he reflected on one aspect of touring: "I was really out there, on ice, reading this book and every time I'd go back to my hotel there'd be a room full of people who I knew I could do what the fuck I wanted to with, there's this power you can hold over them. You feel like you can wield power, at gigs especially, and it's scary. The whole situation became totally absurd really".

There was the normal Mission self-deprecation in the vaudeville style 'She Conjures Me Wings', laughing at their own drunken reputation, and three songs took a side wipe at the music press that had been so vicious to Hussey and The Mission in the past, most directly in 'Sticks and Stones'. The references to love in the track 'Like A Child Again', left Hussey typically honest about the artistic difficulties of the subject matter: "It's very hard to sing about how you're in love without sounding like a prat".

'Masque', like the three previous Mission records, was a personal document of the band's lives at that time; lyrically there was a very clear diversion from its predecessors, as Hussey moved away from the ornamental language he had been noted for. However, it was the musical tone of the record that was the most dramatic departure from previous Mission offerings. Introduced by the sound of a soft waterfall, the two thundering opening tracks 'Never Again' and ''Shades of Green' left the listener in no doubt that the band were fully prepared to confront the eclectic dance scene that was so popular in Britain at this time. The album pursued an incredibly varied course after this, with the bawdy ska-style horns of 'She Conjures Me Wings' being immediately contrasted by the almost funky arabic 'Sticks and Stones' with the intricate violin playing of Abdel Aboud marking the song as a highpoint. Saxophones and fiddles appear continually on the record, but this did not stop the band exploring more eerie themes such as on the disturbing 'Spider and the Fly'. The whole impression was very refreshing and incredibly varied, yet the record still had all the classic trademarks of a Mission album, with Hussey's cunning lyrical artistry maturing even further. In short, the band whose records had once been described as "the most pathetic, uninspired group in Music-dom"[3] had produced a pop album of astonishing quality.

*   *   *

The album took a total of eight months to record, but was a sporadic and relaxed affair, since nobody could face the stress of tight deadlines again so soon. When the tracks were finally finished The Mission were all extremely enthusiastic about the record. Hussey appeared in the press warning people to keep an open mind about the release: "It's not a concept album as such...the songs are much more real as opposed to being based in folk lore and fairy tales. There are a lot of different themes on the LP. We've had the luxury of doing exactly what we want to do, which we haven't been able to do since the very first LP...we've just done whatever we felt the song needed."[4] He also said: "I think it's an eclectic album, but it's got to have helped, not being around the 'biz'. We all knew we had to change, not because of any dictates of fashion, but to satisfy our existence to ourselves. I mean we didn't know if there was going to be another Mission LP, but people will have to open their minds to this record to get past the Mission tag."[5] He also announced that The Mission would not be touring the album at all, largely because of their new personal circumstances and their recent hideous experiences. With the record finally entitled 'Masque' after a Japanese novelette sent to Hussey by a fan,

The Mission prepared themselves for the reaction to their efforts, with Hussey informing the public in no uncertain terms about what to expect:

"If goth really is back, then this record will blow our part in it..."

CHAPTER FIFTEEN

"This record, I see, has now become not merely a chronicle of loneliness – the message of lonely Carlo, due for death five years after his crowning, was really life".

Anthony Burgess: Earthly Powers

WITH the band deeply involved in recording the album along with the difficult political manoeuvres in London, the public only saw one major appearance by The Mission in 1991. As one of the industry's hardest working live bands, this inactivity was most unusual but it was a reflection of their colossal status in their home country that when they did appear it was at a headline show in London's Finsbury Park on June 1st, in front of 18,000 people. With typical honesty, the band admitted that they had resolved not to play any shows that year but simply could not refuse the massive appearance fee they were offered. After rehearsing in Yorkshire, they warmed up for the Finsbury Park date with two shows, one each at Birmingham's Institute and Minsthorpe High School, which had established something of a name as the trendiest Secondary school in the country now that The Mission had played there after similar gigs by The Wonder Stuff and House Of Love. The warm-ups and rehearsals were unusually enjoyable as the new line-up allowed the band to spread their musical wings and work on music which had previously not fitted within the confines of The Mission environment.

The Finsbury show was a showcase for both the new material and two new live members, Martin Allcock and Anthony Thistlewaite. Most notably however, the show saw the return of Simon Hinkler on lead guitar for a one-off appearance. He had been busy with film scores and writing for Rock World magazine, but since relations with the band were now back to the friendly level that had predominated the early days of The Mission he accepted the offer of an emotional, albeit temporary return. The show itself was electric, despite the appallingly cold and wet weather, and the rather dour support bill of New Model Army and Killing Joke. The Mission performed a tremendous gig, despite having so many new elements to the live set up, and the new tracks featured here were well received. The gig also saw a return of the fanatical Mission following as the ranks of the Eskimos took the front area of the arena over. The private joke of a 'duck-on-wheels' T-shirt (there had been such a toy at the Barn recording studio) was a little lost on the followers but still sold well. Away from the actual show, Perrin was confronted by some angry Eskimos who barracked him for including New Model Army, their arch rivals, on the bill and complained of the violence at the front by the stage. The press reaction was somewhat reserved however, and their reception of the new material and new line-up of the band was rather worrying. Melody Maker, a former ally of the band, were most scathing of all: "The Mish have always been a secondhand outfit. Ever since trying to call themselves The Sisterhood they've traded on the inventions of other bands. Please welcome The Waterstuff!" Of Hussey they said "His furious belief amongst all this blustery bollocks is endearing, but he seems increasingly uneasy on the wide-angled material"[1] and went on to criticise the continued presence of what they called the 'pseudo-religion' which clouded The Mission's music. Simon Williams of the NME was equally confused by the new tracks, but less protracted with his criticism: "I can't work out if the Mish are veering towards Hazel O'Connor or Showaddywaddy."[2] Nevertheless, The Mission had long since been used to such press criticism, so with the ecstatic reaction afforded to them at Finsbury indicating the huge corner of the British music scene that was now their very own, the band prepared to release their new record 'Masque' to the public.

*   *   *

The first taste of the new material came on 13th April with the release of 'Never Again', the opening track from the forthcoming album - it's reception was to be indicative of the problem 'Masque' as a project would create, with the press and the public unsure how to respond to the release, despite its quality. In many cases 'Never Again' was never given a fair hearing and was often reviewed jointly with the greatly inferior re-mix of 'Temple of Love' by The Sisters of Mercy, the original of which Adams himself had played on. Both singles were seen as irrefutable evidence of the goth-dance accusations that were being hurled at these bands, notably The Mission. Such was the distaste with which the track was greeted that one had to look as far as the Arbroath Herald for its lone Single of the Week accolade - a worthy journal no doubt, but to be fair not one that the music industry looked to as a gauge of a band's success. Sales were similarly reserved, with the track reaching only No.34. The narrow-minded accusations of goth-gone-dance were repeated when the second single, the classic 'Like A Child Again' was released in June. It had all the ingredients of a superb clip of pop music but because of its origin was classed by the Melody Maker as "damnably impotent."[3] Both band and production staff alike were bitterly disappointed by the performance of this record, which only reached No.30, and soon dropped out of the charts, despite it being the No.1 single in Portugal for over five weeks. Some sections of the media had declared in advance that they did not particularly like what these two singles hinted at.

Their real venom however, was reserved for the release of the album 'Masque' on 22nd June, 1992. Andy Gill in The Independent called it "an overblown concept album featuring lazy, weak-minded battle-of-the-sexes clichés"[4] and Melody Maker was equally uncharitable: "Wayne can't help himself from babbling on, in his habitually clumsy manner, about Eros and Elysian fields, crucifixions, choirs, and ivory towers."[5] Many camps accused the band of trying to capture some of what they called 'cute-goth action' from The Cure, and derided them for going 'baggy' three years after Manchester. The Mission's various projects had frequently been misunderstood but it was these reviews of 'Masque' that saw their detractors completely missing the point of their latest record - to break away from the expected and take the band into new ground. The probability is that these critics were the same people who would have derided The Mission as repetitious self-parody had they released an album with twelve versions on the 'Deliverance' theme.

Ironically, 'Masque' saw some of The Mission's warmest and most enthusiastic press coverage - in some quarters 'Masque' received more positive reactions than any of their previous albums. Many welcomed the change in direction as a breath of fresh air and a sign that The Mission were not prepared to rest on their laurels and churn out the same material time and again, or head down the path of The Cult and become rock dinosaurs. Ironically, it was left to the NME, in the past the band's most virulent critic, to lead the way in fully understanding and praising the release: "It opens with 'Never Again' and 'Shades of Green', both thumping dance rock things that sound a little like Simple Minds with a sense of purpose and a little like an elephantine EMF. It goes on to crash through horror Cure goth waltzes and classy Wayne-isms... It is cute and it's very frightening... It is imaginative in a Mish kind of way. So perhaps 'Masque' is the sound of The Mission lightening up, clearing their throats and throwing open the curtains in the dusty ballrooms of their soul...the clouds of gloom rock are lifted - a tiny bit - to reveal the blue skies of Not Goth."[6] Vox was also enthusiastic: "Revolution. A light bulb flares into life over the band's collective heads...and gone at last are the Hussey tantrums and the ponderous walls of useless riffing - in their place, the camp melodrama...and Waterboy's like jig...(we find Wayne) finally whipping off his plastic shades and shooing the last vestiges of dry ice off the stage. The Thames has not iced over, Lord Lucan is still missing and there's not a single pig cleared for take-off - but The Mission have made a good album."[7]

Unfortunately, such good reactions were not shared by the majority of loyal Mission fans - sales were very laboured and it is perhaps most poignant that the 100,000 sales figure which all three previous albums had raced past was not reached at all, with the record charting at No. 23. Many fans saw the increased band exposure on two Radio 1 Road Shows, along with the more pop-style videos and musical tone as a sign that The Mission had finally succumbed and 'sold out'. It was clear within six weeks of the release that it would struggle to reach the impressive figures set by its predecessors, especially in the UK.

Notably however, the European reaction to the album was much more healthy - Germany saw three times as many copies of 'Masque' snapped up as in the band's home territory, and generally across the Continent the more open-minded attitude which had greeted The Mission in previous years welcomed them once again. Back at home though there was very public disenchantment with 'Masque' by their considerable following - for a band whose last two albums had achieved gold sales within a week of release, and who had purposefully cultivated a warm and intimate relationship with their following, this was all the more disappointing. Having remained out of the public eye for nearly a year and a half, to re-enter the whole music circus and be met by a barrage of criticism, including much from their own fans, was a demoralising and unsettling experience. It would take time for the band to recognise why 'Masque' had provoked such a reaction; fortunately, the one consolation of not touring the album was that time, for once, was something that The Mission had plenty of.

*   *   *

Although there can be manifold reasons why any one album does not succeed as well as hoped, it is perhaps fair to say there were three key reasons evident for the dramatic reduction in sales of 'Masque'. Firstly, all artist album sales were sizeably down over the period, because of the recession which now gripped the country. The figures produced by the industry body, BPI show a dramatic decline in total album sales over the four year period 1989 to 1992. From a figure of 162 million sales in 1989 the figure steadily decreased by approximately 10 million albums per annum to the total in 1992 of only 133 million. Likewise, single sales were down 8.2 million over the same period to 53 million, totals which together reflect the gradual decline of record sales in the UK.[8] The record industry was a victim of the recession as much as any industry, and The Mission were similarly victims as much as any other band. Taking into consideration this 18% decline in total album sales, 'Masque' was in some ways a reasonable seller in absolute terms.

The second reason, and probably the biggest factor on a commercial level, is the fact that the album was not promoted with a tour in any territory. Only two low-key acoustic in-store sets were performed by the band, whereas before each album had been supported by a world tour of at least 100 dates with The Mission being celebrated in some quarters as Britain's greatest live band. In addition, the band only did two major press interview features, partly because of their reluctance to commit themselves to the media circus again, but also for personal reasons - Hussey's wife had lost her father just before the album was released and spending hours talking to journalists was clearly not a priority for the singer. With decreased awareness that all this unavoidably has, there are lower sales. The lack of public awareness, be it through videos, gigs, T-shirts and even bootlegs which this policy of not touring and limited press creates, inevitably has a considerable effect on the record's popularity. These two reasons do not explain the whole picture however, there is one more key factor, the most painful for the band and possibly the most important: the traditional Mission fan simply did not like 'Masque' as much as their previous three outings on vinyl.

This third reason was clearly the most disappointing for the band. After they had worked on the record for eight months it was intensely demoralising to see so many former die-hard fans turn their backs on them, including many of the the Eskimos. To a certain extent, The Mission had been victims of a shift in musical fashion - there were less 'goth' fans around and the recent influx of dance music had captured the hearts of many a record buying music lover. Bands such as Yorkshire's Utah Saints (with whom Hussey made a cameo appearance at the 1992 Slough Festival), were seen as the way forward for many. Some saw The Mission's attempts at marrying these two schools of music as inevitably and helplessly doomed, and accused the album's musical ideas of being under-developed and incomplete. Many frustrated fans saw the departure from their established sound which they had followed The Mission for in the first instance as final evidence that they were a spent force. Essentially, they failed or refused to see past the traditional 'Mish' tag and just as goth as a fashion was now largely impotent, so were The Mission in their eyes. Q Magazine perhaps best summed up this train of thought: "'Masque' pursues a highly eccentric course that will have any remaining Goths crying into their cider and black. Somebody brings out the sax, there's fiddles all over the place and it all begins to sound like The Wonder Stuff, only without the wit or self-loathing...The Mission merely end up sounding small and really rather silly."[9]

At the time the overriding feeling of the band was one of immense disappointment that a record they had held such high hopes for, and one that had been received some of their best press to date, proved to be in their terms at least, a relative commercial failure. Their disappointment was compounded by the poor sales and bad reviews earned by 'Shades of Green' on its release in October 1992, with the press being particularly sceptical of the cross-over hinted at by the collaboration with the Utah Saints, who had re-mixed the single: "This sounds exactly as you'd expect. A cross between Ned's Atomic Dustbin in a head on collision with Slowdive and Sting. Gwar on the 9.17 to Nuneaton with Chris De Burgh."[10] What The Mission had hoped would be seen as a brave, and not too great a departure from their 'normal' material, had been perceived by many fans as a suicidal step, with headlines such as 'Calamity Wayne' confirming their suspicions.

However, despite the low sales and cold public reception of 'Masque', after retiring back to lick their wounds in Herefordshire, The Mission soon began to see the whole episode more philosophically. It was clear that the motives for the record had been correct, but they realised now that it was a case of too much too soon - there was too much diversity on the record and too much change surrounding the whole project. The songs themselves were shorter and of a generally more pop oriented vein. The lack of a tour confused and annoyed large numbers. The more direct lyrical content unsettled those comfortable with the traditionally more flowery and elaborate language which had been so appealing on previous Mission records, despite the fact that on close inspection what sounds like an up-tempo record is actually heavily weighted with very serious and depressed lyrics. There seemed to be an overall change in their image and this unsettled people already unsure of the music itself - even when the band had been 'retrogressive' or 'gothic' at least the public knew what to expect. In summary it was just too different.

With the benefit and distance of time however, Hussey quite rightly believes that it was a quality record, which had many highlights, but admits that maybe he should have opted for his original policy and released it as a solo record: "I think 'Masque' is a great record and has some superb songs on there - on a production level it's our best record by miles. There are mistakes on there but if you're not prepared to acknowledge your errors you'll never progress. A lot of people said it was too much change but because you're so close to it it's difficult to see that. The essential motivation for 'Masque' was very clear cut - we felt we had our backs against the wall creatively and consequently ignored what we were good at in an attempt to shrug off the baggage of history.'Carved in Sand' was reviewed as 'they haven't changed' so when we changed and made 'Masque' the same people said 'What's happened to The Mission we know and love?' It's the whole nature of the British press. Pathetic really".

This awareness of the embarrassingly fickle nature of the British music press had changed The Mission's approach to interviews. Hussey explains why they did this: "In our early days, in terms of how we wanted to be seen by the press, we used to turn up for interviews in pubs and we'd all get drunk and be outrageous, but on 'Masque' we manufactured situations so that this wouldn't happen, so that I wouldn't get drunk and say these things, we deliberately went against that. I'd like to think that we have got some interesting things to say and that we aren't just drunken slobs, but by approaching the interviews in this fashion all they wrote about was the fact that I had cleaned up, where in fact I was only cleaned up for that afternoon. What I learnt from all that was that you can only be yourself and you need to have faith enough in yourself that you're a strong enough personality to carry it off and make a good read. Under no criteria do I see myself as a star, but what I would say was that I'm mouthy enough to make good press, provide a good read and to play up".

"I think in some respects if 'Masque' had come out as a solo record it would definitely have been better received. Every group goes through periods where it's up and down, it's not all plain sailing, but maybe a solo record would have allowed me licence for that diversity. Even though the bottom line is you have a hard core audience who will still buy a record whatever it sounds like, you make an album and hope you'll be proud of it. Lyrically it documents a period of your life, and you can't carry this concern about what your fans will think when you're recording. I don't see 'Masque' as a Mission record really, it's not a bad record at all but I should have had the courage of my convictions and released it as a solo album".

Brown believes that they misjudged the reaction the new direction would evoke amongst even their hardiest of followers: "I think as an album we underestimated how the audience would react, we didn't have a big enough audience to try that amount of diversity on. We didn't feel that it was that diverse, but in a sense it took away from our original fans who saw us as this band that turned out a certain style of track". Tony Perrin, whilst expressing the opinion that 'Masque' is the best Mission record to date, acknowledges the slump but points out the drawbacks had it been a solo record: "Masque is the first time that we've had a downer on record, but any artists records in the last couple of years have taken a dip in sales. If you are going to call it a Mission record I think it's the best one they've done but it should have been a solo record. Having said that, the record company wouldn't have backed the idea though because they know they sell records of the back of The Mission name".

The ultimate irony of 'Masque' is that musically it is by far the most accessible and 'commercial' record The Mission have made. There are pop moments and there are the more epic tracks that The Mission were famed for. It was a brave venture for the band to even attempt, and the result was a remarkable effort. The potential was there to capture large sections of the public who would have found previous albums difficult to listen to. Despite the band's own reservations 'Masque' stands as a testament to The Mission's willingness to change and widen the parameters outside of the tried and tested methods which had brought them so much success. The media dismissed 'Masque' largely as a mistake - this is not the case. The mistake would have been to produce an album of 'Mish-by-numbers', which would have finally condemned The Mission to impotent and repetitious predictability. In their brave efforts to tear down the band's own history, many perceived them as merely losing sight of what had made them so original in the first instance. However, in retrospect, and removed from the poor sales, 'Masque' will eventually prove to be the album that makes The Mission, simply because it erased the suffocating preconceptions which surrounded them and threatened to stifle their creativity. In many sense what was seen by many as the death of The Mission will ultimately prove to be the re-birth of the very same.

CHAPTER SIXTEEN

"The future is not what it used to be".

Robert De Niro in 'Angel Heart'.

THE sense that 'Masque' had ultimately liberated The Mission from the suffocating tendencies which their own popularity had produced, rejuvenated and fuelled a growing optimism and renewed enthusiasm within the camp such that when work began on the band's fifth album, provisionally entitled 'Dog Lover', the overriding feeling was one of excitement and great anticipation for what the new project would bring.

It was thus all the more shocking when Hussey released a statement to the media in November 1992 to the effect that he had sacked Craig Adams and that the bass player would no longer be a part of any future Mission project. On first impression, such moves are usually viewed as the result of deteriorating personal relationships – this was the opposite of the case in this instance – Hussey and Adams had never been on better terms socially, but it was with growing concern that Hussey had viewed what he saw as a decreasing efficiency in their working relationship. Adams and Hussey had worked together for nine years, and had been through all manner of experiences, from the bitter acrimony of their split from The Sisters, through Adam's breakdown on that first American tour, and through the world tour in 1990 when so many factors had threatened to drag them down. They had come through it all as very close friends and with a deep mutual respect for each other – it was clearly not a personal problem.

There were reasons other than their personal relationship for this drastic action, which are probably best explained by Hussey himself: "I just got to the point where I knew it would just fizzle out. We could have made another album, maybe not, but I just thought that was a really sad way to let it all fall to bits. Craig was the sacrifice I suppose and that was the hardest decision I've ever had to make. I'd been with him nine years and we've been through a lot; you can't help but have strong feelings for him but I just felt that I had to make that decision for myself. There was a staleness creeping in. He became very negative about things. Mick and I would be doing speed and we'd have a great idea but Craig just wouldn't be into it, he would always see the down side of things".

"Even though our relationship was sometimes a little turbulent and strained, when we did decide to go our separate ways we were enjoying a personal relationship that was probably better than it had ever been. But, unfortunately, I felt that creatively we were unable to surprise each other any longer. I love him and I shall miss him madly but I am looking forward to facing new challenges and working with new musicians. When I first informed Mick of my decision I hoped and wanted Mick to stay and be part of the new band but I couldn't make that decision for him. Fortunately for me, Mick did decide to stay and because of his decision I felt at least a little vindicated in mind".

Hussey also acknowledged other factors in his decision. In his statement to the press the singer said: "I realise that Simon's departure from the band hurt us a whole lot more than I was prepared to accept or even acknowledge. And like a wounded animal I retired to my lair to lick my wounds and let the healing process take its course. It's taken me two years to realise and accept that when Simon left the band it broke the spirit of what The Mission was and that it would and could never be the same. So we had to create something different but equally as good. This takes time and involves trial and error, and parting company with Craig was, unfortunately part of that process. Making 'Masque' was also a part of that process. You have to destroy to create. I think I'm Craig's least favourite person at the moment, so I'm waiting for the dust to settle."

Brown's decision to support Hussey was bolstered by Joe Gibb, who had engineered 'Masque'. He agreed with the basis of Hussey's motivation for the change: "Craig was an absolutely brilliant bass player but just seemed to lose interest. Mick would be down here all the time we were working on 'Masque', whether he was needed or not, and would be available day and night, but Craig wouldn't always be around, he wasn't into it so much". The vital realism which Adams had contributed to the outlook of the band had apparently edged into cynicism and even negativity – since the lifeblood of The Mission up until this point had always been to ride a wave of enthusiasm and creativity which swept the band relentlessly along, this negative element was something which Hussey did not wish to see. Very often, in order to progress, a band has to remove some of the people or factors that had been central to its progress so far, and nobody had been as essential as Adams in the band's enormous success. Hussey now felt, however, that the momentum which was necessary for the group to further progress might be stifled if the line-up stayed the same.

Nobody was more surprised by the decision than Adams himself, and he was understandably shocked and more than a little angry; however, inactivity was clearly never going to be a problem for him. It is a mark of Adams' continuing reputation within the industry that within weeks of his parting ways with The Mission he was rumoured to be working with the former Sisters and All About Eve guitarist Tim Bricheno's new band CNN, and by May of 1993 he had formally joined The Cult, starting with their summer tour of Europe. The decision to join Astbury's group was only taken after a barrage of offers from many other bands, all of whom eagerly pursued the renowned bass player. By this stage he had already shown that his circumstances would move on regardless and he prefers not to dwell on the split from The Mission. His contribution to both the music and the attitude of The Mission was unmistakable and considerable, and cannot be ignored however. It is indicative of the great respect which they hold for Adams that Hussey and Brown immediately acknowledged his input as unique and irreplaceable, and rather than trying to emulate Adams with their new line-up, they immediately set about establishing something new, different, but equally as good: "I'd like to find a couple of kids who are really enthusiastic, who'll bring a new angle to it and do away with the baggage of history. I want to get back to a more guitar-based thing – not necessarily harder but I think with the last Mission LP I tended to shy away from what I was good at in an attempt to ditch the past. I don't consider 'Masque' as a Mission record in the catalogue of Mission records".

*   *   *

So having taken what was a very difficult and emotional step, The Mission started the new year of 1993 with the new songs Hussey had been working on, which were developing extremely well, so well in fact that he decided to delay no longer and start recording before he had even completed the new band line-up. As before, in the studio The Mission turned to somebody they had worked with previously – Joe Gibb, engineer to Mark Saunders on 'Masque', who was now chosen to co-produce the record with Hussey. The choice of Gibb was interesting itself because he had never seen The Mission live. Since the completion of 'Masque', Gibb and Hussey had become good friends, and over the Christmas period a close working relationship was borne, which was less confrontational than Hussey's relationship with Mark Saunders for the previous album.

Gibb brought with him an enormous knowledge and spirited enthusiasm, even though he had previously described The Mission as 'noise': "I'd come from working with The Kinks who are incredibly hard task masters, so The Mission are a real breath of fresh air. The Kinks would make copies of copies of copies and things were so strenuous – I started off as tea boy and ended up as head engineer at Konk studios, but I'd come to the end of the road there really and although they were inspirational songwriters it was too paranoid an environment all the time to endure for long. I was delighted when Mick and Wayne asked me to get involved".

Gibb's enthusiasm and vast technical knowledge made him an obvious choice; less obvious was the choice about who would fill the roles of guitar, keyboard and bass player. Both Brown and Hussey realised that it would be difficult at first to accommodate the idea of three new members but both were equally excited by the prospect of this new injection of talent, and the opportunity to establish a new 'gang' atmosphere which they had all so enjoyed in previous Mission days. The problems of finding suitable new members did not trouble the band too much however – fairly soon they had settled on Mark Gemini Thwaite on guitar, Rik Carter as The Mission's first full time keyboard player, and Andy Cousins on bass. Carter was a relative unknown as far as major bands were concerned. Thwaite was more aware of the high profile environment he was now joining – after living in Canada and playing in the popular National Velvet, he moved back to the UK where he passed through a series of bands before spending two years in Spear of Destiny, contributing to Kirk Brandon's 'Sod's Law' album, a Theatre of Hate tour aswell as session work for Roger Daltry and Terminal Power Company. The last member to join The Mission's new set-up was also the most experienced – Andy Cousins had been bassist with All About Eve since 1986 and had even toured supporting The Mission in Britain and Europe, after Tony Perrin had started to manage that band aswell. When All About Eve disbanded in early 1993, the offer of a role in The Mission was extended to Cousins by Tony Perrin, and he immediately accepted. The new members thus offered a whole range and variety of experience, and this arrangement appeared to work well, and successfully offered Hussey and Brown the vitality and input they had been searching for.

All the time these new members were integrating into the band, Hussey and Brown were developing the ideas that were to form the majority of the material for the new album. As the summer of 1993 approached, the shape and tone of the album began to evolve – even at an early stage they were very clear where their priorities and goals lay for the record: "In terms of an audience it will be an album to re-establish The Mission, putting our house back in order if you like. It's only calculated in the sense that it's more guitar based – we're sounding like a band again although we haven't played as a band live yet. In the last couple of years I've listened to much more eclectic music, very different to what I listened to in the past, I was much more tunnel visioned, all '70's stuff. There's a lot of good stuff out there and a lot of dross but it plays a part in how you write. This is very much a band record with all five of us working on it. I'm working in the parameters of a band so I can't go off and do different types of tracks here and there as I did on 'Masque'. You need some kind of cohesion, even if it's only tenuous, a sound or attitude that's prevalent all the way through".

Despite the new members, the working atmosphere within the Herefordshire studio soon developed a creative energy which Tony Perrin noticed very early on: "I was amazed at how quickly it started to work like a band again, really for the first time since Simon left. I was sitting in the control room where we were demo-ing the album and I was looking through the window watching the band playing together, really getting it together, and it was a great feeling to see that band atmosphere back again. Very exciting". This freshness was enhanced by Gibb, who immediately felt at home working with The Mission despite never having seen them play live: "That's quite strange when you're recording material, it's always in the back of your mind how it will sound live. But I leave that to Wayne because he knows exactly how things will work live and I go with him in that. When we're in the studio and we get a roll going with Wayne it's very productive and we can get stuff done incredibly quickly. Wayne and Mick are so easy to work with, so open and very professional. They've got great ideas and Wayne's guitar ability is unique – he makes the whole Mission sound which was what was maybe missing on the last album because it was too keyboard orientated. Wayne's guitar technique and ability are quite exceptional and he comes up with some incredibly inventive stuff. His sound, the actual sound of the guitar he plays is weird almost, very original and how he interprets the ideas in his head onto guitar is essentially The Mission's sound. Add to that the fact that Mick's a real vibe merchant and he can get you going so well – he's a great support player if you like, essential to the whole unit".

Hussey and Brown had clearly developed a unique working relationship which had stayed fresh and productive despite all the rigours of touring and being in such a successful band. Brown is not surprised that they are still creating so effectively: "I wouldn't have predicted it but I'm not surprised, we work well musically. We are at different ends of the spectrum but it's like me being as good a guitarist as Wayne because if he likes an idea he'll take it on board completely, and vice versa. Also, we've always credited the songs to all of us so you don't get one song by the drummer on an LP because he wants to get a bit of publishing, that's farcical". Hussey thinks it was always tending towards those two being the most suited to each other: "I don't think it's any accident that me and Mick are still together. In many ways we are very different people but when it comes to music and being excited about what we're doing there's a lot of common ground. We do get very pissed off and very excited at the same time. When Mick's playing drums he can pick up on what I'm trying to say even though I can't play drums, and he can tell me stuff for the guitar. I still find him to be very creative and very into it, there's a lot of support".

The indomitable spirit of The Mission was already returning at this early stage of the project; when the new material began to crystallise more clearly this enthusiasm began to acquire still more momentum. The record headed very much back to a darker sound, with the band recapturing their former emphasis on guitars and with the tracks lending themselves to longer, more forbidding instrumentation. Lyrically, Hussey found the new project very challenging – it was his lyrics which had earned him some of his most vicious criticism in the past, and now as he was four albums further down the line, originality in the vocal expression was the hardest thing he found to capture: "Each record becomes harder lyrically. The first album was a case of not worrying about what they meant as long as they sounded good, then on the next record everything had to mean something, even if it was only to me. Now, I see lyrics as a piece of poetry if you like, which I write completely detached from the music and always a long time after. Usually we'll do a couple of backing tracks and I'll take the tapes away and come up with ideas lyrically and vocally to fit what we've got. To me it has to read well aesthetically, but it can be very difficult because you're trying to get this point across but within the confines of parameters such as meter and rhyme, which you just want to break out of all the time. With this LP, I'm having to look out of myself a lot more, I'm having to be more general because my realm of experience has been a lot more confined recently in the last two years. The music I don't worry about, because there's only so many certain combinations of chords anyway, but more importantly the quality depends on the way you interpret them and your instrumentation of that song and those chord structures. Musically I have no trouble in coming up with tunes, it's really easy, but it's always lyrically I find it takes time".

The general direction of the new record evolved in a very much darker vein. 'Raising Cain' sees a massive rhythmic backbone detailed with violently screeching guitars, with Hussey's vocals heavily treated to disturbing effect, lending the whole track an ominous tone. Still more disturbing is the unsettling but superb 'Daddy's Going To Heaven', a track about Kelly Hussey's father, in which snippets of children playing momentarily harp back to the days of The Mission's second album; any hint of repetition is destroyed however, with this compelling mixture of a delicate vocal articulation against an almost brutal musical backdrop, marking the song as the album's most evocative track. The band's awareness of the eclectic musical environment of recent years is perfectly mixed with their own immediately identifiable style on 'Afterglow', which thunders along with yet more ragged guitar delivery. The whole record is forbidding and even disturbing, fascinating to the listener but unsettling at the same time. The guitar emphasis of the record, the enormous musical landscapes which The Mission re-visit, and the accomplished lyrical direction all produce an album that is overwhelming as a composite – the result is a remarkable collection of songs.

* * *

The Mission find it hard to contain the enthusiasm and excitement they feel for both the new album and the new band line-up; Hussey feels that the new set up has injected a fresh energy into the band and his eagerness to take to the road again is predominant: "We have to rebuild it in every sense. We'll share one bus with the crew and it's a chance for that band camaraderie to build up again. I'd like it to be like that again, so you can face the world as a gang, it's a great feeling. The good feeling is almost a by-product of it all – it's a self-perpetuating thing whereby we're selling records and we all get on. It takes time to trust people and they have to prove to me that they can come up with the goods, but when that happens it's a great thing. With this line-up it's working great already even though the personalities of the new people are yet to be fully realised. For the first time in a while I've got the hunger, the desire back for the whole thing – I've always enjoyed it in principal but you can get distracted, as we did".

I'd like to think that being out for 2 years adds some mystery to us and I think we needed to get some of that back, we'd become too familiar in some ways. For us, the main priority for this record is very clear – we want the fans to like it and we're not too concerned about massive sales. I want it to be seen as recapturing what The Mission are great at without being retrogressive. By kicking against the preconceptions of The Mission we might have alienated a section of our audience, but at least in doing that we have created some space for ourselves. Also it feels like we're the underdogs again, which suits us".

It is also something that The Mission have always been particularly good at...winning against the odds.

*

THE MISSION: DISCOGRAPHY

DATE:	CAT NO/ FORMAT:	TITLES:	HIGHEST POSITION
May 86	CHAP 6 7"	Serpent's Kiss/Wake	70
May 86	12CHAP 6 12" L	As above & Naked & Savage	
July 86	CHAP 7 7"	Garden of Delight/Like A Hurricane	49
July 86	12CHAP 7	Extended versions of above plus Over The Hill And Far Away/The Crystal Ocean	
July 86	L12 CHAP 7	As above but Over The Hills replaced by Dancing Barefoot	
Oct 86	MYTH 1 7"	Stay With Me/Blood Brother	30
Oct 86	MYSG 1 7" L.E.	As above Autographed and gatefold sleeve	
Oct 86	MYTHX 1 12"	As 7" plus Island In A Stream	
Nov 86	MERH 102 LP	GOD'S OWN MEDICINE: Wasteland/Bridges Burning/Garden of Delight/Stay With Me/Let Sleeping Dogs Lie/Sacrilege/Dance On Glass/ And The Dance Goes On/Severina/Love Me To Death	14
Nov 86	MERHC 102 Cassette 830603-2 CD	As Above plus Blood Brother/Island In A Stream	
Jan 87	MYTH 2 7"	Wasteland/Shelter From The Storm	11
Jan 87	MYTHX 2 12"	Shelter From The Storm (Long Version) Wasteland/Dancing Barefoot (Live)	
Jan 87	MYTHB 2 7" L.E.	Single Box Set 7" plus Serpent's Kiss (Live)/1969 (Live) plus photos	
	MYTHX 22	Wasteland (Anniversary Mix)/Live versions of Shelter From The Storm/ 1969/Wake	
Mar 87	MYTH 3 7"	Severina/Tomorrow Never Knows	25
Mar 87	MYTHP 3 7" L.E.	Including Free Poster	
Mar 87	MYTHX 3	Severina (Aqua Marina Mix)/Wishing Well/Tomorrow Never Knows(Amphetamix)	

DATE:	CAT NO/ FORMAT:	TITLES:	HIGHEST POSITION
Mar 87	MYTHL 3 12" L.E.	As Above but large free poster	
Jun 87	MISH 1 LP Cassette CD	THE FIRST CHAPTER: Like A Hurricane/Over The Hills and Far Away/Naked and Savage/Serpents Kiss/Dancing Barefoot/The Crystal Ocean(Extended)/Garden of Delight(Extended)/Wake(RSV)/Like a Hurricane(Extended)	35
Feb 88	MYTH 4 7"	Tower of Strength/Fabienne Breathe (Vocal)	12
Feb 88	MYTHX 4 12"	Tower of Strength/Fabienne Breathe (Instrumental)/Dream On	
Mar 88	MYTHX 422 12"	Tower of Strength(Bombay Mix) Fabienne/Breathe (Vocal)	
Mar 88	MTHCD 4	Tower of Strength (Extended)/Breathe (Vocal)/Fabienne/Dream On	
Feb 88	MISH 2 LP	CHILDREN: Beyond The Pale/A Wing and a Prayer/ Heaven on Earth/Tower of Strength/ Kingdom Come/Breathe/Child's Play/ Shamera Kye/Black Mountain Mist/ Heat/Hymn (For America)	2
Feb 88	MISHC 2 Cassette 8342632 CD	As Above plus Dream On/Fabienne	
Apr 88	MYTH 6 7"	Beyond The Pale/Tadeusz	32
Apr 88	MYTHX 6 12"	Beyond The Pale/Tadeusz (1912-1988)/Love Me To Death (Reprise)/For Ever More	
Apr 88	MYTHX 622 12"	Beyond The Pale (Armageddon Mix) For Ever More/Tadeusz (1912-1988)	
Apr 88	MTHCD 6 CDS	Beyond The Pale/Tadeusz (1912-1988) Love Me To Death (Reprise)/For Ever More	
May 88	MTHCD 62	Beyond The Pale (Armageddon Mix)/ Tower of Strength (Bombay Edit)/ Tadeusz (1912-1988)	
Nov 88	MYTH DJ 712 12" DJ ONLY	Kingdom Come (Heavenly Mix)/ Child's Play (Live) NOT FOR SALE	

DATE:	CAT NO/ FORMAT:	TITLES:	HIGHEST POSITION
an 90	MYTH 8 7"	Butterfly On A Wheel/ The Grip of Disease	12
Jan 90	MYTHX 8	Butterfly On A Wheel (The Magnificent Octopus Mix)/The Grip of Disease/ Kingdom Come (Forever and Again)	
Jan 90	MYTH 8 10 LE/Poster	Butterfly On A Wheel (Magnum Opus Mix)/Kingdom Come (Forever and Again)/ Kingdom Come (Heavenly Mix)	
Jan 90	MTHCD 8	Butterfly On A Wheel/The Grip of Disease/Kingdom Come (Forever and Again)	
Feb 90	842 251-1	CARVED IN SAND: Amelia/into The Blue/Butterfly On A Wheel/Sea of Love/Deliverance/ Grapes of Wrath/Belief/Paradise (Will Shine Like The Moon)/Hungry As The Hunter/Lovely Cassette & CD same as above	7
Feb 90	MYTH 9 7"	Deliverance/Mr.Pleasant	27
Feb 90	MYTHX 9 12"	Deliverance (Sorcerer's Mix)/ Mr.Pleasant/Heaven Sends You	
Feb 90	MYCDB 9 CD Pic. sp	Deliverance (4.08)/Mr.Pleasant/ Heaven Sends You/Deliverance (6.05)/	
Feb 90	MTHMC 9 Cassette sp	Deliverance/Mr.Pleasant	
Feb 90	MTHCD 9 CD sp	Deliverance (4.08)/Mr.Pleasant/ Heaven Sends You/Deliverance (6.05)	
Feb 90	10" Gatefold 12" box	(Deliverance (4.08)/Heaven Sends You (Mr.Pleasant/Virginia Plain (Metal (Guru's) (with 8 page booklet) (Deliverance (Sorcerer's Mix)/ (Blockbuster/Mama We'er All Crazee Now	
	w.poster	((Live - Metal Guru's)	
May 90	MYTH 10 7"	Into the Blue/Bird of Passage	32
	MYTHX 10 12"	Into the Blue (la la sheldon Mix) Divided We Fall/Bird of Passage	
	MYTHCD 10 CD pic sp	Into the Blue/(la la sheldon Mix) Divided We Fall/Bird of Passage	
	MTHMC 10 cassette sp	Into the Blue/Bird of Passage	
	MYTHR 10 12"	Into the Blue (First Avenue Mix)/ Child's Play (Live)/Divided We Fall Gatefold With Poster	

DATE:	CAT NO/ FORMAT:	TITLES:	HIGHEST POSITION
Nov 90	MYTH 11 7"	Hands Across The Ocean/ Amelia/Love (Limited Edition)	28
	MYTHX 11	Hands Across The Ocean/Amelia (Live) Tower of Strength (Casbah Mix)/ Mercenary	
	MTHCD 11 Pic CD	Hands Across The Ocean/Amelia (Live)/ Mercenary/Stay With Me (Demo)	
Oct 90	846937-1 LP	GRAINS OF SAND: Hands Across The Ocean/The Grip Of Disease/Divided We Fall/Mercenary/ Mr.Pleasant/Kingdom Come (Forever & Again/Heaven Sends You/Sweet Smile of A Mystery/Love/ Bird of Passage	28
	846037-4 Cassette	As Above plus Tower of Strength (Casbah Mix)/Butterfly On A Wheel (Troubadour Mix)	
	846937-2 CD	As Cassette	
Apr 92	MYTH 12 7"	Never Again/Beautiful Chaos	34
Apr 92	MYTH 1212 12"	Never Again (F1 Mix)/Beautiful Chaos Never Again (Zero G Mix)/Never Again	
	MYTCD 12	Never Again/Never Again (F1 Mix) Beautiful Chaos/Never Again (Zero G Mix)	
	Pic CD	Ltd Edition Box	
Jun 92	MYTH 13 7"	Like A Child Again(Re-Mix)/ All Tangled Up In You	30
	MYTH 1312	Like A Child Again (Extended)/ Hush-a-Bye Baby (Child Again)/ Like A Child Again (Re-Mix)/ All Tangled Up In You	
	MYTH 1310 10"	Like A Child Again (Extended)/ Like A Child Again (Re-Mix)/ All Tangled Up In You Limited Edition Etched Disc	
	MYTCD 13	Like A Child Again (Re-Mix)/ Like A Child Again (Extended)/ All Tangled Up In You/Hush-a-Bye Baby (Child Again)	

DATE:	CAT NO/ FORMAT:	TITLES:	HIGHEST POSITION
Jun 92	512121-1 LP	MASQUE: Never Again/Shades of Green(Part II) Even You May Shine/Trail of Scarlet/ Spider and the Fly/She Conjures Me Wings/Sticks and Stones/Like A Child Again/Who Will Love Me Tomorrow/You Make Me Breathe/From One Jesus To Another/Until There's Another Sunrise 512121-4 As Above	23
	Cassette 512121-2 CD	As Above	
Oct 92	MYTH 14 7"	Shades of Green (Re-Mix)/Sticks and Stones (Casbah Mix)/Shades of Green (Album version)	49
	MYTH 1412 12"	Shades of Green (Extended 7" Mix) Sticks and Stones (Casbah Mix)/ You Make Me Breathe (The Barn Mix)/ Spider and the Fly (Creepy Crawly Mix) Limited Edition Etched Disc	
	MYTCB 14 Pic CD	Shades of Green (7" Re-Mix)/Sticks and Stones (Casbah Mix)/Trail of Scarlet (Guitar Mix)/You Make Me Breathe (The Barn Mix)	
	MYTCD 14	Shades of Green (Saintly Mix)/Sticks and Stones (Casbah Mix)/Trail of Scarlet (Sitar Mix)/Spider and the Fly (Creepy Crawly Mix) Limited Edition Box CD	

THE MISSION: VIDEOGRAPHY

Channel 5 CFV 06952 May 87	THE MISSION: CRUSADE (LIVE) Wasteland/And The Dance Goes On/ Garden of Delight/Let Sleeping Dogs Lie/Serpents Kiss/Over The Hills And Far Away/The Crystal Ocean/ Sacrilege/Stay With Me/Wake (RSV)/ Blood Brother/1969
PMV 041 685 2	FROM DUSK TO DAWN (video collection) Intro: Tadeusz/Serpent's Kiss/Stay With Me/Wasteland/Severina/Tower of Strength/Beyond The Pale 7"/Kingdom Come/Beyond The Pale 12"/Outro: Forever More
MISH PRODUCTIONS MVD01 Sep 89	SOUTH AMERICA (DOCUMENTARY) Tower of Strength/Shelter From The Storm/Beyond The Pale/Deliverance/The Crystal Ocean/Sacrilege/
PMV 081 776-3	WAVES UPON THE SAND (DOCUMENTARY) Deliverance/Butterfly On A Wheel/ Hungry as the Hunter/Grapes of Wrath/Lovely/Into The Blue/Paradise (Will Shine Like The Moon)/Bird of Passage/Mr.Pleasant/Belief/Sea of Love/Tower of Strength
MVD02	THE METAL GURU'S - ABSOLUTELY LIVE Metal Guru/Mama We'er All Crazee Now/ Blockbuster/Merry Xmas Everybody

PHOTO CREDITS
&
FOOTNOTES:

1 John Blackmore
2 Tony Mottram
3&4 Greg Freeman
5,7,15,18,19,22,23,26,27,28,29,30,32 Mary Scanlon
6,8,9,10,16,17,24,25,34,35,38 Joe Dilworth
11 Bleddyn Butcher
12 Peter Anderson
13 Not Known
14 & 36 Stephen Sweet
20 Not Known
21 Chris Craske
31 H.Photographics
33 Derek Ridgers
37 T.P.Campbell

Front Cover: Mary Scanlon
Back Cover: Peter Anderson

Every effort has been made to credit the photographers' material in this book correctly; however, a few were unobtainable. The publishers would be grateful if any omissions were brought to their attention.

CHAPTER ONE:

1. Melody Maker Pamphlet
2. 'A Family Feud' N.Perry Sounds 22/02/86

CHAPTER TWO:

1. Smash Hits 02/86
2. N.Perry op.cit. 22/02/86
3. R.Gibson Sounds 29/11/86
4. 'His Masters Voice' Melody Maker 05/09/87
5. Live Review M.Smith Melody Maker
6. Live Review Mr.Spencer Sounds

CHAPTER THREE:

1. Live Review T.Staunton NME
2. Melody Maker 19/07/86
3. Short Magazine 19/07/86
4. NME 19/07/86
5. 'Blood Brothers' M.Smith Melody Maker 25/10/86
6. Live Review Roger Holland NME
7. 'Sisters Doin' It For Themselves' W.Leith NME 14/06/86
8. Live Review A.Hughes
9. 'Venice In Peril' Mr.Spencer Sounds 26/07/86
10. 'Brazen Hussey' N.Taylor NME 08/11/86
11. Singles Review M.Snow NME
12. M.Smith op.cit 25/10/86

CHAPTER FOUR:

1. 'Mission Improbable' L.Tilston Record Mirror 06/02/88
2. N.Robinson No.1 Magazine 01/11/86
3. M.Smith op.cit 25/10/86
4. 'Wild In The Country' C.Clerk Melody Maker 29/08/87
5. Album Review C.Clerk Melody Maker
6. Album Review N.Perry Sounds
7. Melody Maker 25/10/86
8. Live Review D.Roskrow 25/11/86
9. Singles Review Sounds 07/03/86
10. R.Gibson op.cit 29/11/86
11. 'Admissions Of A Mummy's Boy' A.Scanlon Sounds 14/03/87

CHAPTER SIX:

1. A.Scanlon Sounds 13/06/87
2. Mr.Spencer Sounds 11/07/87
3. Live Review D.Stubbs Melody Maker 25/07/87

4. N.Perry Sounds 06/02/88
5. 'Shootin' Their Mouths Off' A.Scanlon Sounds 03/03/90
6. Ibid.

CHAPTER SEVEN:

1. 'Wings Of Desire' Stud Brothers Melody Maker 06/01/90
2. Ibid.
3. D.Quantick NME 15/11/86
4. Live Review M.Mercer Melody Maker
5. Live Review R.Holland Sounds 05/09/87
6. Live Review C.Clerk Melody Maker 05/09/87
7. Single of the Week Sounds 31/01/88
8. R.Gibson Sounds 27/02/88
9. T.Mico Melody Maker 05/03/88
10. M.Issue City Limits 26/03/87
11. Live Review M.Smith Melody Maker 18/10/86

CHAPTER EIGHT:

1. Live Review R.Wilkinson Sounds
2. 'A Seminal Man' B.Egan NME 30/04/88
3. M.Minkoff NME
4. B.Egan op.cit 30/04/88
5. Ibid.
6. D.Quantick NME 06/03/88
7. Melody Maker 06/03/88
8. L.Tilston op.cit 06/02/88
9. Melody Maker 06/03/88
10. 'The Hurricane Hits The West Coast' N.Perry Sounds 30/07/88
11. Live Review G.Bent Melody Maker 12/11/88
12. 'Pale Rider' P.Elliott Sounds 23/04/88

CHAPTER NINE:

1. Live Review P.Lester Melody Maker 13/05/89
2. Live Review E.True Melody Maker 09/09/89
3. Live Review S.Williams NME 06/01/90
4. 'The Mission' J.Lewin Making Music 02/90
5. 'Sons Of A Beach' S.Williams NME 03/02/90
6. K.Mellotte Edinburgh Substance 02/90
7. M.Agar Worthing & District Advertiser 27/12/89

CHAPTER TEN:

1. M.Agar op.cit 27/12/89
2. Album Review South Wales Echo 06/01/90
3. Album Review N.Perry Melody Maker 03/02/90

4. Album Review Sounds 03/02/90
5. Album Review Southern Cross 19/02/90
6. Album Review A.Vaughan Music & Video Insight 03/03/90
7. Live Review M.Smith Melody Maker 03/03/90
8. Album Review I.Middleton Record Mirror 10/02/90
9. Sounds op.cit 03/02/90
10. Live Review R.Morton NME 03/03/90
11. Live Review S.Price Melody Maker 31/03/90
12. Live Review P.Elliott 31/03/90
13. 'Scots Mish'd' S.Sutherland Meldoy Maker 26/88/89
14. Live Review A.Collins NME 14/04/90

CHAPTER ELEVEN:

1. Melody Maker 05/05/90
2. Melody Maker 02/06/90

CHAPTER TWELVE:

1. 'Britain's Stupidest Band' R.Morton NME 08/12/90
2. Sounds 26/05/90
3. Live Review D.Simpson Melody Maker 15/12/90
4. Live Review D.Fadele NME 05/01/91

CHAPTER THIRTEEN:

1. Album Review M.Smith Melody Maker 27/10/90
2. The Guardian 02/90
3. Album Review R.Sandall Q 03/90

CHAPTER FOURTEEN:

1. NME 13/10/90
2. Ibid.
3. Live Review D.Fadele NME 05/01/91
4. Melody Maker 02/11/91
5. For The Record 06/92

CHAPTER FIFTEEN:

1. Live Review Melody Maker 09/06/91
2. Live Review S.Williams NME 09/06/91
3. Singles Review E.True Melody Maker 13/06/92
4. Album Review A.Gill The Independent 18/06/92
5. Album Review S.Price Melody Maker 20/06/2
6. Album Review D.Quantick NME 13/06/92
7. Album Review M.Townsend Vox 07/92

8. Figures provided by BPI 05/93
9. Album Review P.Kane Q 07/92
10. Single Review D.Bennun Melody Maker 10/10/92

Lyrics reproduced by kind permission of BMG Music Publishing Ltd.

Every effort has been made to correctly and fully credit the footnotes; however, the publishers would be grateful if any errors or inaccuracies were brought to their attention.